THE FIRST INAUGURATION

The First Inauguration

George Washington and the
Invention of the Republic

STEPHEN HOWARD BROWNE

The Pennsylvania State University Press
University Park, Pennsylvania

An earlier version of chapter 5 was published by Michigan State
University Press as "'Sacred Fire of Liberty': The Constitutional Origins
of Washington's First Address," *Rhetoric and Public Affairs* 19, no. 3 (2016):
397–426.

Library of Congress Cataloging-in-Publication Data

Names: Browne, Stephen H., author.
Title: The first inauguration : George Washington and the invention of the
    republic / Stephen Howard Browne.
Description: University Park, Pennsylvania : The Pennsylvania State
    University Press, [2020] | Includes bibliographical references and index.
Summary: "Examines the first American presidential inauguration,
    including the people, ceremonies, and issues surrounding the event,
    and argues that George Washington's inaugural address provides a
    compelling statement of the values necessary to make the experiment in
    republican government a success"—Provided by publisher.
Identifiers: LCCN 2020034973 | ISBN 9780271087276 (cloth)
Subjects: LCSH: Washington, George, 1732–1799—Inaugurations. |
    Washington, George, 1732–1799. Inaugural address of 1789. | United
    States—Politics and government—1789–1797.
Classification: LCC E311 .B83 2020 | DDC 973.4/1092—dc23
LC record available at https://lccn.loc.gov/2020034973

The Pennsylvania State University Press is a member of the Association of
University Presses.

It is the policy of The Pennsylvania State University Press to use acid-free
paper. Publications on uncoated stock satisfy the minimum requirements
of American National Standard for Information Sciences—Permanence of
Paper for Printed Library Material, ANSI Z39.48–1992.

Frontispiece: detail from *Washington Taking the Oath as President, April 30,
1789, on the Site of the Present Treasury Building, Wall Street, New York City.*
From *Century Magazine*, April 1889. The Miriam and Ira D. Wallach Divisio
of Art, Prints and Photographs: Picture Collection, New York Public
Library Digital Collections, 815048.

For Margaret, Jessica, Maria, Emily, and Elizabeth,
Once and Again, and Always

CONTENTS

ILLUSTRATIONS

ACKNOWLEDGMENTS

I am grateful for the support of Penn State University Press and particularly for the encouragement and direction of Ryan Peterson, Kendra Boileau, and Patrick Alexander. One could not reasonably ask for a better team of professionals committed to the work, the *art*, of scholarly publishing. For their keen eye and helpful insights, I thank Peter Onuf and Robin Rowland; such shortcomings as this book may feature are entirely my own, of course. I was fortunate to receive research assistance and counsel from Haley Schneider, Keren Wang, Benjamin Firgens, and Dominic Manthey. This kind of support is not a given, and I am grateful to Denise Solomon, Head of the Department of Communication Arts and Sciences at Penn State, for affording me the opportunity to pursue my interests.

A special note of acknowledgment is owed to Allison Niebauer, whose rare combination of intrepidity, intelligence, patience, and goodwill assisted materially in the completion of this project. Thank you, Allison.

For their encouragement and wisdom, I am grateful to Mary Stuckey and Curtis Smith. My departmental colleagues have been a source of inspiration and support for many, many years. My thanks to you all.

Introduction

I aim in this book to tell the story of George Washington's journey to New York, of the speech he gave on April 30, 1789, and of the speech's legacy in the American tradition. The first inaugural address is this story's center-piece. My analysis of it is designed to illustrate this simple but necessary thesis: that Washington's performance that day established a resource for the ongoing work of realizing America's greatest ideals. That the address has not been sufficiently recognized or availed of for this end is regrettable but not irremediable. Here, I hope to reassert the inaugural address's claim to place in the American canon of state papers—to remind us that we have in the address and in the circumstances of its delivery a rich and vital fund for thinking about the political situation in our own challenging times.

The First Inauguration is written for a readership concerned with the tenor of political discourse in our own time. Americans have always been a noisy, clamorous people. We do not shy away from debate; indeed, we seem to thrive on it as the very stuff and substance of democracy. When such give-and-take is thought to be productive, sincere, and motivated by rival conceptions of the public good, we applaud; when it appears merely partisan or self-interested, we despair. Thomas Jefferson, James Madison, and Henry Clay; Abraham Lincoln, Elizabeth Cady Stanton, and Martin Luther King Jr.—titans all, and we claim them with pride as our own. Constitutional conventions, civil rights marches, declarations of independence: such eloquence. But more often, and certainly of late, we lament the passing of an age when citizens deliberated *as citizens*, with speeches, not tweets; with crisply argued letters to the editor, pamphlets, orations, and finely tuned sermons. That is nostalgia, but the longing is real. And still, an unmistakable note of despair may be heard, as if we have somehow lost something precious, hard, and fine about our shared humanity. Have we?

We have not. I hope to provide in the following pages a reason to believe again in ourselves, in our leaders, and in the essential dignity of the democratic quest. To those who might wonder whether yet another book on Washington is needed, I respond with a resounding yes. We need to call to mind the story of Washington's inauguration because in it we discover vital resources for the reanimation of civic life; we need, like every generation, to invent a version of the first president to meet our own particular but hardly unique challenges. We need to listen to what he has to say because what he said and how he said it offers us a gift we cannot afford to ignore or cynically dismiss.

We are, I trust, beyond the point where apologies need be made for the Founders. No one now sensibly denies their shortcomings, their racial and gendered assumptions, or their hypocrisy, elitism, and assorted privileges. Few now are inclined to give them a pass, nor should we. They were not saints and ought not to be regarded as such. Neither were they devils. My general approach to Washington is to acknowledge his humanity, and so his sins; to focus on the best of who he was and what he said; and to suggest, along the way, that we may well benefit in our time from paying attention. The first president has always served as a screen on which Americans have projected preferred versions of themselves. In this sense, we can choose our parents. We can summon Washington again to remind us that we can do this, that the American experiment in republican democracy is still worthwhile, and that in his speech and behavior may be found an exemplar of what Americans may sound like again.

Even if one grants that another study of Washington is thus warranted, it may not be evident that a single speech could so significantly shape the political culture of a new nation. This is a genuine consideration, and I will offer several reasons why I think the speech can and should have such an impact. Washington is a rarity in that though he was often thought reserved, he was in fact a man of words—lots of them. We may with confidence presume that when he spoke, he did so to a purpose, and he meant what he said. The inaugural address, written with the assistance of James Madison, was and remains highly sensitive to the exigencies of its time and place of delivery. At the same time, it shares in the Founders' preoccupation with the future; it was thus composed as well for a generation not yet born. By studying it carefully, we learn how to read in its message the fundamental principles of republican government and its call to Americans to become better versions of themselves. The address contains within itself the great and abiding questions of national identity: What values are necessary for a people to launch such a government? What ought its leadership to sound like? What is the place, if any, for such old-fashioned ideas as *virtue* in the new order of things? What, finally, are the ties that bind so strong as to unite a rapidly growing, highly diverse, and aspirant people? These questions will guide our efforts to reclaim Washington and his address for the civic imagination.

What then might we learn by considering Washington's address and the events around it? A great deal, for in these events we glimpse what the creation of the American republic looked and sounded like; we discover a people announcing themselves and affirming their vision of what a truly republican leader ought to look and sound like. This exercise of our political imagination can allow us to see today what all this might have looked like in the process of becoming. The inauguration was not the first or only such natal moment, but it was unquestionably a key phase in the early constitution of what it meant to be an American.

An extraordinary amount of scholarship surrounding Washington is available in biographies, histories, and political theory. I have leaned heavily on it in the pages that follow, including such standards as provided by Douglas Southall Freeman, James Flexner, Joseph Ellis, and James Alden, as well as the marvelous resources to be found in Washington's correspondence. Without presuming too much and hoping to offer the reader a brief but instructive account of the inauguration, I have sought here to ground basic issues of republican government in just a single text—Washington's first inaugural address. The payoff, I hope, is to equip the reader with a deeper sense of what was at stake at the nation's inaugural moment, how Americans chose to participate in it, and ultimately, what we may learn from that moment to forge ahead.

To date, no such work on the inaugural address has appeared in print. Histories of Washington typically include a few pages on the inaugural day and move on to presumably more important matters of statecraft and congressional wrangling over titles, taxes, and others affairs of governance. This is unfortunate given the significance of the event and its dynamic interplay of ideas, personalities, and symbols. My work in rhetorical studies allows me to home in on the rich variety of symbolic and material resources that helped give to this event its abiding importance. In addition, I attend to the rituals of nationhood borrowed and created along the way and to the meaning and force of such popular activities as parades, dances, visual performances, speeches, and balls. At the same time, I will put these ephemera within the context of the political thought and controversy characteristic of the time.

More than anyone alive, George Washington appreciated the utter novelty of the circumstances that would soon usher him into office, far from Mount Vernon's vines and fig trees. No people on earth, *ever*, had dared invent a system of government quite like the one he was now to lead. None dared, not even now, to imagine that it would all work as planned. So many issues remained unresolved; too many of his fellow citizens remained doubtful, some bent, perhaps, on the great experiment's ultimate failure. Forces, only yet glimpsed, threatened, not only at home but also abroad, in a world deeply suspicious of the extraordinary human and natural resources now organized under the sovereign powers of a republican nation. Who now counted as friends? Who now as enemies? These matters would have to be sorted out, and quickly. The presidency itself was without precedent, conjured up in the final weeks of the Constitutional Convention—not an afterthought, to be sure, but commanding surprisingly little in the way of heat or deep reflection. What was to become of him, of his country?

Perhaps—we cannot know this—George Washington asked himself the toughest question of all: Why? Why assume such responsibilities now? On the back side of his fifties now, he had lived several lifetimes in an age when men of his stature had every right to assume the prerogatives of success. Washington's health was sound, providentially so after the endless miles, the battles, and the camp contagions that conspired to lay down most mortals. It was not too much to ask that he now be granted the rewards all agreed were his: some privacy, time to ride, hunt, do a little fishing; dinner with Martha, a glass of Madeira with friends. Like many squires of his station, Washington looked forward to improving his estate—his financial affairs, certainly, but above all Mount Vernon, the house, its farms, the potential that had not yet been brought to fruition. He was never a particularly successful farmer, not really. That could change. His investment schemes had not yielded nearly what he had hoped; that, too, might be improved on. It was all right there—the land, the river, the enslaved and hired help. The general was a reserved man, true, but he needed company and was indeed hardly ever without it. Alexandria was just down the road. Here, too, all was just as he wished: visitors and the curious might circulate through the estate, have a bite, and talk of the day. When that was enough, the patriarch would excuse himself and retire upstairs. Perfect.

Why then? Motive is a notoriously elusive thing, fugitive, and not always to be trusted even when found. The question still seems worth asking, not so much for psychological insight as for what it might suggest about the inauguration and indeed about the national heritage. Perhaps the most efficient route to something approaching an "answer" is through the elimination of standard interests. These, too, are telling. Why does anyone contemplate political office? Ambition, of course, but ambition for what? Power comes first to mind, but that does not tell us much either. It is not clear what about the executive office circa 1789 could possibly have been appealing to a man motivated by power alone. History tells us, too often, that tyrants surely must aspire to more promising heights than this. History tells us, too, that high office can serve as a useful means to wealth, emoluments, the high life! Not here, not now, and not by a long shot. Well, then, military glory: the record will show a long and benighted tradition to this day and doubtless beyond that executives—monarchs, kings, and despots—have always eyed politics as a path to martial ends. Again, America, 1789: *what* military? There was no standing army as such, no navy; a few posts spread along a massive western frontier. Not exactly a tempting object of desire for the would-be Caesar.

Then again, maybe it was just about fame. Granting even the above disincentives, we can readily understand enticements to office for those who see in it a way to satisfy some deep, if otherwise inexplicable, need for the affirmation of others. Celebrity candidates, we might call them today, see office as a kind of extension of their own brand of entertainment. What they cannot deliver by way of ideas may be compensated by pleasures of the spectacle. And yet a man would have to be desperate indeed in the nation's founding age to seek office for such reasons. Fame is complex and historically variable, and it drove men of the time as it has men of all times. Washington was deeply attuned to its chords, and he danced, beautifully, to its call. As strange as it may sound to us now, however, the executive office of a new government, of a fledgling republic, pitched precariously on the edge of the west Atlantic, numbering about three million souls stretched from New Hampshire to Georgia, simply was no place for a man craving attention.

George Washington, Esquire, needed none of this, wanted none. That he was ambitious and made of stern stuff there can be no doubt. He understood power as did few others; he was comfortable with it, used it with little evidence of regret. Men had died at his command; he held hundreds of fellow human beings in bondage. Washington did not seek power, because he already had it; he *was* power. It is inconceivable that he assented to the presidency because he wanted more; if anything, the office could only mean less. As for wealth and its trappings, little needs to be said, because so little was in the offing. Washington was, of course, a very rich man by standard metrics of the day, and money is for the poor, after all. He asked for none in war, and got his way; he will ask again, and be denied. Office will mean for Washington not the way to wealth, but away from it. We may wonder, in turn, what it would even mean to seek after Washington's motives in the way of military ambition. The very question would be absurd if the record were not so grim, the men on horseback so frequently cresting the horizons, ready. That Americans have been spared the trauma of the military coup d'état is owing in no small part to a general insistent on the privilege of civil authority, who, wielding the sword in battle, laid it down in peace and left it there.

If not fame, then, if not power, money, or military might, then why was the master of Mount Vernon pacing its floors on the morning of April 16, 1789, bags packed? The answer, of course, is duty. This much can be no surprise: readers with the most fleeting familiarity of our subject know that Washington had made a career, a life, shaped by the requirements of service to others, to his country above all. He could be imperious, especially in younger days; his appetite for land, especially, was voracious; he would always be exceptionally sensitive to reputation. He had his blind spots. He was human, and then some. But from early manhood in the woods of western Pennsylvania, to the verdant expanses of Virginia's Northern Neck, the fields of battle, and Philadelphia, one constant provided coherence and force to this most singular of men. Duty was for Washington never a choice; it was ingredient to his being.

He left Mount Vernon because that was what it meant to be George Washington. The tautology may be forgiven if we remind ourselves of this fact: for the president-elect, as for his fellow citizens, the prospects of republican success presupposed the triumph of character. Now, character meant above all a capacity to act well on behalf of the public good. It was a virtue and thus an attribute of the individual, but the self alone could by no means circumscribe character. It only had meaning and force when exercised for others, and this required a very serious and very demanding sense of duty. And no one, safe to say, commanded such resources of character, such a commitment to the commonwealth, as the man now clambering into the carriage that would take him, at length, to Federal Hall.

Something of the method at work in this project may be suggested by the image of a road trip. By way of situating the event within its lived experience, I first take the reader on a journey from Mount Vernon to Manhattan in the Spring of 1789. Along the way, we will stop, as Washington did, in Alexandria, Virginia; Baltimore; Wilmington, Delaware; Philadelphia; Elizabeth-Town, New Jersey; and finally accompany him off the boat and into New York City. The point here is to capture in the image of the individual the forward direction of a people at large, to recover the pageantry and anxiety, to listen to the music, oratory, and acclaim, to ask who was left out and why, and to arrive, one hopes, at a more richly textured, nuanced, and instructive perspective on what it means to launch a nation.

The second phase of the project situates us in the New York City of 1789. Here we undertake to discover the various individuals—white elites, African Americans, the laboring poor—who gave to that time and place its distinctive claim on the American imagination. How and why they mobilized to greet and host the new president and government can tell us a great deal about how power in such contexts is articulated, staged, and given maximum persuasive force. The celebrations, parades, dances, music, fashions, food and drink, taverns, ballrooms, churches: all help tell the story of the early, *early* republic.

The third phase entails restaging the inaugural speech itself. Why this address has not received the attention it deserves, I can only speculate. Even if it were thought a poor production, it is after all the *first* such effort in American history; that should be worth *something*. The truth of the matter, however, is that the speech is quite good—indeed, a commanding statement on what the American presidency ought to look and sound like. We will see that the first of our presidential inaugural addresses is, as well, deeply reflective of the man giving it voice, and reflective, too, of the people who made it possible, listened to it, read it, and received its message in trust. The aim here, to be clear, is certainly not to make a case for Washington as a great orator; this he never was, and it would be foolish to claim otherwise. Nor is it to present dramatic new evidence of the speech's abiding influence. The point is rather to demonstrate that it merits and rewards more than we have suspected. There is, I think, considerable yield here if successful: rather than tend exclusively toward either a social or a straight political history of the subject, I hope to synthesize both into a compelling account of how ideas get put into action and of how symbols are made concrete in the service of consolidating power.

Scholarly and popular interest in the founding of America continues to grow, and this project seeks to enter this lively terrain directly. The best work on the subject successfully integrates social, political, historical, and conceptual analysis into comprehensive accounts. Among the most noteworthy treatments, from which I have learned a great deal and for which I remain deeply grateful, are David Waldstreicher's *In the Midst of Perpetual Fetes: The Making of American Nationalism, 1776–1820*; Sandra Gustafson's *Eloquence Is Power: Oratory and Performance in Early America*; Simon Newman's *Parades and the Politics of the Street: Festive Culture in the Early American Republic*; works by Stephen Lucas and by Pauline Maier; and anything by Jack Rakove. These distinguished scholars of the period, so different in approach and design, have materially assisted in my own attempts to give voice to early republican culture. A set of key terms grounds this study. My definitions are, of course, provisional and stipulative, but I think they are responsible to the scholarship and not eccentric to established traditions of usage.

Rhetorical studies strike me as most interesting and useful when they capture something of the noise, drama, and interplay of human agents doing important things in complex circumstances. Drawing on methods of rhetorical studies, this book offers a compelling story of this nation's signal moment of symbolic birth. *Rhetoric* refers to the art of managing symbols in public contexts to persuasive ends. As both a human practice and a study of that practice, rhetoric has enjoyed a long-standing status in Western letters, dating back at least to ancient Athens. The art was understood by its earliest professors in several ways that bear directly on my account of Washington's inaugural address. Although examined in different ways to several ends, early thinkers agreed that rhetoric attended most clearly to the basic act of speaking in contexts of civic life about matters of common concern. Teachers of the craft, including Aristotle, Isocrates, Cicero, and Quintilian, accordingly, sought to train their students in the invention, organization, stylistic treatment, delivery, and memory necessary for effective public speech. All appreciated that language was power or at least that the skillful management of it was, and that such power was crucial for the vitality of life in public contexts.

The Atlantic eighteenth century remained deeply beholden to these classical antecedents. Anglo-American treatises and educational curricula routinely featured precepts handed down from antiquity, especially by Cicero and Quintilian, and even—especially—prominent political, legal, and religious figures looked to them for guidance. The rhetorical landscape, so to speak, was of course dramatically different: white Americans were relatively more literate than most peoples on earth; enjoyed a flourishing, indeed quite remarkable print culture; and expected those who assumed the dais to respect their expectations for the dignity of the art. At the same time, the scope and function of rhetoric expanded to meet the diversifying and increasingly complex demands of early modernity. Today, we include within its ambit any manner of symbolic expression, including visual, material, and sensate artifacts. For the purposes of this study, I examine not only the oratorical performances of Washington and others, but also the persuasive work attendant to festivals, parades, clothing, and related evidence of creative expression designed to persuasive ends. This commitment leads me to our second key term.

Ritual, too, shares with rhetoric a long and rich history and a protean and sometimes elusive set of meanings. From anthropology to religion to politics and beyond, it has been employed across a diverse range of human practices; this, because humans seem if not by nature then by long habit deeply ritualistic animals. We need rituals. Why? Because recurrent form helps stabilize and give shape, meaning, and direction in a world otherwise uncertain and uncontrolled. We know this at the level of individual and private practice: the daily routine that, while seemingly banal, in truth helps establish our rhythms of life and provides the familiar and intelligible terms with which we make sense of the world, of our place within it. It is no wonder, then, that humans under conditions of abjection will seize on apparently trivial rituals of self-care—shaving in solitary confinement—to reaffirm their essential selfhood. We avail ourselves of the powers of ritual because they work.

How do rituals work? For the limited purposes of this study, I employ the term in no especially nuanced way to draw attention to their public functions. These functions help explain at least three persistent features of our story: change, identity, and memory. Students of rituals have long observed that they seem especially conspicuous during moments of transition—liminal episodes in the career of a people confronting change in some fundamental sense. We appeal to rituals under such conditions because they help us over the thresholds, give us a hand, so to speak, give us courage to leave behind what must be left behind, and brace us for the coming time. We need such assistance because these moments put our identity as risk; rituals have always promised to reaffirm who we are between past and future. Not that our shared identity is ever truly certain or fixed; finding ourselves on the other side of that threshold, facing new worlds, we seek confirmation through rituals as a means to remember who we are, and why. Like all peoples, Americans have drawn from and contributed to an enormously rich repertoire of such practices, not least among them inaugurations, festivals, and anniversaries. Now, this does not mean that we respond to such rituals as may be intended, and it seems not merely cynical to observe that our enthusiasm for celebrating shared pasts has waned considerably of late. Is it time for a rejuvenation? I think so.

A third term: *virtue*. We do not use it much these days, not in contexts of public and political life. This is regrettable. Is it surprising? The term is confessedly old-fashioned and frankly has never been used with great precision or consistency. Moral philosophers continue to exercise its potential for explaining, if not actual behavior, then its prospects as a standard for judgment and right action. As a political concept, virtue has been the object of over two thousand years of contemplation, from Aristotle to Alastair McIntyre. But what does it mean? That is, again, an unanswerable question, at least to satisfaction; here, I operate under the assumption that, as with all words, it means what a given people want it to mean. During the period under investigation, most people understood virtue as describing a certain quality of character made intelligible by the willing capacity to superordinate the public good above the private. The term, certainly, presupposes a number of complex assumptions about human agency, the relationship of the subject/citizen to the state, and the nature of political obligation.

I will attempt in this book to honor these premises as they operate in late eighteenth-century American culture. The more specific aim, however, is to focus less on the denotative meaning of virtue than on how it gets performed within the contexts of civic life and how it is ritualized and given rhetorical force. The analysis accordingly seeks to integrate what ought not to be left isolated; seeks, that is, to understand the work of virtue as it is performed by both massed citizens and by their chosen representative. The promise of republican government in 1789, as I understand it, was that America could have it both ways: that it could be governed through an exquisitely designed system without giving up the human element. System without agency is bureaucracy, and no way to run a nation-state; agency without system is tyranny. My thesis, then, is that Washington inaugurated a set of commitments that made it possible to have it both ways. *He did so by instantiating an ideal of political virtue that simultaneously respected the systematic rule of law as established in the Constitution, and embodied the human values giving that system its ultimate rationale.*

A few words, finally, about the man himself. Anyone writing about Washington in our time faces certain challenges, which, if not unique, must be confronted at the outset. Aside from Lincoln, no figure in American history has received more attention; none has been the object of so much hagiography and myth, no one so monumentalized into the collective consciousness as His Excellency. Scholarly treatments of Washington's participation in this process, especially Stephen Brumwell's *George Washington: Gentleman Warrior*, Paul Longmore's *The Invention of George Washington*, Barry Schwartz's *George Washington: The Making of an American Symbol*, and Gary Wills's *Cincinnatus: George Washington and the Enlightenment* have demonstrated to striking effect the creation of Washington as a cultural symbol. There are compelling reasons for this apotheosis; indeed, the not very subtle subtext of this book is its promotion of Washington as a rich and relevant resource for thinking about Washington in the current age. Dangers lie afoot, not only of presentism but also of reproducing the excesses and distortions so long associated with our subject. Then again, we live in a time when it is hardly a given that a slave-owning, white, male elite ought to make any kind of claim on our convictions. Have we not had quite enough of George Washington?

No, we have not. Every generation of Americans needs to figure out its relationship to the past, and Washington is inescapably central to that past. He will not, cannot be made to disappear. The more difficult, pressing question is how to make him matter again. Again, I have tried in the following pages to avoid as much as possible any genuflections to his person on the one hand or any cheap shots at his quite real shortcomings on the other. I can only trust that by now we are beyond such mindless reflexes. My efforts bend rather to identifying the interplay of individual character and ritualized social action; this dynamic in turn helps us understand one of the ways, at least, that Americans inaugurated themselves into nationhood. The values enshrined as Washington's own—his sense of responsibility to the common good, his rectitude and basic decency, his courage and restraint, his love of country—were thus delivered to a common inheritance and made the fit objects of our highest ideals as a republican people.

Considerations of method are seldom as riveting to the reader as to the author. Again, I will be brief. The story of Washington's inauguration is multitextured and admits of no single reading practice. By habit and inclination, I lean toward sustained analysis of speech texts; this appetite is met by the account of the address delivered on April 30, 1789. At the same time, I am insistent that we attend to the many interesting and important modes of articulation that accompany, indeed make possible, the events surrounding that speech. To this end, we will want to look closely at the constituents of ritual, including parades, toasts, music, and so on. The general aim is to take these forms seriously without over reading, let theory inform but not bully the analysis, and fold into the narrative such generalization and arguments as are warranted by the evidence. This approach I take to be appropriate to the basic argument of this book: that Washington's inauguration helped instill into the American story a degree of faith in the essential dignity of republican government that we cannot afford to let lapse. I will return to this matter of faith in the conclusion for further comment and offer briefly a set of reflections borne by the journey to Federal Hall.

CHAPTER 1

The Things He Carried

On Thursday, April 6, 1789, Congress had at last resolved itself into a quorum. Gathered in Senate chambers in the newly refashioned Federal Hall in New York City, the assembly turned to the business at hand: Would John Langdon of New Hampshire please count the votes for president and vice president of the United States of America? He would, and he duly announced that His Excellency George Washington, to the surprise of absolutely no one, had received the unanimous endorsement of his fellow countrymen. As if to make up for lost time, Congress immediately appointed its long-serving secretary Charles Thomson to make the three-hundred-mile trip to Mount Vernon, inform the august Virginian of the "news," and accompany him back to the city to inaugurate the world's first modern republic.[1]

The Irish-born messenger may well have been overqualified for the job. Thomson, sixty now, had endured a calamitous voyage to the American strand orphaned and without means. Talent and perseverance brought in time a fine classical education, securing the young man a teaching post at the Philadelphia Academy. Soon Thomson was on his way, active in the city's mercantile culture and quickly making a name for himself. By the mid-1760s he was deeply immersed in the resistance to British colonial policy; he earned the lasting friendship of Benjamin Franklin and the enduring enmity of Joseph Galloway—all further evidence of his political acumen. In 1774, Thomson, the "Sam Adams of Philadelphia," was appointed Secretary to the Continental Congress, a position in which he served for the entire duration of its existence. During his tenure, Thomson established a reputation for indefatigable commitment to the administration of that body's daily operations, including its journals, correspondence, committee assignments, and foreign communications. No one, not even Thomson, can function in such capacities for so long without making enemies, and this he did. But in time his abilities, steadfastness, and power would make him a valued asset and friend.[2]

On reflection, perhaps this bearer of good news was not at all over-qualified and was indeed the ideal choice for summoning Washington to office as the nation's first executive. For Thomson was in many ways a perfect embodiment of what had already become a distinctly American story: of humble beginnings, hard work and talent, stick-to-it ambition, success eventually, and redemption finally. Our messenger agreed to the challenge, readied his papers, and set off the next morning. The trip was to last eight days and take the rider through New Jersey, Philadelphia, Wilmington, Baltimore, and Alexandria, Virginia—a route with which he was to become all too familiar. "Though much impeded by tempestuous weather, bad roads, and the many large rivers I had to cross," Thomson later reported, "yet, by unremitting diligence I reached Mount Vernon, the seat of his excellency General Washington, on Tuesday, the 14th, about 12 o'clock."[3]

If by chance General Washington was gazing out the window, he would soon have marked the figure of Thomson rounding his way toward the imposing mansion. The guest was not unexpected, nor was the news really news at all, for Washington had been anticipating this moment for a very long time. Whatever elation or relief he may have felt now must have been tempered by equal measures of anxiety over the portents ahead. Ushered inside, Thomson duly informed Washington that he had been elected "President of the United States of America," evidence, if any was necessary, "of your patriotism, and of your readiness to sacrifice domestic ease and private enjoyment to preserve the liberty and promote the happiness of your country." Congress, he assured Washington, harbored no doubt "of your undertaking this great, this important office, to which you are called not only by the unanimous votes of the electors but by the voice of America; I have it therefore in command to accompany you to New York, where the Senate and the House of Representatives are convened for the dispatch of public business. In executing this part of my commission, where personal gratification coincides with duty, I shall await your time, and be wholly governed by your convenience."[4] Thomson concluded his part in the brief ceremony by relaying the sentiments of John Langdon, president pro tempore of the Senate: "Suffer me, Sir, to indulge the hope, that so auspicious a mark of public confidence will meet your approbation, and be considered as a sure pledge of the affection and support you are to expect from a free and enlightened people."[5]

Washington by this time could have no doubts about the "affection and support" of his fellow Americans. That much was self-evident. It was rather the sacrifice of "domestic separation and private enjoyments" that plagued the president-elect, who of all people may have been granted leave to enjoy in peace what days remained to him on this earth. Mount Vernon, the "vine and fig tree" of his imagination, had never ceased to call him home and had sustained him in the darkest hours and furthest reaches of battle for the better part of his adult life. At the end of the War of Independence, the general regained on Christmas Eve the ground lost to him for eight years, and there he aimed to stay. "I am retiring within myself," he wrote the Marquis de Lafayette, "and shall be able to view the solitary walk, and tread the paths of private life with heartfelt satisfaction. Envious of none, I am determined to be pleased with all; and this my dear friend, being the order for my march, I will move gently down the stream of life, until I sleep with my Fathers."[6] There is genuine pathos in these lines, poetry of a sort not commonly associated with their author. Above all, his words suggest a bone-deep exhaustion of body, of course, but also of mind and perhaps of spirit as well. And now this news, and the future it demanded.

So much is a familiar rendering of Washington on the threshold. There is truth to the image, testimony to which may be readily found in the extant record. He was in fact deeply ambivalent about being awakened once again from his Elysian dreams of retreat from the world of politics, society, and public life. His "movements to the chair of Government," Washington claimed, "will be accompanied by feelings not unlike those of a culprit who is going to his place of execution."[7] These and many other demurrals suggest not merely a gentleman's diffidence but a mind in some ways at war with itself, pulled on the one hand by an earnest wish to remain within the embrace of home and on the other by the imperatives of civic duty. If we are to understand the full import of his journey north to Federal Hall, if we are to track in that journey its symbolic resonance and legacy, we need then to grasp what it meant for Washington to leave Mount Vernon and all that it represented to him. The matter is not altogether as straightforward as may be thought. One way to get at the question is to dwell not so much on what the traveler chooses to leave but on what he chooses to bring with him for the journey. And what were these things? Mount Vernon and the moral order it was made to embody, a finely tuned balance of pragmatic and principled judgment, and a distinctive commitment to the requisites of power rightly exercised. We will treat each in turn and prepare ourselves thereby for the trip ahead.

"STILL AND PLACID WALKS": MOUNT VERNON AS MORAL ORDER

Late in December 1783, the commander in chief of the United States Army handed over his sword to Congress, turned his mount south, and headed for home. That much was astonishing enough, but Washington was more interested in what lay ahead than behind. Before him, not too far away, awaited his beloved Mount Vernon, and to it he must go. Eight years and a war of independence had separated the man from his ancestral lands. The general had laid down his plow once, willingly; not again during the conflict would he indulge himself in an extended rest. He might have; he chose otherwise. But now, Washington confided to George Clinton, "The Scene is at last closed. I feel myself eased of a load of public Care. I hope to spend the remainder of my Days in cultivating the affections of Good men, and in the practice of domestic Virtues." For the next six years the general made good on his intentions, returning now to his crops, the oversight of his enslaved labor, recalling to striking effect the mansion, the world, he had left so many years ago. "I am at length become a private citizen of America," he exulted, "on the banks of the Patowmac; where under my own Vine and my own Fig-tree, free from the bustle of a camp and the intrigues of a court, I shall view the busy world, 'in the calm light of mild philosophy,' and with that serenity of mind, which the Soldier in his pursuits of glory, and the Statesman of fame, have not time to enjoy. I am not only retired from all public employments; but am retiring within myself and shall tread the private walks of life with heartfelt satisfaction."[8]

A charming image and sentiments well earned—but in the end, a mirage, conjured by a desperate need to restore to his world some nearly

FIGURE 1 Benjamin Henry Latrobe, *View of Mount Vernon Looking to the North. July 17, 1796. The Portico Faces to the East.* Watercolor. Courtesy of the Maryland Historical Society, 1960.108.1.2.13.

lost sense of place and moral order. For the forces Washington had helped unleash and then direct were not yet spent; they were indeed merely at rest before resuming a course that would change this world forever. Washington had every intention of "hastening with unspeakable delight to the still and placid walks of domestic life."[9] History, in its way, had different plans and made of Washington's hopes no more than the dreams of a very tired and homesick man.

Mount Vernon and its several farms sit above the Potomac River a few miles south of Alexandria, Virginia (fig. 1). Today it is rightfully appreciated as one of the nation's great landmarks, visited by millions, impressive in its stately presentment and staid formality. Jacques-Pierre Brissot de Warville thought the estate "elegant, though simple, and of pleasing aspect"; its surrounding lands, David Humphreys recalled, affording "philosophic shades to which the late commander in chief of the American armies retired from the tumultuous scenes of a busy world." For all its apparent stasis and serenity, however, the "Mansion House Farm" was in truth itself a very busy world, home to the free and the enslaved, alive with the sounds, smells, and sights of human production, consumption, and trade. And then there were the visitors: an endless stream, it seemed, of old friends and the merely curious, dignitaries and the importunate, so much so that Washington cried at one point that his home might well be "compared to a well-resorted tavern, as scarcely any strangers who are going from north to south or south to north do not spend a day or two at it." Not that he or Martha ever put a stop to it, of course. They cherished domestic life together amid the bustle, and if Washington could make himself scarce enough when he felt like it, no visitor ever seems to have gone away hungry for attention or a hot meal. All this was just as it should be, just what he imagined: for now, he happily informed Lafayette, "The noon-tide of life is now passed with Mrs Washington and myself, and all we have to do is to spend the evening of our days in tranquility, and glide gently down a stream which no human effort can ascend."[10]

The meridian of one's life is yet only its half. Washington might then look with some confidence to his hard-earned "days in tranquility." His fellow citizens, however, were finding such repose hard to come by. While he tended his gardens, they sought to make sense of what independence had wrought, and many, though grateful for its arrival, struggled to contain and direct the energies it loosened. The years between war's end and the launching of a national government were accordingly fraught with political, social, and economic problems, the solutions to which conspired to end Washington's peace of mind once again. Soon enough, he would be called on to leave Mount Vernon again—for Philadelphia in 1787—and for New York City in the spring of 1789. In both instances, the summons was to battle of a different kind: not armed resistance against the enemy but on behalf of a nation that was not yet a nation. Yet it was to be a battle, nonetheless. If we are to understand his role in its conduct, we need to consider what Washington brought with him to the field—what he armed himself with, so to speak, as he prepared to meet this, his final and greatest call to duty.

Mount Vernon meant to Washington more than almost anything in the world. At times in his life, it *was* his world. It strains credulity, therefore, to assume that when called away, he truly left it behind. He did not. The estate could no more be alienated from his affections—from his very being—than his deepest aspirations, values, and ideals. No one, and certainly not

Washington, invests so much of himself in something for so long without becoming an indelible part of it. Mount Vernon was but the materialization of Washington's own interior architecture, the public expression of his most private structure of convictions. It was one of the three great models he composed during his life so far. Mount Vernon, like his conception of military command and ultimately like his own character, was built, maintained, and set on display as the very embodiment of what it meant to be George Washington, an exemplar at once of the man and the world he would fashion. To understand Mount Vernon is thus to understand Washington, and this much takes us no small distance toward understanding the inauguration of America itself.

It was for Washington not a house but a home. "Signature and self-portrait," in the words of Robert Dalzell and Lee Dalzell, Mount Vernon "was a tangible emblem of his character, his personality, his hopes, his dreams." An English visitor in the autumn of 1786 found it a "handsome seat, delightfully situated on the banks of the Potowmack, a few miles below Alexandria; the house commanding a fine and extensive view up and down the river, and over into Maryland." The estate, originally built in the early eighteenth century, had come into Washington's possession by way of a lease on the death of his beloved step-brother Lawrence Washington in 1754. Owner now of five hundred acres spread over five farms and twenty-seven human beings, Washington set about in short order to expand and improve on his fortunes. There was much to do for the new master, above all conceiving how his holdings might assert themselves into what Jessica Kross has referred to as the "social geography"[11] of the planter South. By the time Washington came to full ownership in 1761, he had raised the mansion house to two floors, tripled the number of slaves, and initiated extensive renovations both inside and out. Palladian in design, though roughly so, Mount Vernon fixed the epicenter to an estate devoted to agricultural production, social comity, and, eventually, the swirling politics of colonial and early national life.

To such idyllic pleasures Washington had retreated at war's end, and here he planned to stay. Abandoning tobacco as a hopeless enterprise, he diversified his crops, undertook extensive landscaping projects, and threw himself happily into the daily management of land and humans. Yet another visitor observed that here Washington proved himself "quite a Cincinnatus, and often works with his men himself—strips off his coat and labors like a common man." The general, he noted, "has a great turn for mechanics," and the visitor found it "astonishing with what niceness he directs everything in the building way, that all may be perfectly uniform."[12]

"In the building way": the diarist perfectly captures the image we may derive from the sight of Washington at home. It is, moreover, suggestive of those qualities of character and mind, of habit and preference that this Cincinnatus was eventually to carry forward to New York City. Mount Vernon was certainly a site of material and psychological comfort to Washington. But it was never a place of actual repose. More verb than noun, the estate was designed to accommodate an unceasing buzz of activity: in production, exchange, and consumption; arrivals and farewells; expanding and retracting, building, razing, and rebuilding. Here, the master brokered deals and resolved conflicts; experimented, failed, and tried again. Mount Vernon gave, and it took; there, Virginia squires plotted freedom among the enslaved. For all its fame as a plantation home—a village, really—it never truly thrived as an economic entity. It functioned more importantly as a quasi-public site of controlled human interaction, where even retreat from the affairs of business and politics meant endless guests, entertaining, and sport. Except in degree, perhaps, this much may be observed of many planter homes similarly situated, but Mount Vernon was not just a plantation home. It was George Washington's home, and like him it slept little and hit the day early.

Humphreys was not a very good poet, but he loved George Washington and served him long and well. In the summer of 1786, he published an ode to Mount Vernon while in residence there. "To thee, my friend," Humphreys wrote, "the lays belong / Thy happy seat inspires my song / With gay, perennial, blooms / With fruitage fair, and cool retreats / Whose bow'rd wilderness of sweets / The ambient air perfumes." Untold others of his country similarly imagined the pastoral scenes into which their hero had apparently settled. There must have been comfort in such renditions. But in truth, Mount Vernon was much more than just a retreat. Like its owner, the house and lands embodied a complex set of tensions; these tensions in turn gave structure, energy, direction, and value to the whole. This much will be key to our understanding of the journey Washington would soon undertake, its public meaning and acclaim, and allow us to see more clearly the distinctive qualities with which he imbued the new nation's chief executive office.[13]

We have observed that Mount Vernon presents to the eye an image of total control, uniformity, decorum, and above all, moral authority. The impression is at once entirely reasonable and indeed precisely what its builder intended. We must be mindful, however, that such placidity can only be the result of prodigious labors, vexed by circumstances, negotiated, compromised, falsified (visitors today know that those exterior walls are in fact made of wood and painted to appear as stone), stylized, and staged. At the risk of being overly schematic, we can summarize the many such tensions that prefigure the Mount Vernon / George Washington homology thus:

Inheritance–Improvement
Material–Symbolic
Private–Public
Agriculture–Commerce
Nature–Art
Native–European
Independence–Debt
Simplicity–Complexity
Fixed–Transient
Freedom–Slavery

Kross has suggested that "colonial mansions were both mirrors of and metaphors for colonial society."[14] We have reason to both stretch her point and to give it greater specificity by thinking of Mount Vernon and George Washington along similar lines. I will argue, indeed, that we can plausibly extend the image to include America itself. All were constructed from certain givens, conceived, as it were, to carry a message; shaped by the competing seductions of forest and city; intensely localist but straining ever outward, ever *toward*; stubbornly independent, always in debt; preoccupied with place but restless, expanding, changing; hell-bent on freedom, owners of others. These kinds of tensions are, to say the obvious, profound and powerful; unmanaged, they may tear a people apart, and have. It was Washington's unique gift to so embody these tensions as to give them productive and not destructive potential. In the case of slavery, of course, this much was and is to be lamented; for that matter, none of these need be taken as goods unto themselves. The point is rather that

Washington was able to transfer the values encoded into Mount Vernon because those values we associate with the building were *his* values, as complex, brilliant, faltering, inconsistent, tragic, and ultimately redemptive as we know them to be. Mount Vernon teaches us, then, that its owner was able to subsume such tensions within himself and therefore to resolve their opposing energies—not by eliminating one or the other but by so disposing and balancing them as to create something new in the world, something real, lasting, and finally, redeemed by tragedy, worth it all.

BETWEEN THE REAL AND THE IDEAL: PRACTICAL INTELLIGENCE AND THE ART OF POWER

Mount Vernon was at once the source and effect of Washington's most personal ambitions. It afforded solace even when—especially when— he was elsewhere; it was the symbolic expression of material success and the material embodiment of cherished ideals. We have reason, then, to suppose that it must take a great deal to move a man from such a home; so much was Mount Vernon a part of Washington that leaving it meant leaving something of himself behind, a sacrifice of self for a purpose greater that oneself. He had been thus summoned before, of course, several times, and for the same reason—because he owed it to his country. And just because Washington was willing, in effect, to leave a part of himself behind, he remained open to the ineffable, the unpredictable, to change. For all its beauty and comforts, indeed for all its hubbub, Mount Vernon could never really be anything but a place of splendid repose. And Washington, need it be said, was not a man given to repose. Like most, he grew, learned, struggled, and prospered most away from home; like few others, this process helped shape decisively the origins and growth of early American nationhood.

We continue our search for the things Washington brought along for the journey north, the resources of mind and character, experience, and habit that came bundled for the trip. Among these must be reckoned the values displayed so conspicuously on the banks of the Chesapeake Bay. We are thus able to now move Washington off his ground, to observe him operating far from its placid waters on the very threshold of war, independence, and nationhood. Even the brief glimpse that follows makes plain that among the qualities forged by military experience was the general's capacity for taking what was given, discerning its potential, and transforming it into something greater than it might have been.[15]

Such a talent presupposes a rare but powerful insight into what we might today call the social psychology of leadership. To exercise it effectively is to understand that the real and the ideal are not fated to their juxtaposition; that indeed, each may be made the condition of the other's fullest realization. Most genuinely great military leaders evince this habit of mind, notably Napoléon Bonaparte, Ulysses S. Grant, and George Marshall. Washington, it must be said, was not a great military leader, at least on the level of these august figures. But what he exemplified on his arrival in Boston in the summer of 1775 is entirely consistent with their shared refusal to sunder the *is* from the *ought*. Like them, Washington confronted what was real, in all its messiness, disappointment, and uncertainty; judged therein what might be possible; and sought to make it happen. He possessed, that is, a kind of pragmatic idealism, and though seemingly given by nature, he learned through experience, failure, and success to negotiate its competing demands to expert effect. Neither did he allow the pragmatic to descend into cynicism, nor the ideal ascend to irrelevance. This is at least one mark of real leadership, and this, too, he carried with him to the nation's inaugural moment.

A strikingly clear illustration of Washington's pragmatic idealism may be seen at work as he assumed command in Boston. The story has been told often and well and need not be detailed at length here. There is nevertheless some gain in reminding ourselves of what Washington was about that summer. Clearly, he thought himself unready for the task ahead; he made mistakes, and he might have exploited the circumstances to greater effect. This is true. But he also proved himself a quick learner and admitted his faults. Most importantly, the new commander in chief strove relentlessly to grasp what exactly he had at hand, identified its inherent promise, and then set about creating the conditions for successful action. Along the way, he set in place a model of executive authority extending to both civic and military ends. The process was not always satisfying and seldom tidy or truly predictable, but it worked, and in time came to represent a standard for political life as compelling today as it was in that very different world of revolutionary America.[16]

The outbreak of armed hostilities in April of 1775 appalled loyal Americans, exhilarated the impatient, and confounded the honest. A great deal could be and was made of the Lexington business, and reasonably so: it offered up to the king's friends damning evidence of colonial intentions, and to the patriots it confirmed suspicions of ministerial tyranny. But as so often happens after such eruptions, all parties came quickly to realize that nothing had been resolved, and virtually everything was now open to question. For the good Whigs of Boston, at least, chief among these questions was this: what now? Townspeople woke on the morning of April 19 to the sight of thousands of troops—the number would grow to around 15,000 in the months ahead—circling their fair city. Young men from Massachusetts, Connecticut, New Hampshire, and Rhode Island—most bound by militia ties, but not all—had dashed to the area in an impressive show of patriot zeal. And now they stood at the ready, arcing from Cambridge to Dorchester, eyeing a roughly equal number of British regulars ensconced in the town proper. That is to say, there were twice as many military personnel in and around Boston as there were actual Bostonians. America's third largest city had become a garrison.

The American "army" was in truth not much to look at. Nominally under the charge of the ineffectual Artemas Ward, the soldiery was great in number, rather less so in terms of skill, experience, or discipline. This is not to imply, as is sometimes suggested, that it was a mob, or drawn from the dregs of the social order, or hungry and diseased. Not true. But they were getting bored, and if there is one truth that must obtain across all space and time, it is that lots of bored young men, armed, sequestered, and often quite drunk, will create problems. Aside from the immediate threat to the peace, these conditions have always imperiled the proper alignment of civic and military authority. No one could predict what might happen next; none saw the battles of Bunker Hill and of Breed's Hill coming a few months away. But enough grasped the seriousness of the situation to extend an official request for help. Someone needed to get in command of this situation and do it in a manner consistent with the best of America's common law traditions. And who might that be?

On June 15, 1775, members of the second Continental Congress gathered to decide on just this question. The pool from which they could draw was not conspicuously broad and certainly not deep. It did not take long, then, for all eyes to settle on the formidable figure of the tall, austere, and appropriately uniformed delegate from Virginia. It had been a long time—twenty years—since Washington had led troops into battle; he had never commanded an especially large force, and indeed he had never attained rank as a regular in His Majesty's service. But no one doubted his powers of command, not within earshot of those who mattered. The general could not have been surprised at his appointment, although he confided to friends his anxieties over what failure might mean for his reputation. Still, he wrote Martha, as "it has been a kind of destiny that has thrown upon me this service, I shall hope that my undertaking it is designed to answer some good service."[17]

Congress proved rather less ambivalent on the matter. The new commander in chief was officially charged with nothing less than "the maintenance and preservation of American liberty" and sent packing. Those selected to assist him included Major Generals Artemas Ward, Charles Lee, and Philip Schuyler; Brigadier Horatio Gates; and aides Joseph Reed and Thomas Mifflin. From Philadelphia, Washington set off on June 23 and made his way to New York City. There he received an address from the New York Provincial Congress, who saw fit to remind this man on horseback of a very important obligation. When peace came, as surely it must, "You will cheerfully resign the important Deposit committed into your Hands, and reassume the Character of our worthiest Citizen." Anyone at all familiar with the benighted record of conquering heroes, then and now, will find no need to search for any subtext in this language. Washington did not, and he replied in words even more resonant: "When we assumed the Soldier," he promised, "we did not [lay aside the] Citizen, and we shall most sincerely rejoice [with you in] that happy Hour, when the Establishment [of American] L[iber]ty on the most firm, and solid Foundat[ions, shall enable us] to return to our private Station in [the bosom of a] free, peaceful, and happy Country." A noble sentiment, this, and one about to be tested on many fronts.[18]

Turning north, Washington and company arrived in Watertown, seat of the Massachusetts Provincial Congress, on Sunday, July 2, and headed shortly thereafter to set quarters in Cambridge. Town and army were edged by fear; the severe action on Bunker Hill and Breed's Hill not a week before might well be followed by reprisals, and it was not at all clear that the army was in any shape to meet such demands as may be placed on it. The paperwork, for starters, was a mess: reports on provisions and supply proved hopelessly inaccurate, and men and families circulated in and out of camp and no one knew, really, how many troops stood in fact ready to serve. The situation was not entirely out of control, but just as importantly, it was not entirely under control either. The problem, explained an abashed Provincial Congress, was more owing to circumstances than to character. The men—amateurs all—were in truth "naturally brave and of good understanding, yet for want of Experience in military Life, have but little knowledge of divers things most essential to the preservation of Health and even of Life."[19]

That much might be said of all young men, of course, but it cannot remain true of young men in the military if the military hopes to remain in being for long. Washington, who was to famously remind his fellow citizens that discipline was the very soul of the army, was predictably mortified by what he now saw. Again, the local authorities conceded the reality: "The Youth in the Army are not as possessed of the absolute Necessity of Cleanliness in their Dress, and Lodging, continual Exercise and strict Temperance to preserve them from Diseases frequently prevailing in Camps." With this Washington could only agree, and he replied with typical restraint that he understood how singular the situation was: "The Course of human Affairs," he wrote, "forbids an Expectation, that Troops form'd under such circumstances, should at once possess the Order, Regularity, and Discipline of Veterans." Still, he trusted that the energy of his officers and obedience of the men would soon make up for these deficits, and these "Quali[ties,] united with their native Bravery, and Spirit will afford a happy Presage of Success, and put a final Period to those Distresses which now overwhelm this once happy Country."[20]

Optimism on this order begs to be challenged; it would not be useful or interesting without being tested. It is ultimately an expression of faith, an abiding conviction that the world as given might in spite of itself be transformed into a better version of itself. This is Washington's faith, forged by experience and alloyed with such principles of the common good that, taken together, enabled him to see the possible in the circumstances at hand. And thus seeing, he learned to act on behalf of that vision, to make kinetic that which might otherwise remain latent. To see what this process looks like on the ground, we might well visit Washington as he set about putting his new house in order in that summer of 1775. Several indicators of Washington's makeup will thereby suggest themselves. These in turn may serve as prompts for thinking about the art of discerning potential under less-than-promising circumstances. They are cast in the form of propositions for ease in shipping to the future.

First: it is easier to teach a civilian to be a soldier than it is to teach a soldier to be civil. In the context of America's emerging republicanism, this fact could not be clearer or more important, and Washington knew it. With the manifold horrors of the twentieth-century wars behind us, we might now take such things as obvious. Washington, on the other hand, never allowed himself, his officers, or his men to forget the stakes involved, no matter how apparently small the immediate issue. The commander in chief was staring at 15,000 mostly young men, many as far as they would ever get from home, and all of whom had by now scented blood. From the earliest General Orders, consequently, Washington insisted time and again that officers and men were to behave, in effect, as citizens.

And, second, what did this mean? It meant above all the assumption and exercise of a certain attitude, a manner of understanding oneself as a fit object of republican citizenship. This much achieved, it also meant crucially acting toward other citizens in ways that affirmed the bonds of mutual obligation and rights. A fair amount of all this may be counted the stuff of camp law. Still, Washington knew there was more to it than cider house rules; ultimately, it was a matter of self-respect. That is why, for example, he was so insistent on chapel attendance, temperance, and cleanliness. Within a week they were being ordered to take care of the "Necessaries [outhouses]," to clear the grounds of "all Offal and Carrion," and "all Filth & Dirt removed from about the houses." Soldiers were whipped for drunkenness and directed to observe Congress's fast day declaration through confession, prayer, and appeal for divine assistance "to avert the Desolation and Calamities of an unnatural war."[21]

With the enemy well positioned in town and in harbor, its intentions unclear, we might wonder at this attention to detail. In the event, of course, Washington and staff were wrestling with everything from provisioning plans to military justice to the construction of siege machines. And yet among the orders and correspondence, we cannot help but marvel at such seeming minutiae; this is, after all, the commander in chief of the American army. Again, the answer must lie near to hand, where he saw in the daily comportment of his men the makings of greatness—or indeed of failure on an epic scale. To recall the citizen within the soldier was first to teach him to acknowledge and respect himself as a citizen; it was, second, to extend that knowledge in recognition of the essential citizenship of others. This recognition was in turn to be embodied through acts of respect for the rights of others; there was nothing airy, whimsical, or otherworldly about it. It meant this: leave the farmer's cows alone; ask first; stay out of the orchard; and for the sake of God and the fair sex of Boston, stop swimming buck naked in the Charles River!

This ethic of practice seems key to understanding Washington's distinctive contribution to republican thought generally and to his brand of pragmatic idealism. The following passage so perfectly captures its tenor and import that it must be quoted at some length. It may help the overall analysis to keep this question in mind as the language unfolds: could the sentiments here expressed conceivably be mistaken as those of any other major military figure between the time of its utterance and our own?

> General Orders
> Head Quarters, Cambridge, July 5th, 1775.
> Parole, Bedford.
> C. Sign, Cambridge.
> The General most earnestly recommends, and requires of all the Officers, that they be exceeding diligent and strict in preventing all Invasions and Abuse of private property in their quarters, or elsewhere[. H]e hopes, and indeed flatters himself, that every private soldier will detest, and abhor such practices, when he considers, that it is for the preservation of his own Rights, Liberty and Property, and those of his Fellow Countryman, that he is now called into service; that it is unmanly and sully's the dignity of the great cause, in which we are all engaged, to violate that property, he is called to protect, and especially, that it is most cruel and inconsistent, thus to add to the Distresses of those of their Countrymen, who are suffering under the Iron hand of oppression.[22]

Washington did not discover the concept of the citizen soldier and was neither the first nor the last to seek after its best realization. But he did assist materially in the invention of a modern ideal: the citizen, who, on becoming the soldier, becomes a better citizen for it. Superintending this ideal was a commitment to civil-military relations both frankly instrumental and deeply principled; armies fight better when they are supported by the people, and through such support the people remain something worth fighting for. Did the principle and the practice always bear each out?

Certainly not; they never do. But Washington installed from the very beginning a set of expectations that they should, and he communicated them forcefully and often; he punished men who violated them and rewarded those who abided by them, and he never forgot that these were American boys. "If he had been demanding and stern when necessary," Don Higginbotham concludes, Washington "had nonetheless treated their sons and neighbors as free men rather than as European mercenaries. He had, in addition, paid strict 'attention to the civil constitution of this colony.' The latter, even more than the former, was an incredible accomplishment in the morning of a war and a revolution."[23]

None of this is to suggest anything close to perfect equipoise. When it comes to civil-military relations, at least, that much is fantasy. And indeed, the realities on the ground continued to exasperate Washington throughout the summer, into the fall, and well beyond. By August he complained to Richard Henry Lee of "an unaccountable kind of stupidity in the lower class of these people," lamenting that "there is no such thing as getting Officers of this stamp to exert themselves in carrying orders into execution." The general would take some heat for letting such views get aired publicly; he regretted as much, said so, and moved on. That does not mean he ceased to think similar thoughts, of course; safe to say, every commanding officer in the history of warfare has groused about the men. The important point is that Washington never abandoned faith in the capacity of soldiers to act as good citizens and of citizens to wage war effectively.[24]

The months fell away busily that summer and fall. Thomas Gage, feeling much put on, ceded authority to William Howe in October; Washington and Benedict Arnold set their sights on Canada; an America navy was contemplated; and men looked forward to the termination of their tours at year's end. By early March of 1776, the firing would begin from Brooklyn Heights and continue until the British guests, having long overstayed their welcome, exited Boston Harbor in search of more accommodating hosts. In less than a year, then, New Englanders had gathered themselves as a fighting force, if not an army, exactly; had been disciplined and taught to thinks as soldiers—and therefore as citizens; and in the end had managed to expel the greatest imperial power on earth from its midst. Now, that is a remarkable fact, made possible by a kind of leadership best exercised in the art of transformation; it is an art that establishes its ethical grounds by bending change to the service of the common weal. Effecting these ends required both a kind of instrumental intelligence and a super-intending faith in the republican experiment. The American Revolution, the historian John Shy once wrote, offered up a "political education conducted by military means." If so, Washington may be counted a founding teacher, perhaps, and the lessons he learned in that summer of 1775 he was to carry with him to the end.[25]

REPUBLICAN FRIENDSHIP AND THE POLITICS OF AUTHORITY

The story is probably not true, but it must be told again. A small group of distinguished delegates are gathered at a reception capping the day's work of constitution making during the summer of 1787. Nearby: His Excellency. Casting their eyes at the august Virginian, several members comment on his austerity and reserve. Gouverneur Morris objects that such a view, though widespread, does his friend an injustice. Alexander Hamilton, quick as ever to mischief, calls Morris on the point and wagers drinks and dinner if he, Morris, will engage his new friend in a casual exchange of pleasantries. The affable New Yorker takes the bet and crosses the room. After the requisite pleasantries, Morris rests his hand on Washington's shoulder, and says, "My dear General, I am very happy to see you look so well." The dear general is not amused and says nothing; the hand is withdrawn, and Morris retreats a wiser man.[26]

If not true, it should be, because the story captures so efficiently the curious matter of Washington's interpersonal relations, his capacity for friendship and its attendant rituals for a man at once wholly self-contained and deeply attuned to public life. There he is, after all, at a reception, glass of Madeira in hand; then, too, Morris really was a friend, and so for that matter was Hamilton. In short, it takes no great stretch to imagine such a scene unfolding. More importantly, it helps us ask after the nature of Washington's habits of comportment with others, how and why he forged the relationships he did, and to what effect. These questions are worth asking here because they matter to our understanding of what he brought at length to Federal Hall and the nation's first office. We will find answers most readily and, I will suggest, most convincingly, by seeking first to locate the structure of convictions on which these relations are based. That structure has everything to do with authority.

The truly powerful are not much like most of us. For them, authority is less a way of acting than a way of being. It is ingredient to who they are; authority helps them make sense of themselves and the world in which they must operate. Power orders, sanctions, and puts itself on display; it is given effective expression when such expression sustains the conditions of its own possibility. This is why power is in many respects deeply conservative: such change as it seeks to exercise presupposes an already established set of personal and cultural affordances. These abstractions may be forgiven if they help us see Washington from a certain and telling perspective, where friendship and other forms of interpersonal relations are extensions of his deeper commitment to power and ultimately to the kind of authority such power makes possible. Washington's case is complicated, as it must be, by the unique sources of his authority, his personality and Virginia heritage, and his military and political experiences.

In the following section, I suggest how we might use friendship to think through Washington's conception of authority and how it helped fund his gift to American republicanism. After establishing a few general considerations, we will turn to a brief case study having to do with our subject and the redoubtable Nathanael Greene. In this way, I hope to demonstrate that Washington brought to the presidency a distinctively republican vision of how power ought to function, on what authority, and for whom it is legitimately exercised.

FRIENDSHIP, REPUBLICAN STYLE

He was, noted Edmund Morgan, "the aloof American," a man who for all the dance lessons, civility handbooks, levees, and endless visitors and prodigious correspondence seems fated to a legacy of Stoic remove. Unfailingly polite, Washington was yet, confided the Pennsylvanian William Maclay, "a cold, formal man. No cheering ray of convivial sunshine broke through the cloudy gloom of his settled seriousness." No one doubted his dignity, of course, but even Abigail Adams thought it "forbids familiarity," and Timothy Pickering could not help but note that he possessed a "steady, firm, and grave countenance and an unusual share of reserve, forbidding all familiarity." We might indeed and with some reason admit from the start that George Washington had only one real friend in his life; he loved her as he did no one else, through it all, and until the day he died. But reserving to

Martha a place of her own, we can still arrive at a set of modest but illustrative generalizations about those to whom he was close, those men who wished, perhaps, to claim something like a special place in the general's large but formidable heart.[27]

Washington could not claim many truly close friends, and he seemed to like it that way. After forty years of civil and political action in the field, he arrived in New York City in the spring of 1789 with remarkably few intimate relations; these, in turn, would predictably constitute the core around which his administration would operate. Not that the center was especially stable: key figures entered and exited, several deeply disaffected—if not with the president, then certainly with his Federalist counsel and each other. We are thus obliged to note that not all Washington's friendships prospered and grew. Among those luminaries who for various reasons fell from the orbit included George Mason, Charles Lee, Jefferson, Madison, James Monroe, Joseph Reed, and, for more obvious reasons, Benedict Arnold. Through the years, Washington had learned to be more patient with the shortcomings, failures, and excesses of others and had developed, even, a certain fondness for faults recognized in younger versions of himself. But like most great men, he had absolutely no tolerance for what he perceived as betrayal: this he never forgave, whether it came in the form of outright treason, as in the case of Arnold, or in the political apostasy of a Mason or a Patrick Henry.

What can we say more positively about those with whom Washington did manage to sustain long and productive relationships? A rough profile illuminates at least a few characteristics worth noting; we need not make more of them than necessary, and it will not be difficult to cite exceptions. Together they may yet carry some explanatory force. We note, for example, that he tended to draw younger men, most at least ten years and some a generation his junior. Put another way: can we think of a single individual during Washington's adulthood who might count as a confidant, mentor, or authority figure as old or older than he? Even Marshall had his General John Pershing. His Excellency rather took energy, insight, and love of a kind from men much younger and less experienced, more unsettled and less feted, but men who, to a one, aspired to greatness in ways he understood and indeed cherished.

A second trait seems equally suggestive. If we locate, say, Daniel Morgan, the great battlefield tactician of the war, on one end of a social spectrum and Lafayette on the other, it becomes readily evident that Washington's version of friendship was not in any apparent way distorted by considerations of what we might now refer to as class. One needs to be careful, to be sure, given our profoundly varying views on these matters. In context, however, it bears acknowledging that his closest associates included a wagon trainer, a Boston bookseller, a Rhode Island iron forger, several lawyers, Virginian squires, a French nobleman, and a "bastard brat of a Scots pedlar." This much seems not trivial, but what are we to make of it? The point is not to imply that Washington was particularly ecumenical in his choice of confederates; that is not true at all. Nor is it to invoke notions of sociability, sympathy, or democratic inclinations that may help soften the adamantine features of our aloof American. That is false romanticism, merely. The question insists that we look more closely at the composite portrait of Washington's fellowship and then to a set of conclusions about the habits of character he brought with him to the nation's first inaugural moment.[28]

They tended to be young or younger, these friends. What else can we discern of this small coterie that may help advance our account? Notably, several had been raised in the absence of one or both parents; a few had experienced decisive breaks with their elders over matters of faith or career. Washington lost his father at age eleven and was never close to his mother, who not once appeared to have found joy in her son's achievements. What effects this may or may not have had on Washington is unclear, but we do know that those who remained closest—Henry Knox, Greene, Lafayette, and Hamilton—arrived in a time of profound unrest and forged their relationships on the fields of war. More than any other theater of shared experience, battle tightens the sinews of mutual commitment, shared vision, and sacrifice. These are ancient truths grown clichéd, perhaps, but nonetheless relevant. We simply cannot understand the character of America's first civil magistrate without appreciating the fact that he was and remained the country's commander in chief.

For all the obvious differences in background and temperament, Washington's team demonstrated from the very beginning a strikingly similar set of traits. No student of the war, nor indeed of the early republic, can fail to be struck by how amateur it all was, how improvised, sometimes reckless, at times brilliant, how contingent and accidental it could all seem. This much can be said of all wars, to be sure, and has, but the sheer amateurishness of the American host remains a matter of astonishment. Equally remarkable were the individuals who, possessing scarcely anything in the way of military experience or formal training, managed to insinuate themselves into the requisite leadership positions. Here, too, the role of accident must be given its due, but there are reasons why it did not just all fall apart—a prospect not a bit implausible at the time. Chief among them is the happy convergence of two forces: the commander in chief knew talent when he saw it, and those with talent knew how it might best be developed, directed, and rewarded. How else to account for an obese bookworm emerging as the patriots' chief artillerist, and a very good one at that? A disaffected Quaker with a bum knee racing Charles Cornwallis to the Dan, winning, and turning the south for good? An illegitimate Caribbean aide-de-camp, soon to be mastermind of the new nation's financial system? A twenty-year-old Frenchman with a halting command of the English language and eventual namesake of counties and towns throughout the land? Among them, Knox, Greene, Hamilton, and Lafayette could boast no more actual military experience than today's Reserve Officer Training Corps student. What then did they have that Washington perceived, and what did they offer in turn?

In a sense, of course, the answer cannot surprise. Washington's comrades possessed precisely those traits we would expect a beleaguered leader in any arena to find desirable, indeed absolutely necessary. They were self-evidently talented, as if by nature equipped to exercise native intelligence and ready acumen despite limited experience. Knox, Greene, Hamilton, and Lafayette were autodidacts; Hamilton alone was the beneficiary of any real formal education. Within a decade, each became experts in the crafts of war and civil government through reading, trial and error, persistence, and sheer hard work. None of this is likely, moreover, without unwavering ambition. These were bright men who believed themselves destined to great things, and they had every intention and used every means to make sure that they were granted the opportunity to succeed.

There were moments of struggle, certainly; when tensions arose, it was almost always because one or another thought his path unfairly blocked— Greene straining against the bit imposed by appointment as quartermaster, Hamilton squirming as a mere aide to the general, or the Frenchman pining for command on the field. They felt the sting of others' promotions, as officers will; resented slights, real and imagined; and grasped after the next chance as a matter of habit. Such ambition is often, though not always, driven by the need to overcome. Greene lamented his want of a liberal education, Knox his inexperience, Hamilton his ancestry, and Lafayette his youth. They did overcome, however, because they capitalized on raw talent through self-discipline, prodigious capacity for hard work, and old-fashioned grit. If we are tempted to think such qualities as a given, a brief reminder of how the British leadership comported itself on the ground may help sharpen the point. Washington's command structure involved no mistresses on the side, destructive personal animosities, drunken farewell parties, or court intrigues. When problems along these lines arose, as they must over eight years of conflict, they were dealt with summarily: either by eliminating the source altogether, as with Charles Lee; removal from command, as with Horatio Gates; or cool distancing, as with Anthony Wayne, Monroe, and Mifflin. For all their initial lack of experience, the group that held fast and closest to the general remained trusted leaders because, in the end, they earned it. That is how real meritocracy works.

A final set of observations on the nature of Washington's friendships and its relation to authority will help conclude this phase of our account. Here we are concerned to identify some generalizations about how such friendship gets communicated and about how Washington and his men typically interacted, spoke, and wrote to each other. This, too, is important, because we know that such language use is scarcely incidental to the creation and maintenance of such relations. More broadly, it has significant implications for certain ideals of republican power that we ignore at our peril.

Today's readers can be startled—perhaps dismayed—by the vast amount of correspondence and other writings produced by major figures of the age. This is not altogether an unreasonable response; the published volumes stretch across the library shelves at formidable length. On the other hand, they provide a movable feast—and the temptation to pluck from such rich offerings is probably irresistible. Either way, generalizations must be extended carefully and with due respect for limits. That said, a finite number of characterizations about the habits of interaction between and among members of our group do seem warranted by the sources. For purposes of efficiency, we will take Nathanael Greene as a case in point, with the understanding that with variations, much the same may be observed about the others. Together, Washington's friends show themselves to be loyal without truckling; frankly ambitious but within culturally acceptable limits; physically tough and often courageous, though seldom reckless; prickly at times, prideful, and demanding. These very human qualities, some rare, some not, invariably find expression as the generals navigate their way through the war and its aftermath.

There is predictably the requisite formality and rituals attendant to eighteenth-century epistolary practice, the crisp directives, reports, and general orders we expect of sound military prose. Many of Washington's missives, or at least those written under his name, are nearly perfect specimens of the genre. Here is a brief note to Greene early in the Arnold business: "Dr Sir: I request that You will put the Division on the left in motion as soon as possible, with orders to proceed to Kings ferry where [or before] they will be met by further Orders. The Division will come on light, leaving their heavy baggage to follow. You will also hold all the Troops in readiness to move on the shortest notice. Transactions of a most interesting nature and such as will astonish You have been just discovered. I am etc."[29] Washington was no Grant when it comes to the language of battle—no one is—but this is a marvel of concision, information, and even drama. And it is not unusual; modern readers may be pleasantly surprised to find how riveting, for example, can be General Orders. To the extent that Greene, like the others, found himself on the receiving end of such communications, he found Washington to be unfailingly direct, clear, terse; without ornament, pleonasm, or gossip; humorless, utterly without sentimentality; and genuinely respectful. In lieu of hundreds, in fact thousands of such examples bearing on the point, the following passage will perhaps suffice. It, too, is a gem of sorts, for reasons that will carry us into some concluding remarks. The year is 1780, very late. Major General Greene has just been appointed, at his commander's request, to assume responsibilities for the southern campaign. It had not been a good year: the usual financial problems, only worse; Arnold's treason; Lincoln's fiasco in Charlestown; and Gates's at Camden. With all eyes, including British eyes, now turned south, Washington writes from his New Windsor camp on the Hudson to Greene. After assuring Greene of his support and that of his countrymen, Washington writes: "You have no doubt an arduous task in hand, but where is the man charged with conducting public business in these days of public calamity that is exempt from it? Your difficulties I am perswaded are great; they may be insurmountable; but you see them now through a different medium than you have ever done before, because the embarrassment of every department is now concentered or combined in the Commanding Officer; exhibiting at one view a prospect of our complicated distresses."[30]

We need not read too much into the text to note its tone and implication. Greene was by near consensus Washington's most talented general in the field. The Rhode Islander had in the brief five years since first meeting his commander risen through the ranks with remarkable alacrity; his counsel, though not always successful, was prized above all. He had demonstrated a tactical brilliance without rival and was poised now to seal his fame in the Carolina backcountry. Greene admired Washington as did no other man, and that is saying something; indeed, he named not one but two of his children after the general. Some believed him Washington's pet; he probably was. Greene certainly thought so, indeed basked in the prospect. But here we are brought up short; for as historians have elsewhere noted, Washington never really returned such effusions in kind. Though clearly impressed by Greene's talents and always ready to defend and promote him, there yet remains in Washington's communication a sense of reserve. Washington no doubt loved Greene, after his fashion, and grieved deeply at his premature death in 1786. But there appears something missing here. Or is there? An answer may be had, perhaps, by returning to the above passage. On one reading, we find virtually no evidence that these two men shared a close and binding intimacy; Washington's words speak of a stern and wholly unsympathetic reminder to his subordinate to buck up and get going.

On another reading, more plausible in context, this message could only have been sent to someone held in the greatest esteem; only Washington could write to Greene in this manner. The distance felt is not to be taken as an absence of regard; it is rather the achievement of that regard. If there is friendship in this, it is friendship of a very special kind, shaped by office and duty, vertically arranged, and sanctioned by their respective authority. Here, sentiment and affability are not missing; they are irrelevant. More broadly, Washington's relationship to those closest to him on the battlefield or in deliberative settings embodied what we might call a version of republican friendship. In a world heretofore marked by ancient traditions of patronage, nepotism, and clientage, Washington insisted now and later on a radically new model for the exercise of power. By the terms of this

model, a certain distance, sustained by a shared responsibility to principle, was necessary for the proper and prudent performance of authority.
Failing that distance, indeed, authority—republican authority—lost any
claim to legitimacy, and ceased, in fact, to be authority at all but instead
an especially viral form of old-world corruption. That, Washington would
not abide.

Authority thus conceived must inhere in a specifically republican disposition. Neither despotic nor democratic, it could only find its proper
ends free from the tyranny of the one or of the many. In this way, we can
think of such republican friendship as obtained between Washington
and his men as an instance of a more general structure of obligations. At
the heart of the republican experiment was a quest to discover a politics
located between the excesses of monarchy and of democracy. At their
classical extremes, both are, as Hannah Arendt reminded us, forms of cor-
rupted love—they operate by adumbrating the space necessary for free
and rational thought.[31] Republicanism of the kind Washington was fighting for, and would in time install politically, promised a solution to this
ancient dilemma. As with all great republican leaders, Washington loved
his country as he loved his men: so much that he would not make them,
however cherished, his own.

CHAPTER 2

On the Road to Philadelphia

Today's New Jersey Turnpike takes us from Mount Vernon to Manhattan in four or five hours. The Global Positioning System reckons the distance at 238 miles, alerts us to traffic ahead, and helpfully steers the driver around such problems as may be reliably counted on along this very crowded, very busy stretch of American real estate. Should we take our eyes off the road ahead, we might glimpse through the housing and industrial base pleasing enough hints of verdant lands and gentle swells; this can be green, even lush country, where big water of some sort is never that far away. Neither is town, center, or city. The route takes us up to Baltimore, from there to Philadelphia and through the Garden State, and deposits us in the heart of the nation's greatest metropolis. Breakfast in Alexandria, lunch in Manhattan: a promising start to the day!

By the time Charles Thomson at length rounded his way toward the front doors of Mount Vernon, he had been in the saddle for a week. In a few days, he would double back along the same route with the president-elect and his aide David Humphreys. This time, however, the trip would be punctuated by a series of remarkable performances, orchestrated rituals of affirmation that contributed powerfully to the sense of shared identity and aspiration on which the very idea of America depended. "We are a young nation," Washington had written to Lafayette, "and have a character to establish. It behooves us therefore to set out right, for first impressions will be lasting." His Excellency was by this point highly skilled in the craft of shaping both

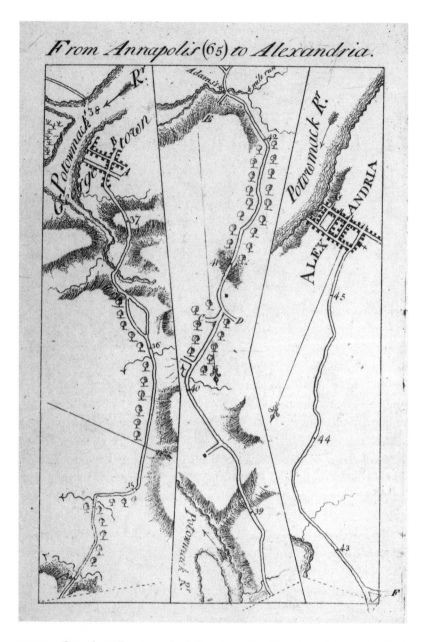

FIGURE 2 Christopher Colles, survey of roads from Annapolis to Alexandria, in *A Survey of the Roads of the United States of America* (New York: Christopher Colles, 1789). Geography and Maps Division, Library of Congress, Washington, DC, LCCN 84675230.

first and last impressions; now he aimed "to set out right" by playing to perfection his role in a conspicuously republican version of the royal procession. Along the way, but hardly by chance, Washington catalyzed a kind of chain reaction, where many Americans—so different, so raw—could be reconstituted as one people all turned in the right direction.[1]

What this process looked like and what it might mean to Americans at the time are the subjects of this and ensuing chapters. I hope to demonstrate that such rituals of nationhood, far from being empty gestures or mere ephemera, were rather decisive. They mattered because nationhood mattered to most and because no one mattered more to the nation's prospects than the figure now being feted along the journey to Federal Hall. But because this was to be a republic and because Washington was its exemplum, he must not matter *too* much. Put another way: just how does a people, presumably devoted not to men but to measures, resistant by nature and habit to cults of personality, go about the work of acclamation? In the ritualized and exquisitely rhetorical exchanges that mark the road to Philadelphia and beyond, we discover some answers to the question; they will be worth further reflection later, but for now let us get Washington on his way. Which route to take? Who to bring with him, whom to meet here and there? Where to sleep? What to say?

First, the route. At around 10:00 a.m., April 16, 1789, Washington, Humphreys, and Thomson will depart Mount Vernon and head to nearby Alexandria for lunch at Wise's Tavern; that night, our party takes its rest at Spurrier's Tavern in Georgetown (fig. 2). The next day finds them in Baltimore, but not for long; next morning, on April 18, it's up and out at 5:00 a.m. for Wilmington, Delaware. By 7:00 a.m. on Monday, April 20, they have arrived in Chester, Pennsylvania; then to Gray's Ferry on the Schuylkill, across the river, and into Philadelphia, a massive parade ushering its hero down Market Street and depositing him by early afternoon at the doors of City Tavern. That night, Washington will stay with his old friend Robert Morris and be off again in the morning, bound for Trenton and beyond.[2]

TOWARD DELAWARE

He would travel light, as always. No massive retinue or trains of baggage and hangers-on (fig. 3). Only two companions will make the trip: Thomson and Humphreys, both of whom we have already met. Tobias Lear, always

FIGURE 3 One of George Washington's coaches. Courtesy of Mount Vernon Ladies' Association. Photo: Robert C. Lautman.

essential, will remain at Mount Vernon to help with the others. Washington very likely had hoped to bring with him the redoubtable William Lee, his slave property and longtime servant dating back to prewar days. "Mulatto Will" quickly emerged as his owner's favorite, by all accounts a forceful, gifted, and physically tough character about whom we do not know enough. Lee had been at Washington's side during the first Continental Congress and through much of the war itself; lately, he had teamed up with Washington regularly on the hunt. But time, injury, and drink were taking their toll, as they do. Will's knees were worn out and he could make it no further than Philadelphia, where his owner delivered him to the ministrations of the Pennsylvania Hospital for care and rehabilitation. He will outlive the general and, emancipated by will, ease out his days on the grounds of Mount Vernon.

In the meantime, matters needed attention. For one who professed such longing for vines and fig trees, Washington managed to spend a good deal of time away from home and was thus practiced in the arts of preparation and leave-taking. There was, of course, the complex and often exasperating business of business: money, loans, land deals and investment schemes, lawsuits, and debts to be paid or called in. Estate-rich and cash-poor, like so many others of his station, now Washington faced the prospect of leaving Mount Vernon—who knew for how long?—uncertain of his financial affairs and, indeed, whether he had enough pocket money to get him to New York City.

Although it must have pained him terribly, the most famous man in America was finally reduced to hitting up a friend in town to ease his palpably felt "want of money." To Richard Conway he confessed that poor harvests and other problems had left him short, and he proposed "what I never expected to be reduced to the necessity of doing, that is, to borrow money upon interest." Would five hundred pounds be possible? It was. Several days later, however, Washington was obliged to write again. Could Mr. Conway see his way to an extra hundred on top of that? The original amount helped cover some debts but proved not enough to meet "expences of my Journey to New York if I go thither." Conway would come through for him; others would not, and Washington, his "necessities growing more and more pressing," was at length forced to threaten legal action to call in further resources. Such financial irritations, together with innumerable details attendant to a large and complex estate, crowded and often vexed the final months prior to departure. But they must be taken of, and responsibly; that much, at least, was expected of a chief executive.[3]

Not all was quite so grave. There was the question most travelers must face at some point: what to wear? Washington, we know, was a very serious man, as literal, self-possessed, and task oriented an occupant of the office as ever seen. Still, the man knew how to wear a suit, and that, too, mattered. Just a few weeks before heading north, he offered up a bit of advice to his nephew George Steptoe Washington. The letter itself is of the genre but telling for several reasons. "First impressions are generally the most lasting," the elder Washington observes. "It is therefore absolutely necessary if you mean to make any figure upon the stage, that you should take the first steps right." The general, let it be said, ought to know. There follow the expected urgings about minding one's education, friends, and morals. More space than might be expected is devoted to the protocols of dress; evidence, perhaps, that the author's youthful exercises in civility remained vital to his sense of self and others. George Steptoe, in any case, was spending too much money on clothes trying to impress others. Not necessary. "Decency and cleanliness will always be the first object in the dress of a judicious and sensible man," the older man advised, though "a conformity to the prevailing fashion in a certain degree is necessary; but it does not from thence follow that a man should always get a new Coat, or other clothes, upon every trifling change in the mode, when perhaps he has two or three very good ones by him."[4]

Why, during all the ado and dust of preparing for the greatest journey of his career, Washington paused to offer his wisdom on the matter of attire is perhaps not self-evident. It becomes rather more evident, however, when we recall the gentry from which he came, the work of self-fashioning of those who would arrive and remain at the table of the great, and the finely wrought sense of the symbolic he carried with him, always. We note, too, the republican emphasis on style, yes, but style of a kind: suits well-made, but not many; in the mode, dignified, but never garish; not rustic, but simple, elegant; republican.

These standards amount to a politics of dress, the importance of which cannot be stressed enough for understanding both the period generally and our story. More will accordingly be said about these politics later. Here it is enough to lean over Washington's shoulder in late January as he writes to his old friend and future secretary of war Henry Knox with a favor to ask. It seems from an ad in the paper that a good deal may be had on some "superfine American Broad Cloths." Would Knox procure enough for a suit of clothes? About the color Washington is indifferent, but he hoped that the materials were of good American stock. Knox made the arrangements as requested, and within a week before departure they were at Mount Vernon. The "cloth and Buttons," he told Knox, "really do credit to the manufactures of this Country." It was to be the suit, plain, brown, and well-made, in which the president-elect performed the rituals of inauguration.[5]

Such restraint ought not to be taken for false modesty. Washington was exceptionally well attuned to the expectations of others, and no one better understood the symbolic dimensions of power—republican power—than he. Whether it was the architectural and landscape design of Mount Vernon, the rituals of camp life, or the very clothes on his back, the president-elect grasped through instinct and experience that right appearances were essential to the experiment under way. Fellow Americans were in effect being asked to behold what they had wrought and so bear testimony to the promises of republican government. What they hoped to see thereby was a version of themselves, properly done up: simple dignity, strength and forbearance, and purpose and the discipline to carry it out. In the image of their leader the people would flatter themselves.

What would all this mean in terms of the trip itself? A royal procession? Here was a long and colorful tradition, to be sure, but one scarcely befitting the circumstances. On the other hand, Americans have always enjoyed a party, the parade, the festivities, food, drink, and rodomontade marking accession to office. Decisions must be made, though such planning guaranteed little. Thus it is with all travel plans, of course. "If I must go on to New York," Washington confided to a Philadelphian in early April, "and my wishes and inclinations were consulted on the occasion, they would lead me to proceed in as quiet and peaceable manner as possible." Little chance of that, and he knew it. On the same day, he responded to James McHenry's offer to put up our travelers in his Baltimore quarters along the way. Several such courtesies were to be extended, though few accepted. Washington thanked McHenry for the gesture but explained that he could not in good conscience impose his public self on the private station of fellow citizens. Besides, noted Washington, "The party that may possibly attend me, the crowd that always gather on novel occasions, and the compliment of visiting (which some may incline to pay to a new character) all contribute to render a public house the fittest place for scenes of bustle and trouble."[6]

And so it was that the nation's first chief executive spent nights on the way to his inauguration in "public houses," taverns scrubbed and done up, but taverns still. Washington seems not to have been able to resist quarters at the splendid home of Robert Morris in Philadelphia, but for the most part he held firm to his strategy of dignified restraint. The plan made a certain amount of sense on the road, but what about his ultimate arrival? More on this later, but here it merits brief mention for what it suggests about Washington's republican sensibilities. Back in March of 1789, Governor George Clinton had offered Washington the use of his home in the city until permanent accommodations could be secured. Again, the demurral: thank you, but "I shall make it a point to take hired lodgings, or Rooms in a tavern until some House can be provided." This, because "it would be wrong, in my real Judgment, to impose such a burden on any private family, as must unavoidably be occasioned by my company: and because I think it would be generally expected, that, being supported by the public at large, I should not be burdensome to Individuals." Better to leave all that alone, Washington reasoned, and keep the lines of commitment and obligation as simple and uncompromised as possible. To that end he sought Madison's help in arranging for quarters in the city. If a residence was not yet ready, a nice tavern would do fine. "I shall only add," Washington wrote, "that as I mean to avoid private families on the one hand, so on the other, I am not desirous of being placed early in a situation for entertaining. Therefore, hired (private) lodgings would not only be more agreeable to my own wishes, but, possibly, more consistent with the dictates of sound policy."[7]

Thus might republican style, among its other virtues, make for a little peace and quiet. Might, but not likely, and certainly not now. Of all the logistical problems besetting Washington on the eve of his journey, none posed such vexations of spirit as aspirants looking for work in the new administration. Here was a phenomenon as old as government itself, and he could not possibly have been surprised at the requests, scores of them, hundreds of them, that soon enough landed on his table. They came from near and far, from old friends and total strangers, and from down-and-out veterans of the war and fellow elites. They came from fathers on behalf of sons, former employers, rich and poor. They might be presumptuous or groveling, officious, pathetic, or, sometimes, all of these in the same letter of importunity. And still the letters came. "Scarcely a day passes," Washington complained, "in which applications of one kind or another do not arrive."[8]

Safe to say, no incoming executive has ever been free from such claims, and they never will. But though appeals for position may follow office taking as night follows the day, they represent an abiding test of political character. Most fail, or at least strain hard against the rigor of its terms; Americans, too, and little wonder. For all its familiarity, the seemingly humble application for office in truth codes within itself a very long, very complex history of power and its disposition. From ancient structures of affinity to the labyrinths of eighteenth-century patronage, spoils systems, Tammany Hall and beyond, until today, there seems always to have been readily available rationales for putting one's favorites close and keeping them close. If these affinitive practices work—and they do, often, for a while—it is because they provide the connective tissue through which power is kept intact. And what kind of power is this? At its heart, such systems are fundamentally personal in nature and function; they operate either through blood or kith relations, and, crucially, impose obligations and benefits on those who bestow as well as on those on whom the gift is laid. In practice, it is designed, when necessary, to override the circuitry of law. That is at once its genius and its most enduring, most toxic effect. In Arendt's terms, systems of affinity collapse the spaces of difference requisite to political judgment properly rendered. Republican politics depend rather on a structure of commitments closer to friendship than love: hence "measures, not men."[9]

Soon enough Washington would tire of explaining at much length his reasons for rejecting the endless pleas. But he did make the effort to respond to each source, however humble or exalted. In these brief accountings can be found a distinctively republican answer to why indeed such appeals cannot be met, indeed must not be met. In general, Washington's missives may be another expression of anti-European habits of political affinity. More specifically, he is insistent that the spaces of judgment—his own and that of the citizens'—be respected, kept open and unchained by obligations irrelevant to constitutional republicanism. Thus to Samuel Vaughn, who would seek a position for his son, Washington was as explicit as he was adamant. First: if elected to office, "I would go into it, without being under any possible engagements of any nature whatsoever." Second: "I would not be in the remotest degree influenced, in making nominations, by motives arising from the ties of amity or blood." Third: only these things genuinely pertain—"the fitness of character to fill offices, the comparative

claims from the former merits and sufferings in service of the different candidates, and the distribution of appointments in as equal a proportion as
might be to persons belonging to the different States of the Union." Without these criteria fixed as standards of appointment, he warned, the new
nation would have a very rough time of it indeed. Feelings will no doubt
be hurt and egos bruised. But for himself, Washington concludes, "a due
concern for my own reputation not less decisively than a sacred regard to
the interest of the community, required that I should hold myself absolutely at liberty to act, while in office, with a sole reference to justice and
the public good."[10] We shall bear these sentiments in mind. For now, it is
time to get on the road.

George Washington was fifty-seven years of age, and the years were
beginning to tell. He could feel it, as old soldiers always do when the energy
and ambitions no longer make themselves so vividly present. Vine and fig
tree. "The first wish of my soul," he had written a few months ago, "is to
spend the evening of my days in the lot of a private citizen on my farm."
By then he must have known—everyone else did—that this was fantasy.
The tally of electoral votes in early April confirmed the inevitable, and
the time had arrived for Washington to depart, once more. He was ready;
the flood of late business and details had been taken care of, mostly, and
besides, there was work to do. "Upon considering how long a time some
of the gentlemen of both Houses of Congress have been at New York," he
told Thomson, "how anxiously desirous they must be to proceed to business, and how deeply the public mind appears to be impressed with the
necessity of doing it speedily, I can not find myself at liberty to delay my
journey."[11]

By midmorning on April 16, the president-elect, Thomson, and Humphreys were off (fig. 4). They would not go far: Alexandria lay just a dozen
miles away, and here they must stop, for the town claimed Washington at
its own. He had grown up in its embrace, knew the people well, conducted
business there, socialized at its taverns, and bought and sold property.
The town was not large, numbering about 5,000 whites, free blacks, and
enslaved, but even before its official founding in 1748, Alexandria had been
and would continue to be a bustling and prosperous center of commerce,
shipping, and exchange. Scottish settlers had early displaced indigenous
peoples in favor of the tobacco market and related enterprises, including but
not limited to traffic in human bondage. During the War of Independence,

FIGURE 4   Howard Pyle (artist) and F. M. Kellington (engraver), *Washington Met by His Neighbors on His Way to the Inauguration*, 1889. The Miriam and Ira D. Wallach Division of Art, Prints and Photographs: Picture Collection, New York Public Library Digital Collections, 815006.

the town protected itself by positioning the *George Washington* offshore and had welcomed him on his way home in December of 1783. If, as Washington notes in his diary, he left Mount Vernon "with a mind oppressed with more anxious and painful sensations than I have words to express," here he might find solace of a special and welcome kind.[12]

At the heart of Alexandria lay an assortment of commercial and residential structures, neatly organized for maximum usage. Travelers, traders, and townspeople took their refreshment at one of the several well-known taverns located in its midst, including Wise's at Fairfax and Cameron Streets. Here Washington was received and so initiated a series of rituals that was to be rehearsed time and again, varying by place and people, never by sentiment. On hand to superintend the event was Mayor Dennis Ramsay, son of the venerable Scotsman William Ramsay, a local worthy and old friend of Washington. His Honor was himself a tobacco merchant and had served as an officer in the late war; ten years later, he would serve his commander in chief again—as a pallbearer. Today, he must assume the bittersweet responsibility of at once feting and bidding farewell to the town's celebrated son. First, of course, toasts must be downed—thirteen in all—and then a few words. Ramsay's address is not long, but it is heart-felt and even today moving, in its way. A few lines may suggest something of the tone and sentiment:

> Again your country demands your care. Obedient to it's [sic] wishes, unmindful of your own ease, we see you again relinquish-ing the bliss of retirement; and this, too, at a period of life, when nature itself seems to authorize a preference of repose. . . . Fare-well! Go, and make a grateful People happy; a People, who will be doubly grateful when they contemplate this recent sacrifice for their interest. To that Being, who maketh and unmaketh at his will we commend you—and, after the accomplishment of the arduous business, to which you are called, may He restore to us again the best of men, and most beloved fellow-citizen.[13]

Ramsay's paean to the town's favorite son set the tone and substance for many that would greet Washington on the road ahead. At once effusive and heartfelt, the address captures the pathos of separation and pride, as if in handing over one's prodigy to those he is destined to serve. Thus Ramsay rehearses the Cincinnatus theme and extolls Washington's achievements as soldier, patriot, and citizen—exemplar to the young, patron of learning and the arts, and, not at all incidentally, promoter of local interests. Alex-andria had done well by Washington, and it would be a long time before its citizens would, once again, welcome him home. "It may truly be said," wrote one correspondent, "that a more melancholy scene was never exhib-ited, than was now apparent on every countenance. . . . May ye! Who in future times shall aspire to the honor of being enrolled in the catalogue of American heroes, make it generally your aim to secure the love of your neighbors, and be equally fortunate in annexing the appellation of a good man, in their esteem, to the more dazzling one, of that, of the great!"[14]

It was now Washington's turn to stand before the crowd. He will deliver, orally or in writing, many similar responses in the week ahead. A brief com-ment, then, on his rhetorical powers may be appropriate at this early point. Washington was not nor ever claimed to be an orator, and no one then or now would ever have reason to put him in the same class as Henry, Rich-ard Henry Lee, John Hancock, or James Warren. The great man seemed not especially comfortable in front of audiences; he preferred the camp meeting, General Orders, and written missives as means for communicating what needed to be said. By nature and practice, Washington was reserved, sometimes to the point of appearing to others distant, cold, and disapproving. More positively, we may say that he was modest, as aware of his shortcomings as he was of his gifts.

At the same time, we are referring here to the nominal author of some of America's great testimonies to the civic tradition. Washington cannot be said to have composed these texts alone; he asked for—required—the pens of Humphreys, Hamilton, Madison, and others. Whatever his role in their creation, to Washington must nevertheless be assigned the source and delivery of, among other statements, the Newburgh Address, the 1783 Circular to the States, first inaugural address, and the Farewell Address of 1796. That is by any measure a record worth taking seriously. We may note, finally, that most of these statements function in the mode of what students of rhetoric refer to as *epideictic* address, that is, speech designed less to argue than to give maximum expression to what really matters in a given case. The artistry here is to provide through the effective use of language a means to disclose before others those essential values that may be otherwise occluded by events, issues, or other ephemera. Hence the address to the mayor and citizens of Alexandria and all those to follow will bend themselves toward a shared commitment to the fundamentals of civic life and republican government. In no sense can or ought such performances be dismissed as empty rituals.

And so he spoke. As Washington seems never to have said anything he did not believe, we may assume the sentiments thus expressed were his own, and they were, like Ramsay's, from the heart. The address in Alexandria, as with the others, is relatively short—six paragraphs—and may be found in its entirety in the *Papers of George Washington* and will not be reproduced fully here. A few passages will in any case help establish the commonplaces and tenor of the whole.

> Gentlemen: Although I ought not to conceal, yet I cannot describe, the painful emotions which I felt in being called upon to determine whether I would accept or refuse the Presidency of the United States. . . .
>
> Those, who have known me best (and you, my fellow citizens, are from your situation, in that number) know better than others

that my love of retirement is so great, that no earthly consideration, short of conviction of duty, could have prevailed upon me to depart from my resolution "never more to take any share in transactions of a public nature." . . .

All that remains now for me is to commit myself and you to the protection of that beneficent Being, who, on a former occasion has happily brought us together, after a long and distressing separation. Perhaps the same gracious Providence will again indulge us with the same heartfelt felicity. But words, my fellow-citizens, fail me: Unutterable sensations must then be left to more expressive silence: while, from an aching heart, I bid you all, my affectionate friends and kind neighbors, farewell![15]

It is worth reminding ourselves again of the novelty marking this occasion. Royal processions, of course, and the various ceremonies attendant to office taking, ministerial appointments, and the administrations of faith have been familiar to the texture of public life since time out of mind. But this was different: here was a native Virginian not a decade from camp, setting out to assume official responsibilities as the chief executive of a constitutional republic. Under the circumstances, then, it is also worth noting what the speaker does not say, for this, too, matters. We find nothing in the way of partisan aside or comments on the election; no appeal to residual anxieties or popular anger; religious sentiment is flattened by appeal to Providence; no reference to regional pride. The rhetorical craft rests, rather, in somehow constructing an image of oneself as compelling but not self-indulgent, of the audience as special but not unique, and of their collective convictions as one but not so abstracted as to be meaningless. This is art of a distinctive kind, designed on the spot, as it were, to invest what might otherwise be faux royalism with a fully republican, fully American sense of shared values.

Not everyone, in the event, was convinced. Although any explicit criticism of His Excellency was conspicuously muted, some felt the military cast of his receptions along the way a bit much. One Marylander took a dim view of such things and said so publicly. "The measure of conducting our beloved President through this state, by a military guard, to be fed out of the public treasury," he complained, "becomes everyday more odious and unpopular." Even James I "was conducted to the throne of England without a military parade—nor is military parade part of the splendor of a coronation in Great-Britain." But these killjoys proved rare; the people would have their parade, their militia, and horse out to escort "the first citizen of the union." For all their professed contempt of European-style pageantry, Americans were never above a good show, and the locals were not about to let the occasion pass without a bit of civil display. Such rituals of collective self-affirmation have always been integral to the creation and maintenance of shared identity, never more so then at the beginning of great things.[16]

Onward. The next leg of the journey would not be long: Alexandria to Georgetown, southwest of Baltimore, was about twenty miles. Escorted out of town by a host of well-wishers, Washington and company were in turn received by an escort that evening and settled into Spurrier's Tavern for the night. Today a sign on its former premises boasts that he found repose there "at least twenty-five times between 1789 and 1798"; if so, we may assume that on this night Washington found the accommodations satisfactory. Taverns in general were undergoing something of a renaissance in late eighteenth-century America. Though not what we would recognize as hotels as such, many were being built or renovated to welcome a more demanding class of travelers. New York, Philadelphia, and Boston would see major construction in the years ahead, and even down market establishments were paying more attention to the menu, drink, bedding, and entertainment expectations of such customers. Certainly on this night the proprietors of Spurrier's Tavern could be counted on to fluff the pillows and air the room for the illustrious company.

Early next morning, on April 17, the party was up and on the way to Baltimore. With a population of 13,000, Baltimore was the country's fifth largest "city." As with most other commercial centers, however, it was growing fast, and its boosters were anxious to make the most of Washington's arrival. If the president-elect really believed he might enjoy a quiet time of it on the way to New York, by now such hopes must have seemed delusory. Civic leaders had arranged for a "number of respectable Inhabitants of Baltimore" to meet and usher their guest to his quarters, cannons roaring, and from there to the Fountain Inn.[17]

On this very day, men were busy in New York conspiring to provide the greatest spectacle of them all. The Senate had already asked John Langdon, William Samuel Johnson, and William Few to make the requisite arrangements. The House added to its reception committee Elias Boudinot, Theodorick Bland, Thomas Tudor Tucker, Egbert Benson, and John Lawrence. Together, they were assigned to "receive the President, at such place as he shall embark from New-Jersey for this city, and conduct him without form to the House lately occupied by the president of Congress; and that at such time thereafter the President shall signify, it will be most convenient for him, to be formally received by both Houses." Of all this Washington was perhaps vaguely aware, but a letter on this day from John Jay assured him that at least a residence had been secured in the capital city.[18]

Back in Baltimore, meanwhile, the festivities were already well away. The city could not match New York's resources, but it could certainly try, and did. Washington was informed by authorities that he was to be met by a party on horseback who were in turn directed to organize themselves into files, and, meeting their guest, "will open to the right, and left; And, if your Excellency will please to pass through, they will wheel into the rear, and follow your suite to town." By six o'clock that evening a select gathering sat down for dinner at the Fountain Inn for what would become the second verse of America's republican procession. The meal was no doubt long, diverse, and of prodigious quantity; the drink probably Madeira, and plenty of it; the conversation animated and, perhaps, a bit self-conscious. At length an address must be made, and it was. We do not know who delivered it, but the text was signed by the Irish-born physician and delegate James McHenry; prominent merchant and veteran Nicholas Rogers; the famed naval officer Joshua Barney; former cavalry captain Paul Bentalou; local lawyer Robert Smith; former brigadier general and first commissioner of the Port of Baltimore, Otho H. Williams; future mayor of the city Thorogood Smith; former major John Swan; former major and regimental paymaster John Bankson; and William Clemen.[19]

These were men of consequence, representing a formidable combination of military, political, and commercial achievements. Now they were gathered to acknowledge, in a sense, their collective reason for being, or at least for being a collective. We are reminded again, accordingly, that while it may be tempting to wave away their words as mere fustian, it would not be wise. We need only bend ourselves to the sentiments expressed and appreciate their context to quickly see their import. A brief selection will perhaps encourage us along these lines.

The good citizens of Baltimore had every reason to conclude that

under the administration of a Washington the useful and ingenious arts of peace, the agriculture, commerce, and manufactures
of the United States will be duly favored and improved, as being
far more certain sources of national wealth than the richest mines,
and surer means to promote the felicity of a People, than the most
successful war.

Thus, Sir, we behold a new era springing out of our independence, and a field displayed where your talents for government
will not be obscured by the splendor of your military exploits. We
behold, too, an extraordinary thing in the annals of mankind, a free
and enlightened People chusing by a free election, without one
dissenting voice, the late Commander in chief of their Armies, to
watch over and guard their civil rights and privileges.[20]

These were not idle sentiments. Baltimore's citizens were keenly attuned
to the commercial and political stakes inherent to the republican experiment; they knew, too, that there could be no absolute guarantees against
its potential for abuse. Not the least of these, of course, was the fact that
Washington had been thought by most to be America's man on horseback,
and history did not favor the odds of such an arrangement. Only six years
separated the inaugural from the near miss at Newburgh, when he was
obliged to quell a near mutiny among the officers. True, the commander
in chief had effectively defanged that threat to civil authority. Could he
be counted on to do so again should a similar threat arise? Yes, he could:
"And now, Sir," his hosts declared, "by accepting the high authorities of
President of the United States, you teach us to expect every blessing that
Can result from the wisest recommendations to Congress, and the most
prudent and judicious exercise of those authorities." The commonwealth
had been secured by arms, they understood, but it could be kept only by
civil means. And they trusted Washington to act on this principle—they
trusted him because it was "from the tenor of your whole life, and your
uniform and upright political principles and conduct that we derive the
fullest confirmation of our hopes."[21]

We might in our time refer to all this as the politics of character. In
the context of his time and circumstances, Washington's character *was*

his politics. The rest—policies, laws, appointments, and so on—were, not merely, but primarily expressions of that character. In this as in other attributes, Washington was unmistakably a man of the eighteenth century. Presidential politics have always been to a greater or lesser extent about character, of course, but never again so explicitly and with such agreed-on norms of what counted for probity, decency, and authority of a just and sanctioned kind.

The textual record of his addresses on the way to Federal Hall provides us with an exceptionally rich resource for seeing how Washington hoped others would see him; that is, how, in part, character in this sense worked. As Aristotle insisted in his treatise on the art of rhetoric, ethos—intelligence, character, goodwill—was not the property of the speaker alone; indeed, it could only make sense, could only be effective, if others collaborated in the process of its formation. Insofar as one's character defined who one was, then *to be* really was to be perceived. This was, at the time, often referred to as one's "reputation," a matter Washington took very seriously indeed. This, too, is why these speeches of response subordinate issues of workaday politics to more general considerations of principle and, always, character.[22]

Principle and character: the stuff of republican politics, as least in its natal moment. With virtually no precedents, the slate before Washington, his audience, and American citizens was essentially clean. This is rare enough. What one chooses to say under such conditions would seem then unavoidably telling of what the speaker holds to matter most. So it is with Washington: "It appears to me," he explains, "that little more than common sense and common honesty, in the transactions of the community at large, would be necessary to make us a great and happy Nation. For if the General Government, lately adopted, shall be arranged and administered in such a manner as to acquire the full confidence of the American People, I sincerely believe, they will have greater advantages, from their Natural, moral and political circumstances, for public felicity, than any other People ever possessed."[23]

To whom so much is given, so much is expected. Washington, though not of course Washington alone, helped write the code of "American exceptionalism" that was already winding itself into the new nation's genetic makeup. Much has been said ever since about the sources and effects of this trait; that is as it should be. At the same time, we can see readily enough in these performances a persistent concern for the moral capacity, rights, and obligations attendant to those so gifted by Providence. Rhetorically, the speeches operate by putting virtue on display, by thus instantiating the kind of character necessary for redeeming the republican promise. Hence what will become a recurrent theme: Washington has reconciled himself to the pull of obligation and fears himself incompetent to the demands of public office. "In the contemplation of those advantages, now soon to be realized, I have reconciled myself to the sacrifice of my fondest wishes, so far as to enter again upon the state of Public life. I know the delicate nature of the duties incident to the part which I am called to perform; and I feel my incompetence. . . . But having undertaken the task, from a sense of duty, no fear of encountering difficulties and no dread of losing popularity, shall ever deter me from pursuing what I conceive to be the true interests of my Country."

It would be a miracle if he were to leave office as esteemed as when he went in, he notes with no little prescience. "But in the present instance, that circumstance would be accounted by me of little moment, provided, in the meantime, I shall have been in the smallest degree instrumental in securing the liberties and promoting the happiness of the American people."[24]

In short order these brief replies to the local elite and, by abstraction, to the citizens at large will offer up a modest but important contribution to American public discourse. They have largely receded from the record today, but Washington's contemporaries understood, and appreciated, the sentiments thus expressed. "His replies to the various addresses of his fellow citizens," remarked a Bay State writer, "do the highest honour to his character in the complex view of a citizen and a statesman; it being difficult to determine, whether he appears most engaging in the amiable display of his feelings as a man, or of his virtues as a patriot." Most of the local addresses and responses were published in leading papers throughout the colonies, where readers from New Hampshire to Georgia might keep track of their new president's celebrated progress. For all the pageantry and unblushing encomia, this was still to be taken, emphatically, as a republican fete. Washington's fame, as one Pennsylvanian explained, "results entirely from the love of his country." Americans understood, as did their new leader, "that he is the first citizen of the union; and will experience more solid satisfaction in presiding over a willing nation, than the conqueror of his country could have felt when he faintly rejected the diadem, offered him by a servile and injudicious senate."[25]

Though no Caesar, Washington yet had rivers to cross and hastened from Baltimore Saturday morning north toward Wilmington and hence to Philadelphia. Here was familiar terrain, too, low and lush vales winding among the verdant hills. A pleasant leg, then, though longer than most. After forty or fifty miles the travelers decided to call it a day and spent the night in the environs of Havre-de-Grace, Maryland. Another long stretch greeted them Sunday, but the party managed to get into Wilmington by late Sunday night. Delaware's complex history and centralized location meant that, as today, it was at once well populated but could boast of no particularly large centers of population. The entire region was and remains rich in agriculture, trade, and human innovation. Geographically only Rhode Island is smaller, but like its diminutive cousin, the state maintained a proud and independent aspect that belied its size. The good people of Wilmington, in any case, were more than happy to host this product of a constitution they had been first (they would remind us, again) to ratify. A native Blue Hen on the scene of Washington's arrival reported that "all were on tiptoe of expectation, when his chariot appeared, driving slowly through the crowd, he, with hat in hand, bowing to the people, who responded by waving cloth handkerchiefs, and every face flashing, and eyes sparkling with joy, paying their respects in this rustic way to the Father of their Country."[26]

On Sunday evening, Washington, Lee, Humphreys, and Thomson were ushered into town "accompanied by a number of gentlemen of this State." At some point between his arrival and next morning the "President-General" was presented with two speeches of welcome, one by the local burgesses and members of the Common Council, another by the Delaware Society for Promoting Domestic Manufacturers. The commercial priorities of the region were made evident by both groups: civic and business leaders alike were anxious but hoped that the new order of things would so stabilize the region as to accelerate its claim on the nation's attentions and appetites. Wilmington's representatives looked to the future with some optimism; they put behind them the "disadvantages we have long experienced for want of a good and efficient government" and contemplated with satisfaction "the happiness and prosperity the citizens of this country will enjoy under a government so wisely planned, and which we flatter ourselves will be so well administered under your direction." The Society, in turn, promised to wear clothing of domestic manufacture only from here on out as testimony to the "federal and patriotic sentiments of the citizens of Delaware." Organized as a kind of early day booster club for local business interests, the Society similarly looked with confidence to the advent of a truly national government, their hearts now "elevated with pleasing prospects of a glorious reformation, especially when we contemplate the approaching period which will afford us the benefit of your superior abilities, disinterested virtue, sage direction, and illustrious example."[27]

Here we might pause and call to mind again the image of Washington's inauguration suit. Well-tailored and fashionable but made of sturdy homespun, it may stand in as a token of sorts for the symbolic and the material message Washington hoped to convey. Then again, it was no fleeting gesture at that; as his Delaware hosts together made perfectly clear, the promises of nationhood very much included economic revitalization. It would not be easy to achieve, as the decade ahead would prove; indeed, could not be wholly realized until after the country's second war with their British rivals in the early nineteenth century. For now, however, Washington could at least assure his audiences that the message was received loud and clear. Indeed, he told the Society, the "promotion of domestic manufactures will, in my conception, be among the first consequences which may naturally be expected to flow from an energetic government." That such economic gains must be underwritten by certain habits of virtue Washington thought a given. The aims of the Society were in any case "highly commendable," he concluded, and he proposed "to demonstrate the sincerity of my opinion on this subject, by the uniformity of my practice, in giving a decided preference to the produce and fabrics of America, whenever it may be done without involving unreasonable expenses, or very great inconveniences."[28]

TOWARD PHILADELPHIA

A fair amount of struggle then and now may be predicted in the final lines above; for now, there were miles to cover and ever more receptions to attend. By early the next morning of April 20, the crew was being escorted out of town and to the Pennsylvania line. From there they were received by several veterans who in turn directed their former commander in chief to breakfast at the Washington House in Chester. This was wise; Philadelphia still lay twenty miles away, and a very long day was stretching ahead of him. Wishing to make the most of the occasion, local citizens crowded the dining hall to "congratulate themselves upon this opportunity being afforded them to pay their respects to, and to assure you of the unfeigned joy that swells in their bosoms. . . . From this event they entertain the most pleasing expectations of the future greatness of the western world; indeed, they cannot but observe to your Excellency that the torpid resources of our country, already discover signs of life and motion from the adoption of the Federal Constitution." After a few words of thanks, Washington then pushed off for the largest, most elaborate and colorful such reception yet. Ahead—Philadelphia.[29]

The journey thus far had been a relatively restrained affair. Not entirely, to be sure; townspeople and civic leaders hoped to exploit the good fortune of hosting the national hero and enjoyed every bit of it. Washington was quite willing to play his part. This he did with his usual exquisite feel for the right gesture, the appropriate word, and conspicuous nod. Certainly, he was by now well-practiced in that special performance of the minuet so distinctly American. That these rituals of affirmation were in fact American—that is, not European—was important. Observers all along the way made a point of insisting that for all the hoopla here was no royal indulgence but a truly republican spectacle. "Patriotism appears no longer a dream—and the disinterested spirit of Washington," one exclaimed, "gives new luster to the dignity of human nature."[30]

Some, as we have seen earlier, proved less than enthusiastic about the military pageantry attending arrivals and departures, but not many. Washington's procession was more generally taken to be of a piece with a new chapter in history. The war of independence, the Constitution, the election, and indeed Washington himself—these were new things of the world, to be feted accordingly, that is to say in the republican style. A New Yorker surveyed the scene unfolding and could not help but remind himself that "the first magistrates of the Nations of Europe assume the titles of Gods, and treat their subjects like an inferior race of animals." Not so in America: Washington rather "delights to show, that he is a man, and, instead of assuming the pomp of Master, acts as if he considered himself a friend of the people." That so much could be said of a deeply conservative, enormously wealthy, slave-owning, Virginia squire will strike modern sensibilities as a bit much, and then some. But these things are relative; in context they are best understood as much as the projection of popular hopes as the reflection of hard realities.[31]

Philadelphians, in any case, loved a good party. They still do, but few celebrations were to rival the one being readied for our entourage heading into the city late morning on Monday, April 20, 1789. Philadelphians, too, are inclined to boast of their festival habits, and with good reason. By the late eighteenth century, the city had become expert at the arts of public address and had made their views known through street riots, marches, funerals, illuminations, salutes of artillery, and formal processions. More will be said of this in a bit, but here it is enough to register, as did one local, the "general joy that was displayed on this occasion." Like many others, he was convinced that such an effusion of popular sentiment "furnished a triumph, which surpasses all the pomp and pageantry of the most absolute monarch." Americans must prove themselves good republicans, yes, but they would out-celebrate their European rivals in the process.[32]

Washington knew that Philadelphia well knew its people and its ways, and he knew what was coming. To the rear went the carriage. Up came the magnificent white stallion that would take him the twenty miles to the bridge at Gray's Ferry, across the Schuylkill River, and from there to Second and Market Streets. Such time as he may have enjoyed on the trip for quiet reflection was over and would not return. Troops of horse quickly pulled up: they came from any number of areas in the region, bidding no doubt to put on display their own special claim to Washington's affections and respect. Soon Arthur St. Clair—veteran officer, former president of Congress, and current governor of the Northwest Territory—drew up beside the general. Theirs was and would continue to be a complex relationship; presumably, for the moment, they focused on the coming time. In this they shared in a pervasive, highly orchestrated, and necessarily transient ritual of unanimity. The travelers, as well as Philadelphians, and indeed all Americans were in effect rehearsing for a role in the spectacle of republican citizenship. Now, spectacles are nothing unless they command spectators, who in turn exercise the several means through which a republican people bear testimony to what they had themselves created. To the extent that such performances could be seen to succeed, could be given witness and sanction, then here was proof that the experiment was working. Thus a New Yorker reported of the day's events that the "fears of many honest, but scrupulous republicans, that the energy of the new government, might render it unfavorable to liberty, are at length subsided." Any such anxieties as Americans might have suffered over the prospects of monarchism, he rather optimistically concluded, "have been removed, by the election of their beloved Washington."[33]

Those of a more Spartan aesthetic might wince at the excess; more would stare and applaud the offering rising before the general's line of sight. "Such a scene presented itself," recalled one admirer, "than even the pencil of Raphael could not delineate." Again, local pride—but it is perhaps fair to say that though the Schuylkill had been ferried, spanned, bridged, and otherwise rigged for passage since the late seventeenth century, never had its crossing looked quite like this. The Gray brothers, bearing now the name of the pontoon bridge as well as the ferry, had enlisted the help of Charles Willson Peale and his daughter Angelica to design the structure. Drawings and eyewitness records, widely circulated through the print culture of the period, give us a brief but telling description. At either end of the bridge—he will enter east and exit west—Washington beheld "magnificent arches, composed of laurel, emblematic of the ancient arches used by the Romans," these arches in turn complemented by more laurel shrubbery running alongside, the effect of which "seemed to challenge even Nature herself for simplicity, ease, and elegance" (fig. 5). With studied dignity and pace properly restrained, the visiting hero nudged his mount to the boards and made his way across the waters.[34]

At about 140 miles long and several hundred yards wide, the Schuylkill is not an especially large river by continental standards. Where it begins and where it empties into the Delaware, however, has made it a very important waterway since well before European settlement in the area. Washington himself had crossed it as a matter of course before, during, and well after the war. But not like this. For this occasion, "eleven columns were plastered on the north side of the bridge," ran a report in the *Columbia Magazine*, "in allusion to those states which have ratified the constitution; on the south were two others, one emblematical of a new era, the other representing Pennsylvania." The resourceful Mr. Peale and daughter had saved their best for last, however, for perched above in the laurel-covered arches hid young Angelica. As Washington passed under to exit (fig. 6), so it was reported, "a civic crown was suspended from one of the temporary arches . . . and so contrived as to fall, by the aid of a little boy [*sic*] dressed in white, within a short distance of his Excellency's head as he passed under it." Legend tells us that he modestly avoided the laurel crown—naturally—nodded indulgently to the girl, and made his way finally to the familiar cobblestones of Market Street.[35]

FIGURE 5   James Trenchard and Charles Willson Peale, *An East View of GRAY'S FERRY, Near Philadelphia, with the TRIUMPHAL ARCHES, &c. Erected for the Reception of General Washington, April 20, 1789*. Prints and Photographs Division, Library of Congress, Washington, DC, LC-USZ62-342.

The city into which Washington rode that spring day was singularly well-disposed to welcome its illustrious guest. Colonial Americans and now citizens up and down the seaboard were by century's end veteran celebrants, heir to the rich and colorful traditions of folk rituals that had migrated with them to America's shores. Bostonians and New Yorkers would inevitably challenge the point, but as the new nation's largest city and, for now, busiest port, Philadelphia could boast of being the most vital—the most *interesting*—city in America. So its citizens said, at least, and did they not have a point? When something truly big needed doing—say, convening a continental congress, or forging the world's first modern constitution, or, soon enough, serving as the first permanent home to the federal government—then Americans turned to Philadelphia, did they not?

The city was about to undergo an extraordinary population spike in the coming decade, although it would cede first place to New York City as the country's largest. Then as now it was exceptionally diverse, though in different ways. Squeezed largely within a relatively compact space, the dominant English, Germans, and Scots-Irish lived near free and enslaved Africans, Irish, Welsh, and other immigrant groups. "Just strolling or riding a horse

FIGURE 6 *President-Elect Washington Crosses Floating Bridge (Gray's Ferry) on Inaugural Journey, Philadelphia, April 20, 1789.* The Miriam and Ira D. Wallach Division of Art, Prints and Photographs: Picture Collection, New York Public Library Digital Collections, ps_mmpc_042.

through the city's streets," concludes a team of city historians, "would have provided a linguistic adventure. Philadelphians heard a medley of tongues—not just different dialects of English but also Dutch, German, French, Spanish, Portuguese, Swedish, and Gaelic, as well as a smattering of African and Native American languages." Not surprisingly, this kind of admixture can make for a lively public culture, not all of it especially decorous or even legal. But they could put on a show when they wanted.[36]

When Philadelphians came together in the late eighteenth century, they took by habit to the streets. In this they were scarcely unique, and like other towns and cities they relied on European folk practices ranging from royal processions to public funerals, from guild marches to Lord Mayor's Day parades. These were by design fleeting affairs, momentary occasions where and when "ordinary" people—largely but not exclusively white and male—might assemble in public, cheer on the hero, protest the villain, listen to some music, eat and drink what one might, and with luck raise a little hell. Not too much, however, for these events were best conducted "in the utmost order and harmony." No festival better illustrates this convergence of folk memory and ritual, nascent democracy and emerging public sphere than the Grand Federal Procession of July 4, 1788. Like its sister cities, Philadelphia aimed to celebrate like no other the ratification of the federal Constitution. Not just a big bash—nothing less would do than "the most brilliant and interesting spectacle that ever occurred in the annals of the new world." To that end, civic organizers put on parade an estimated 5,000 members of various guilds, trades, professions, sects, faiths, schools, and offices. Music played, of course, and artillery boomed; James Wilson delivered a magnificent oration; and to wrap it all up, supper was served to 17,000 in an elaborate feast of thanks.[37]

Does all this suggest that Philadelphians were of one mind on the Constitution? By no means, and no one in their right mind would have assumed as much. Festivals such as the Grand Federal Procession—they were repeated from Portsmouth to Charleston—functioned precisely to conjure, if only for this day, a vision of what unity might look like in these unprecedented circumstances. Humans by nature or habit need to mark moments of birth through ritual; this need in turn bespeaks a profound desire for sanctioned community in the face of uncertainty, danger, and disintegration. As it was on July 4, 1788, it was now in April the following year, here in Philadelphia, then New York, and indeed every four years of inaugural celebrations thereafter. Albrecht Koschnik, an especially astute historian of such rituals, captures the point just right: "The ritualistic observances of national celebrations," Koschnik writes, "were attempts to legitimate the participants' aspirations to represent the nation by using a means that created an image of their own unity, and, ultimately, of national unity."[38] That is, we have reason to see in the reception accorded to Washington evidence of people habitually ambitious, bumptious, diverse, grasping, partisan, often violent, often generous, hypocritical and sincere who, at this time and in this place, had found in Washington a reason to believe that they, for all their ways, *just might* make it as a republican people after all.

Philadelphia was ready and indeed had been all day. Accounts vary as to how many of its 40,000 residents crowded the short route to City Tavern, but it is safe to say thousands. New Yorkers, keen as always to know what the competition was up to, read that the "number of spectators who filled the doors, windows and streets," had to have been "greater than on any other occasion we remember." And noise: there must be noise, and lots of it. And so "bells were rung thru' the day and night, and a feu-de-joy was fired" as Washington "moved down Market and Second Streets to the City Tavern." Riding with him now was Governor Mifflin, Arthur St. Clair, Attorney-General William Bradford, Chief Justice Thomas McKean, and Speaker of the Assembly Richard Peters. On the waters stood the *Alliance*, brilliantly festooned, and a Spanish ship "was handsomely decorated with colours of different nations." More noise! Artillery reports added a certain martial emphasis to the city's enthusiasm, while Christ Church pealed its welcome; "brilliant fireworks were exhibited in the Evening, at the upper end of Market-street, by that very ingenious and indefatigable artist, Mr. Anthony Wright, Sargent-Major of the battalion of Artillery."[39]

Here was Philadelphia on display, a role she had surely become accustomed to by now. More reason to stress, as observers did time and again, that such revelry was yet "extremely elegant and conducted with great propriety and decorum." Such restraint was not to be assumed and was never a given; this could be a riotous city, the nation's largest with a diverse population packed into a small zone on the river. Now would be the worst possible time for any show of excess, violence, or partisan spirit. To the Tavern then, where Washington and the chosen stepped out of sight for the scheduled 3:00 p.m. dinner. Judged by standards of the time, we may be confident that the food was hearty, ample, and washed down with plenty of wine and similar refreshments. And then, inevitably, would come the toasts. A writer for the *Pennsylvania Packet* reported that the diners raised their glasses to the following:

1. The United States
2. The Federal Constitution
3. The Senate and Representatives of the United States
4. His Most Christian Majesty, our great and good Ally
5. His Catholic Majesty
6. The United Netherlands
7. The State of Virginia
8. The Vice-President of the United States
9. The State of Pennsylvania
10. The immortal memory of those Heroes, who fell in defence of the liberties of America
11. The Members of the state General Convention

12. The Agriculture, Commerce, and Manufactures of the United States
13. May those who have opposed the New Constitution be converts, by the experience of its happy effects
14. Government without oppression, and liberty without licentiousness.[40]

Early Americans were a hearty breed of drinkers, when they could get at the stuff, and they usually could, one way or another. On such occasions as might be appropriate, and no doubt some that were not, celebrants often employed the toast as a way of giving voice to shared values and hopes. It is a homely ritual, not infrequently ending in squinted eyes and boozy sentiment; still, these dinner-table performances may offer up a kind of spontaneous testimony to what a given assemblage holds dear and what needs to be said before others and affirmed by all. We may with profit, then, read these fourteen toasts as a rough but reasonable index of what mattered to these people.

George Washington was still a formidably physical man, toughened by war and the road. He may be forgiven, however, if he at length put down the glass, pushed away from the table, and made for bed. He would stay not at the tavern but at the home of his friend Robert Morris, the renowned financier and Federalist. It had been a long day, as expected—the miles, the crowds, and dinner and drink. In the Morris mansion he would find repose and gather himself for the road to New York City. If he was of a mind, which is exceedingly doubtful, Washington may have given some thought to the requests for patronage that continued to pour in. Sharp Delaney, an Irish veteran and local businessman, hoped to be appointed Collector for the Port of Philadelphia; Benjamin Franklin's royalist grandson William Temple Franklin had the nerve to ask after a diplomatic position; and a local clock maker by the name of Robert Leslie thought he might be of service. From New Haven, Isaac Sherman wrote that he would take almost anything available, and Richard Bache, father of the future publisher of the *Aurora*, sought something in the way of the Post Office. And so it went on and on, well into his eventual administration. To them all Washington could only respond as he had to the others: he must be free of such obligations and offer such rewards based on merit alone.

On a more positive note, Washington might well have reflected on the addresses that had been extended during his brief stay in the city.

Among them, several must have been especially gratifying, and to them he had made a special effort to reply in kind. Seven years had passed since Henry Knox and others established the Society of the Cincinnati in Newburgh at war's end. Conceived as a fraternal organization of fellow and soon to be ex-officers, the Society had encountered unexpected censor from Americans suspicious of its allegedly aristocratic and secretive tendencies. Washington had then been as a matter of course selected its first president, but he was obliged in the ensuing dust-up to distance himself from its vaguely anti-republican ways. He nonetheless remained close to its members and knew many of them personally. How could he not? Presiding over the Constitutional Convention in this very city only a few years ago, Washington must have registered the presence of the Society that summer; more than a few of the entire assembly of delegates were known members of the Society.

The ubiquitous Thomas McKean, vice president of the local organization, offered on behalf of the Cincinnati a short but piquant welcome to its most distinguished guest. Members had good reason to claim him as their own, in a way. Together they had fought for independence, and together they had fought to exemplify and hold in trust those values worth the costs of freedom. "We have now the most perfect assurance," declared the Society, "that the inestimable rights and liberties of human nature, for which we have toiled, fought, and bled under your command, will be preserved inviolate." To their fellow citizens were likewise due congratulations, certain as they were that "their national safety and dignity are secure, and that they have the best grounded prospects of all that happiness, which a good Constitution, under a wise and virtuous administration can afford."[41]

The recipient of these kind words may have felt some satisfaction—and relief—in being thus welcomed by an organization whose leadership he had been so ambivalent in assuming. Pressed to caution by Jefferson and others, Washington had on the eve of the 1787 Constitutional Convention skipped the Society's annual convention in Philadelphia. At the moment, he confessed that "my mind has been deeply affected with a grateful sense of the attachment and aid which I have experienced from them, during the Course of our arduous Struggle for Liberty." Promising only to do his best, His Excellency concluded by thanking his old comrades "for the interest you so kindly take in my personal Comfort and Honor, as well as in the prosperity and Glory of the General Government."[42]

Exactly how these addresses and replies were staged remains unclear. It seems unlikely, though possible, that they were delivered orally; we can well imagine such an exchange, say, during a long meal as at the City Tavern. More plausibly, the address arrived in manuscript, and Humphreys in turn arranged to have Washington's sentiments returned in kind. This is speculation. But we can very clearly see that they functioned as a kind of two-step dance, where each party both leads and follows; ritually acknowledging and taking cues from the others, they perform an important if highly stylized version of what such communication ought to look and sound like in the early republic.

We may note, as well, that the addresses issued from institutions would continue to help define the shape of American culture. Thus to the military origins of nationhood was added its foundations in law, here expressed in the body and words of the Pennsylvania Supreme Court. It was an impressive roster: the apparently tireless Thomas McKean (1734–1817), who would go on to become the state's governor a decade from then; William Atlee (1735–1793), a prominent Whig before the war and now trustee of the University of Pennsylvania; Jacob Rush (1747–1811), the intensely conservative but faithful Federalist and brother of the more renowned Benjamin; and George Bryan (1731–1791), the Irish-born jurist and former president of the commonwealth. Like their cousins in the Society of the Cincinnati, these men were older, experienced, accomplished, and tough—a fact worth keeping in mind today as we read what might otherwise be seen a mere blandishment. No real cipher is required when we note the Society underscoring their military heritage; we hear these veteran officers saying that war mattered and so do they. And when we hear the Pennsylvania Supreme Court reflect on the meaning of Washington's arrival, we know them to be urging something more than polite applause: "We are duly impressed with the mercies of God in preserving you hither, in so many public and private dangers to which your person hath been exposed, and we hope and pray the same Providence will carry you through the great work (which seems reserved for you) of establishing justice, ensuring tranquility, promoting the general welfare, and securing the blessings of Liberty and Independence to the good people of your native country and their latest posterity."[43]

The cadence and phrasing of this passage was surely familiar to this veteran of 1787. Whether he was reading or listening to it, Washington must have understood with absolute clarity that he was being reminded that for

all the homage and noise attending the journey to Federal Hall, expectations would remain very high indeed. Did he need to be thus reminded? Of
course not—in one sense. In another, yes, because every chief magistrate,
no matter how exalted (especially the exalted), needs to be thus ritually
fixed within a sanctioned order and constrained by the rule of law. George
Washington was not an especially well-educated man; he was not much of
a farmer, really, and as a field commander the record is decidedly mixed.
A case can be made that even as president he was something less than one
might hope. But Washington understood power, as we have noted, and he
understood power in its republican aspect as did no one else at the time.
What does this mean? It means that he grasped its inherently paradoxical
nature: that though born of war, power enabled peace; that such freedom
as it granted must be governed by force; and that its fullest expression could
only be realized when restrained by the protocols of constitutional law.

It came down to winning the peace. The historical track record on this
score has been grim; nothing at the time, certainly, suggested that Americans
would somehow escape the fatal seductions of a Caesar or a Cromwell. But
they had every intention of bucking the odds, had in fact asserted a claim of
unprecedented strength on the future. For this they needed an agent or cat-
alyst to superintend the transition from Yorktown to Federal Hall. George
Washington was obviously that agent. For all the self-fashioning invested in
creating this role, however, we know that monuments do not build themselves. They are constructed from the needs, aspirations, delusions, fictions,
and dreams of those who might gain from their power. Stories get told of
these heroes, and if all goes well, they get told again, and then again, until
it is impossible to tell them apart—the hero and the story. This much is the
work of rituals in fastening the ties that bind a people—to family or faith,
to tribe or team, perhaps even to nationhood.

No Americans then or since have been more assiduous in this telling
than the good people of Philadelphia. They had been in the thick of things
well before the advent of war and would remain there during and after it;
they would indeed host the new nation's government as the capital city
for a decade. On this day, April 20, its civic leaders, notable among them
Mayor Samuel Powell and the city's Common Council, chose the occasion
of their guest's arrival to rehearse, once more, the essential plotline. When
freedom demanded battle, they recalled, the people answered, but they
were weak and the foe mighty. There arose then a Washington, and the way

seemed clear: "under your auspices they fought, they bled, and through unparalleled distress of war, you led them to freedom, the choicest gift of Heaven." The real victory, however, was yet to come; for it is one thing to prevail on the fields of battle, rather another to make good on the promises of a war thus conceived. Now came the crucial chapter in this story of republican nationhood. "Scarce had you retired to the calm retreat of domestic peace—when the civil rule which we had suddenly established, amidst the busy tumult of war, proved unequal to secure the blessings to be derived from a well digested constitution." And so the general was summoned again, "and presiding over our wisest councils, have handed to your Country a system of civil policy, happily uniting civil liberty with effective government. What then remained undone is now accomplished."[44]

Almost. Washington and company still had another four days on the road ahead, with the inauguration ceremony more than a week away. These miles and days, too, would be busy with the sights, sounds, and general to-do that crowded the course to lower Manhattan. For now it was enough to perform his part of the duet, to acknowledge the respect paid the person and office with his own simple gesture of republican good will: "When I contemplate the Interposition of Providence, as it was visibly Manifested, in guiding us thro' the Revolution in preparing us for the Reception of a General Government," Washington reflected, "and in conciliating the Good will of the People of America, towards one another after its Adoption, I feel myself oppressed and almost overwhelmed by the sense of the Divine Munificence."[45]

More addresses were to be offered that day and more responses delivered along similar lines. Though ritualized, they were not routine; though expected, such speeches had work to do. Thus the president and faculty of the University of Pennsylvania reminded Washington that it had bestowed on him an honorary degree at war's end: July 4. Now the assembled scholars hoped that he would remember that the "influence of sound learning on religion and manners, on government, liberty, and laws, will make it a favorite object in every civilized society: and the sciences, having experienced your protection amidst the convulsions of war, reasonably expect a distinguished patronage in the calm of peace." The president-elect could only stress his support for higher education, as indeed he would, not very successfully, in the decade ahead. He believed, in any case, that "we are on the eve of a very enlightened Era," and that ultimately "the same unremitting exertions, which, under all the blasting storms of war, caused all the sciences to flourish in America, will doubtless bring them nearer to maturity, when they shall have been sufficiently invigorated by the milder rays of peace."[46]

The "milder rays of peace" would prove rare enough in the coming time. Yet the men of the college were giving voice to a prominent and entirely understandable anxiety that the transition from war to peace—going on a while now, after all—be finally secured to republican advantage. For most of the interim it was not at all self-evident that a "United States of America" was possible or indeed even desirable. Now that it proved both, at least to enough, there remained the self-imposed obligation to tell the proper story of what just happened. Why? Because, as history tells us time and again, a people who do not know how to tell the right story about themselves at length cease being a people. Such an imperative in turn explains why it was so important to get straight the legacy of this war for the prospects of this peace. War must be made sense of, one way or another, and the stakes will always be very high. What was the American Revolution supposed to be about? What did it *mean*? These addresses allow us to see how cultural elites of the time sought to arrive at a convincing answer to these questions—convincing, that is, to themselves, to their immediate audience, and to their fellow citizens at large.

A rainy April morning in Philadelphia, and the crew must be off. As Washington left the city and headed east toward New Jersey, he received one last such communication from the Pennsylvania Legislature. Its members expressed themselves as grateful for the general's leadership during the war, and "by that impression we are taught to expect that the exercise of the same virtues and abilities, which have been thus happily employed in obtaining the prize of Liberty and Independence, must be effectually instrumental in securing to your fellow-Citizens and their posterity the permanent blessings of a free and efficient government." To which Washington replied in language at once familiar and deeply suggestive: "If under favor of the divine Providence, and with the assistance of my fellow-citizens it was my fortune to have been in any degree instrumental in vindicating the liberty and confirming the independence of my country, I now find a full compensation for my services in a belief that those blessings will be permanently secured by the establishment of a free and efficient government." Thus is nationhood composed in the call and response of a people and their past.[47]

CHAPTER 3

Between Past and Future

Trenton and Beyond

Tuesday morning, April 21, 1789. George Washington awakened in the home of Robert Morris to a Philadelphia rain. For five days now he had been on the road, feted, fed, sang to, and fed again. For a man so allegedly averse to ceremony, he must have felt trapped in an endless loop of hoopla, but he was yet a long way from Federal Hall, and he must have known there was more, much more, of this to come. The way ahead pointed first to Trenton, New Jersey, some thirty-five miles northeast of Philadelphia. Though a small town of under 2,000, Trenton and its environs must have loomed large in Washington's memory, indeed in that of the nation's itself. Here, in that otherwise wretched year not so long ago, he had prevailed over a Hessian post in the dead of a Christmas storm in his finest tactical work of the war. Washington may not have been a great general, but on December 26, 1776, he was very great indeed, and everyone knew it. Thirteen years later, His Excellency was to make a most triumphal return. The Ladies of Trenton would see to that.

The plan was to depart from Morris's impressive estate by 10:00 a.m. under the usual horse and escort. Washington must have chafed at the late hour—once a soldier, always—itching to get under way and put the miles behind him. The post road would carry the crew up along the Delaware River, through Frankford and Bristol, then past Bordentown and into Trenton, hopefully, by early afternoon. Not a blistering pace, but purposeful, and Washington wanted to get on with it. He had time then to rewrite the agenda, offering a plausible excuse: "As the weather is likely to prove unfavorable," he explained to Governor Mifflin, Washington "must absolutely insist that the military Gentlemen of Philadelphia will not attend him in the manner they had proposed." No offense intended, of course. Washington was in fact "so perfectly satisfied with their good intentions, that it would be impossible for them, by taking any unnecessary trouble, to make any addition to the proofs of their attachment, or the motives of his gratitude." Mifflin may or may not have passed on the message, but a newspaper account notes that the horse escort turned out at ten o'clock anyway. Too late: Washington and company were already on their way "before that hour, from a desire," it was said, "to avoid even the appearance of pomp or vain parade."[1]

Vain or not, pomp and parade were to be Washington's lot for the foreseeable future. We will accordingly track his progress in this chapter to Trenton and beyond and conclude by attending him to the Elizabeth-Town Point. From here he will embark on a custom-made barge and make way over the waters to Murray's Wharf on the tip of Manhattan Island. The relative peace and quiet of this leg through the Jersey farmland will happily provide us with occasion to pause for a moment, allow the aging soldier a nap, perhaps, and reflect on certain themes thus far unaddressed but important to our story. They include the role of religion and faith in Washington's thought and action; questions as to what, if anything, he may have thought about "the people" and "democracy" as constituent features of this strange new government called a republic; an opportunity, too, to check in on the portly, wise, and irascible John Adams, for he too has an appointment in the City. These are great and often complex matters and no pretensions to a full treatment are offered. At the same time, however, these matters can scarcely be avoided. More positively, they may provide interesting and important prompts to further reflection on what it meant, and means, as Thomas Paine wrote, to begin the world again. Although these considerations will not be explicitly invoked, they may be discerned hovering very close to the foreground of the inaugural ceremonies.

Revolutionaries are not as a rule given to irony; neither are Stoics and investors in massive land deals. Being all three, Washington was by nature and design a quite literal man. Though apparently not entirely humorless, he could be, as we saw with the Knox story, a bit aware of himself as a personage. Even so, he must have appreciated the historical twists and turns that led him on this post road to Trenton. In truth, Washington and his army, such as it was, had had a time of it in New Jersey. The retreat from New York was painful in almost every way; the region's loyalties could be pliable, and no other state hosted as many armed engagements as did New Jersey. On the other hand, her postwar record was brightened by early support for ratification and the federal cause in general. It was and remains an agriculturally rich state, flat and temperate, with its people distributed widely rather than centrally in any especially large towns. Trenton itself had survived the war more or less intact and was to prosper in the decades to come. For now, its citizens leaned to the task of making this return trip his most memorable.

They certainly tried. Not long after noon the party arrived and made its way across the Delaware at Calvin's Ferry, once more though less desperately a welcome sight. As Washington alit on Jersey soil, "he was welcomed with three huzzas, which made the shores re-echo the cheerful sounds." There followed an orchestrated reception that at least rivaled, if not surpassed, the competition from Gray's Ferry (fig. 7); it, too, has settled into a set piece for historians of the subject. And for good reason, and all in good fun, as long as "no one will suppose, that the greatest feast of so good a man, is that of adulation!" warned a New Yorker. "No, it oppresses him . . . he is an American. Americans have gloriously, by his aid, shaken off dependence upon the tools of a monarch—idolaters of gorgeous palaces and splendid equipage."[2]

Not entirely, in the event, but duly noted. For some time now, in any case, a number of women and their daughters had been hard at work over on Assunpink Creek a little south of town; there the army had pulled off a bit of magic in 1776, and here the Ladies conjured some of their own. This time, the general would cross the small stream over an arch about eighteen feet high, fifteen feet wide, and ten feet long (fig. 8). Thirteen pillars festooned with laurels and foliage helped create "a scene," recalled an observer, "which no description can do justice." This much had been said about the events in Philadelphia. The Ladies had more in mind than that: ushering the general through the arch was a large sign declaring "The Defender of the Mothers will also Protect their Daughters." And on top of it all, another: "TO YOU ALONE." As if to assure the stern New Yorker cited above, mothers and daughters were reported to have exercised due economy throughout the project: "the materials were the most plain and

FIGURE 7   Sheet music for "The Favorite New Federal Song, Adapted to the President's March," also known as "Hail Columbia." Words by J. Hopkinson, 1793. This was reported to have been sung to Washington as he passed through Trenton. Notated Music, Library of Congress, Washington, DC, M1630.3.H31798 b3.

FIGURE 8 Washington's reception at Trenton, New Jersey, on April 21, 1789. From *Columbian Magazine*, May 1789. The Miriam and Ira D. Wallach Division of Art, Prints and Photographs: Print Collection, New York Public Library Digital Collections, 424680.

unpolished, until so superbly decorated by the hands of the ladies." The returning soldier now made his way over the bridge, guided by white petals and the voices of thirteen girls in white. To the tune of "See the Conquering Hero Comes," Trenton's daughters sang out:

> *Virgins fair and Matrons grave,*
> *These thy conquering arm did save,*
> *Build for thee, triumphal bowers,*
> *Strew ye fair his way with flowers*
> *Strew your hero's way with flowers.*[3]

Presumably even Washington's habitual gravity relaxed just a little; how could it not? A witness wrote soon after that "if ever power was grateful to his heart, I believe it was at that moment when youth, beauty and innocence besought his protection." At some point before leaving the town, we know, Washington made sure to thank the "matrons and Young Ladies who received him in so novel and grateful a manner at the Triumphal Arch in Trenton." Here, too, the sweetened irony of the scene was unmistakable, for "The astonishing contrast between his former and actual situation on the same spot—The elegant taste with which it was adorned for the present occasion—and the innocent appearance of the white-robed Choir who met him with the gratulatory song, have made such impressions on his remembrance, as, he assures them, will never be effaced." Later that day came the usual rounds of toasts and sumptuous courses at Samuel Henry's City Tavern. Safe to say, however, that Washington's day had reached its meridian on the bridge. Men will prefer to celebrate with more noise and crash; this, because they are men. "It yet remains for the ladies," concluded the *Columbian Magazine*, "to meet their defender with sentiments, and touch the tender feelings of the HERO's heart."[4]

Where the travelers spent the night is not altogether clear; perhaps they had moved on to Princeton to the home of John Witherspoon or perhaps stayed put in Trenton. We do know that they were able to make breakfast in the small college town and receive an address from Witherspoon and John Beatty on behalf of the faculty and residents. In it, they had duly acknowledged Washington's "self-denial and devotedness to the public good." He assured them in turn that "if the sacrifice has been great, the occasion was still greater," and he prayed "that Almighty God will have you all in his holy keeping." Though Princeton—both town and college—had been the site of intensive and dramatic action shortly after the battle of Trenton, Washington had little time for reflection or, for that matter, much else. Before midday they were off for the twenty-mile leg to New Brunswick. Waiting for the company was Governor William Livingston, the mayor, and others of note to usher them into town. Here again was spectacle, ritualized into a recurrent but highly functional affirmation of shared sentiment. The *Pennsylvania Packet*, keeping a close eye on all this, reported on the military escort, the music, the crowds, and of course "a great number of the fair daughters of Columbia." Washington's stay would be brief, but for the moment, "Joy sparked in every eye, and perfect satisfaction was demonstrated by the countenance and behavior of all degrees and conditions of the people, when they beheld the object of their esteem and confidence again coming into public life."[5]

The townspeople would not glimpse their hero for long; after dinner at the home of Thomas Egbert, it was on to Woodbridge for the night. Tomorrow would be Thursday, April 23, 1789. By dawn the company would depart Woodbridge, make its way through Bridgetown, and arrive at last in Elizabeth-Town by nine o'clock that morning. Here we will leave

Washington, Thomson, and Humphreys to their thoughts for a short while and let them gather themselves before embarking for the final hop to lower Manhattan. Their pause will provide us with an opportunity for reflections of our own on matters that must be brought to account. That accomplished, we will rejoin the crew for the welcoming party of all welcoming parties.

WASHINGTON AND THE RELIGION QUESTION

Every revolution is a matter of faith. This is not to say that all revolutions are about faith or that faith is always sustained or rewarded. Sometimes, indeed, revolutions are mobilized against faith. At certain historical moments, they are undertaken on behalf of faith of a kind, a practice, or its prophet. Whatever its role and however it all turns out, revolution must always demand of its members a degree of conviction far in excess of more sensible realities. The great American experiment in republican government, singular in so many ways, was from its outset entirely recognizable within this tradition. The faith of these Americans was particularly outrageous, for it asked of them belief in the power of ideas and ideals and in the capacity of a geographically dispersed and diverse people to unite in common cause. It demanded faith in farm boys, local militia, and a largely amateur officer corps to take on the most formidable and professional war machine on the planet and in the wisdom of its commander in chief not to leverage victory into a despot's peace.[6]

But faith is not the same thing as religion. And revolutions over and about creedal identity are not of the same nature as those on behalf of civil rights. Indeed, the very concept of such rights as we understand them today is the product of a series of revolutions in the West to free the political from the religious. The American experience in the age of Washington must stand as a pivotal moment, then, when the very idea of a revolution on behalf of civic government was conceived and executed largely independent of religious imperatives. Did some or perhaps many soldiers die with a prayer? Of course. Did clergy summon the millennium, call for God's assistance, and renounce Satan? Yes, and frequently. But we cannot say that the War of Independence, any more than the constitutional establishment of the republic thereafter, was *about* religion. It was, however, very much about faith.

Still, the question of religion persists. This is as it should be. Why? Heaven knows the subject is unwieldy and often vexed, made indeed impossibly complex when folding both the war and the founding into the account. Leaving issues of faith and religion out of such an account, on the other hand, must result in a regrettably distorted picture of the period generally and of our story in particular. With no pretensions to solving the problem, we can begin by rather severely circumscribing the terrain of analysis; that is, by grounding such insights as might be afforded in what our travelers and their hosts had to say about ways of God and man. This approach will necessarily preclude broader generalization or summary statements on religion and the founding; still, it may reward us with a small but useful set of conclusions. These in turn will help situate and deepen our view of Washington and the nation's first inaugural moment.

Bluntly put, this is the question: what role, if any, did religion play in Washington's assumption to the presidency? More specifically, are there elements of religious thought, language, and imagery that need to be acknowledged as we approach Murray's Wharf? The answers, if that is the proper term, may be stated with equal simplicity. First, religion did in fact operate as a force in the creation and establishment of the executive office, and Washington's election to it was shaped by those forces. Second, the journey from Mount Vernon to Federal Hall was richly symbolic of religious rituals, themes, and public vocabularies; we cannot and would not want to ignore these elements, and certainly Washington did not. At the risk of deferring their treatment just a bit longer, we need to center and directly confront the question of how best to understand Washington and religion.

No other figure in American history save Lincoln has so captured the interest or devotion as that accorded George Washington. The *Papers of George Washington*, under the general editorship of W. W. Abbot, Dorothy Twohig, and others, is itself a monument of astonishing scholarship, as are the multivolume biographies by Freeman and Flexner. Sculptors, painters, and miniaturists have banked careers on his image; the Ladies of Mount Vernon are unrivaled, period. One could go on, as indeed many have. For all this, for all the extraordinary effort and sometimes brilliance in making meaningful this most remarkable life, how is it that after more than two centuries we have so few serious and comprehensive studies of Washington and religion? This is curious. Several explanations, admittedly glancing, may help explain this state of affairs and, in the process, set our coordinates more firmly toward New York.

For starters, it was not, nor is it yet, altogether clear exactly what Washington believed about this or that faith practice, organized religion, or creedal position. He had little time or inclination for theological niceties and seems to have been perfectly satisfied with the state of his soul; little to work with, then, for those who would seek spiritual reflection, struggle, or public declarations. Then again, he has been liable to patently sectarian claims on his religious views from very early on; some of these, such as those issuing from the lively pen of "Parson" [he was no parson] Weems, are absurd on their face—not all, of course, but many to this day are just a few steps from the local letter to the editor insisting on the nation's Christian origins. Scholars, popularizers, and acolytes have wrangled over the great one's favorite vestry and whether he received the sacrament, stood, kneeled, or sang. Was he really a Deist? Surely not! Time and again throughout the war he bade the men in General Orders to attend chapel, pray for protection, and give thanks. A God-fearing and proper Episcopalian, then? Perhaps, but why no reference—ever—to Jesus Christ? What kind of Christian never mentions his own Savior? These lines of approach seldom yield much of substance and can seem interminable. The historiography is marked by a fatal combination of massive contextual documentation, very little material from Washington himself, and vested appropriation; best to leave it alone and move on to more promising grounds of inquiry.[7]

We take our cue from the rhetorical tradition. Its students remind us that language is less a repository of meaning than a type of symbolic action. When put to use, words are turned into verbs, so to speak; they do, they operate, they function, and they act in the world. Language use takes place in situ; it is purposeful, pragmatic, never innocent, and always selective. Given certain contextual determinants, it allows us to make probabilistic claims as to intention and effect. Sometimes, such usage gives us a reason to suspect that an invitation is being extended to a certain and preferred attitude; it seeks to prompt action of a kind. The interpretation of language thus construed will always be provisional and qualified, as it must; precisely because rhetoric traffics in public and contingent affairs, so we are warned away from posing anything in the way of absolutes or summary conclusions. We can, nevertheless, render a plausible account of such scenes of discursive action by paying attention to what is given by the source, the text, the audience, and the circumstances of its appearance. These abstractions may be forgiven, perhaps, if they help us better understand the relationship between Washington and religion on the eve of nationhood.

We need first to delimit the space and time of our inquiry: Mount Vernon to Manhattan, April 16 to April 23, 1789. The circumscription is admittedly but necessarily severe, and while granting ourselves permission to strain ahead or behind on occasion, we will remain for the most part within this field of action. Now the basics: did religious speech make itself heard during the trip, and if so, in what ways? Yes, it did, and in very interesting ways indeed. As an indication of how this language played out on the road, we might start with this limited profile: between Thomson's formal representation to Washington on April 14 and his arrival at Elizabeth-Town on April 23, a total of twelve addresses were presented to His Excellency; he in turn issued a like number of replies in kind. Of the former, eight include no religious language at all and four do; of the latter, nine of Washington's replies feature such usage and three do not. At no point do either the local hosts or the visiting hero mention Christ, Christianity, or any particular denomination. The addresses to Washington appeal variously to "God," "Providence," "Being," "Ruler of the Universe," and "Throne of Grace." Washington will invoke the divinity fourteen times, ranging from "Providence" (six times), to "Being," "Heaven," and "God" (twice each), to "Divine Munificence" and "Throne of Grace" (once each).

This kind of counting does not take us very far, true enough, but it is a place to start. The fact that so many reception addresses chose not to mention the divine at all, for example, seems not insignificant. Thomson made no such reference; neither did the Baltimore committee, Wilmington's civic or business organization, the Society of the Cincinnati, the mayor's office in Philadelphia, the Pennsylvania legislators, and the Ladies of Trenton—not a word. The total absence of reference to sectarian or explicitly Christian imagery is telling; those wishing to make a case for the strength and reach of Deistic thought have found this kind of evidence compelling, as indeed it is. Washington did incline very much in that direction; again, for our story, this much is both true and not especially relevant. We are concerned rather to ask after the work such allusions are made to perform and how they articulate and assist in the task of making America make sense.[8]

What then does the divine being actually *do* in these addresses? Those feting Washington apparently hold that Providence "maketh and unmaketh at his will"; he may "restore to us the best of men" and grant "great deliverance," protection, guidance, rewards, and blessings. Nothing exceptional here, then, and none intended; the language is cast at a rather general level of reference where few could find offense and fewer still any real spiritual inspiration. Again, however, perhaps the most notable feature of these addresses is just how few and how light are the religious touches. Washington, on the other hand, invokes some variation on the theme of divine being much more frequently than his hosts. This, too, is interesting and warrants more illustration. Since the references are not that many or long, they may be represented here in full, or nearly so:

> **Alexandria**: "All that remains for me is to commit myself and you to the protection of that beneficent Being, who on a former occasion hath happily brought us together, after a long and distressing separation. Perhaps the same gracious Providence will again indulge us with the same heartfelt felicity."
>
> **Baltimore:** "I know the delicate nature of the duties incident to the part which I am called out to perform: and I feel my incompetence, without the singular assistance of Providence to discharge them in a satisfactory manner."
>
> **Wilmington:** "Heaven and my own heart are witnesses for me . . . with a reliance upon that gracious Providence, which sustained us through our struggle for Liberty."
>
> **Philadelphia [Mayor et al.]:** "When I contemplate the Interposition of Providence . . . I feel myself oppressed and almost overwhelmed with a sense of the Divine Munificence."
>
> **Philadelphia [Court]:** "Almighty God hath been pleased, in some sort, to make use of me as his instrument."
>
> **Princeton**: "I pray that Almighty God will have you all in his holy keeping."[9]

Late in life, James Madison recalled that his fellow Virginian "had never attended to the arguments for Christianity, and for the different systems of religion, or in the fact that he had formed definite opinions on the subject." Washington seemed instead to "take these things as he found them existing," happy, in the main, to abide by the elemental rituals of faith familiar to those of family, class, and community.[10] As a description of the president-elect's religious comportment, this will do, and it is better than most. It does not take us very far, however, as an account of how Washington managed the symbolic resources afforded by religious tradition. For this we must pay closer attention to the rhetorical craft embedded in these exchanges with the electorate and their representatives. At a minimum, we can readily see that Washington views Providence as an active force in human affairs: it protects, restores, and indulges; aids, superintends, and sustains; and humbles and invests human agency. Providence appears then not, as certain Deistic views would have it, a distant and especially clever watchmaker; on the contrary, it seems heavily involved in the conduct of men and nations and essentially benign, merciful, and eager to reward righteousness.

The propositions are commonplace; the conditions under which they are mobilized emphatically are not. Words indeed have no meaning or force independent of context, and here context is everything. Washington's addresses of reply thus inscribe to distinctively American and republican ends a story of ancient lineage and power, of a chosen people in covenant with an omnipotent, jealous, but ultimately rational God. Much later, citizens would come to speak easily of American exceptionalism, civil religion, and its many variants: in Washington's journey to Federal Hall, we may see up close what this story looks like as it is being written, quite literally, on the ground. We cannot really know his fixed religious convictions in any doctrinal sense, assuming he had any. It is impossible, however, to miss and unwise to gloss over what he did to activate the language of faith to political ends.

And just what were these political ends? The point of these addresses cannot have been only to confirm the role of faith in civic affairs; they worked as well, indeed crucially, to insist on the integrity of republican values in religious community. Here was a challenge of enormous importance, the historical record of which was not especially inspiring. The new nation featured a religious landscape of unprecedented diversity and range of faith practices; at the same time, its constitution was conspicuously absent any references to divinity whatsoever. We may chalk up this anomaly—and it was very much an anomaly in the world of the eighteenth century—to high principle, expedience, or ambivalence about establishments edging on hostility. So many different personalities, experiences, and regional traditions were at work in the making of the document that it is probably pointless to speculate along these lines. Everyone must have understood, in any case, that the faithful and their churches were not going anywhere; that they, too, were to be counted—some only generations later—as Americans, and that they, too, mattered.

But how did they matter? What kinds of claims might citizens of faith make on this new American state? Conversely, what claims can such a state make on its citizens of faith? Americans are still trying to figure out a satisfactory answer to these questions. Here, too, the event of Washington's assumption to the first presidency offers a brief but suggestive perspective on this vexed subject. To get at this view with some clarity we will need to stretch the temporal frame of the analysis just a bit to include texts composed and delivered during the later stages of the trip and into the very early days of the presidency. During this phase of transitions within transitions, several leading churches and their representatives saw fit to deliver statements to Washington, offering, as might be expected, words of congratulations and good will; inevitably, too, they offered polite reminders about the importance of God in the affairs of man. The addresses—from German Lutherans, Methodists, Presbyterians, and Virginia Baptists— accordingly provide a telling analogue to the civic texts treated above. Together, they prompted Washington to some of the most interesting commentary we have on the relationship between the civil and the religious in the life of the republic.

The addresses are short and restrained, as we may expect, and thus readily profiled. All bear testimony to the military origins of the nation and its new leader; again, not surprising, but not unimportant either. Pennsylvania's Lutherans acknowledged the happy state of "affairs in which Your Excellency bore so illustrious a part from the very beginning of a most arduous Contest," certain now that "the present crisis sheds a luster on the past events of our union." So, too, agreed the Methodist Bishops, who place their confidence "in your wisdom and integrity, for the preservation of those civil and religious liberties which have been transmitted to us by the providence of GOD and the glorious revolution." The General Assembly of the Presbyterian Church, having recently convened in Philadelphia, declared its gratitude to "Almighty GOD the Author of every perfect gift" for giving to the nation a Washington, whose "military achievements ensured the safety and glory to America, in the late arduous conflict for freedom." From the Virginia Baptists came heartfelt satisfaction that with success in war and the "grand object obtained; the Independence of the States acknowledged; free from ambition and a sanguine thirst for blood, our Hero returned with those whom he commanded, and yielded up his sword to those who gave it him." No appeals to special treatment are made; nothing in the way of lobbying or sectarian evangelizing is evident. Together, they represent a modest but highly articulated restatement of their shared hope for fair treatment and the protection of rights as duly organized assemblies of the faithful.[11]

The first president was a child of the Enlightenment, no question. To the extent that the term means anything, it signifies a historical preoccupation with questions of rights—their source, sovereignty, and ends. Washington, though no political theorist, was deeply shaped by the values coded into this massively influential, exasperatingly elusive concept. We miss something very basic, however, about his thought and action and legacy by leaving it at that. Everything we know about the man—his early life and formative experiences, adulthood, the war, home life, and beyond—argues strongly that Right only made sense as it was realized through Duty. Within the dialectic of self and other lay the twin inheritances of the Enlightenment and Protestant Christianity that he and many other Americans could claim. Unlike Madison and Jefferson, for example, Washington could never bring himself to endorse a given conception of rights for its own sake; for its fullest expression, a right needed to be realized in obligation as a means to an end. Those to whom a right was extended were accordingly expected, indeed obligated, to exercise it on behalf of others for the general good. Rights are in this sense an individual good realized on behalf of the community.[12]

What these assumptions portended in the context of religion, Washington, and the early republic is a complex but central question. For help in formulating a response, we cannot do better than turn to Vincent Muñoz, who has provided us with expert examination of the matter. After surveying much of the material noted above, and more, Muñoz concludes that Washington held firmly to the principle that "a condition of civil society, and thus of a government capable of protecting the rights of conscience, is that individuals must conduct themselves as good citizens." By extension, such a government "may legitimately expect all citizens to perform the reasonable duties of citizenship, even those that religious citizens find objectionable." Now, Washington was inclined to leave such prescriptions at a rather general level, although he was to let his Quaker friends hear in no uncertain terms his disappointment in their wartime record. And he was prepared, when circumstances allowed, to be tolerant enough of religious expressions that pushed the limits now and then. But of these things he was convinced: the prospects of American republicanism hinged on a virtuous people; religion helped to shape and encourage a virtuous citizenry; and the right to profess one's religion was therefore to be protected by the government, and this Washington pledged to do.[13]

Rights are necessary because the ends to which they must be put are necessary. The state thus takes on the responsibility to protect rights with deep seriousness. In return, however, Americans of faith assumed a covenantal obligation to act in such a way as to sustain the conditions of their own possibility; that is, to act as citizens. No more poignant expression of this view, in all its generosity and toughness, can be found than in Washington's 1790 statement to Rhode Island's Hebrew congregation: "For happily the Government of the United States, which gives to bigotry no sanction, to persecution no assistance requires only that they who live under its protection should demean themselves as good citizens, in giving it on all occasions their effectual support." Here is the very lifeblood of the republican compact.[14]

When we say, then, that the best way to approach Washington and the religion question is to ask what he does, we mean that he sees faith as a rationale for optimal action. Providence works in the world for those who earn its blessings; "it is visible," he claims before his Lutheran audience, "in every stage of our progress to this interesting crisis." And they have earned it, not because they are Lutherans but because of "the excellent character for diligence, sobriety, and virtue, which the Germans in general, who are settled in America, have ever maintained." Thus he assures the Methodists of his commitment to "the civil and religious liberties of the American People," even as he reminds them that "the people of every denomination, who demean themselves as good citizens, will have occasion to be convinced that I shall always strive to prove a faithful and impartial Patron of genuine, vital religion." Washington is happy to thank his Presbyterian friends commending Heaven's favor, but he will stress, too, that "piety, philanthropy, honesty, industry, and economy seems, in the ordinary course of human affairs," especially "necessary for advancing and confirming the happiness of our country."[15]

The point is that it works—or can be made to work—both ways. Religion may serve the purposes of a healthy and vital commonwealth, and government may meet its obligations by protecting the rights of conscience requisite to these ends. That is the republican ideal, at least in no small part, to have it both ways, for religion promotes virtue, and virtue promotes good government. This is, so to speak, the reason of state and why even the Virginia Baptists, who had more reason than most to flinch at the order of things, eventually came around. To them Washington promises to "establish effectual barriers against the horrors of spiritual tyranny, and every species of religious persecution." In return, he must assume that they "will be the faithful Supporters of a free, yet efficient general Government." To all the congregations, sects, and faith communities, Washington pledges not just tolerance but vigilance and the power of his office. However, "it is rationally to be expected from them in return, that they give proof by life and actions," this because "no man, who is profligate in his morals, or a bad member of the civil community, can possibly be a true Christian, or a credit to his own religious society."[16]

We shall leave these reflections soon and rejoin our travelers as they proceed to their appointment in Manhattan. If our time has been used wisely, we will have seen, if only at a glance, something of Washington's religious predilections; and seen, more importantly, something of the convictions he seems to have held for most of his life and that he will bring to office before the month is out. If so, this pause will appear less as a detour than a chance to explore an understudied stretch of the road to Federal Hall. Just as clearly, we can see that Washington's thoughts on religion and its role in republican government are of a piece with resources he brought along: his sense of order and the happy arrangement of otherwise conflicting elements that we have glimpsed at Mount Vernon; the kind of judgment he exercised in the war's early months, with its insistence on taking principle from the expedient and the expedient from principle; and the commitment to republican authority evidenced in his friendships, where power was a matter not of personal fealty but of commitment to justified ideals. If Washington was a religious man, it was because he had an unshakable faith in the republican prospect, and if faith is not the same as religion, he was convinced that the latter could serve the former to mutual advantage.

WHAT DID "THE PEOPLE" MEAN TO WASHINGTON?

Scholars of the subject teach us that the modern national state was designed for war. The state's origin and prospects, that is, may be said to depend crucially on at least three requirements. These are (1) that it possess a military that is capable of sustaining a defensive posture at least and preferably capable, as well, of offensive operations; (2) that it successfully devise a system of extraction to pay for its military, conventionally in the form of taxation and manpower; and (3) that it maintain a centralized system of authority to administer the whole business. In the main, this explanation seems to square with the realities of the last several centuries. But we know, too, that there is more to it; some kind of epoxy is necessary to keep a people stuck together fast enough and long enough to make a plausible claim on nationhood. Surely we know by now that this sense of collective identity cannot be enforced at the end of a musket—not for long, in any case.

People, to be a people, need a reason to invest in each other's fortunes as well as their own—some sense of promise, reward, and affective satisfaction from considering oneself part of something greater than oneself. This is the task of what today we call "culture," an elusive enough term that here suggests something of the symbolic, institutional, and artistic labor demanded for such a task. At no time is this labor more important or more conspicuous than in its formative moments, and so we are led to ask after Washington's role in shaping this structure of commitments that is the American promise. We need to ask, that is, what he might have thought about these people celebrating him along the way, and more generally, what his relationship was to "the people," conceived as the basis and warrant for the very government he was about to lead.

When Washington leaned back in his carriage and thought of the days past and to come, what can we suppose he saw in the mind's eye? What kind of people did he think he was dealing with, these Americans? And what possibly could have been the source of any confidence that they—he and they—might be able to pull off this actually quite outrageous venture in republican government? We may consider the odds; they certainly did, and they knew that historically, people stuck together for a finite set of reasons. These might include blood, faith, common danger, physical survival, enforced subjectivity under absolutist regimes, and geographical intimacy. Now, our traveler would have seen none of this; he never had and never would. These "united" states were, like the New Jersey through which he now rode, extraordinarily diverse ethnically and with respect to faith practices; they shared no common enemy, at least now at the gates. No one appeared desperate, abject, or bowed by the yoke (blindness and insight being conditions of each other). This sense of disparity and diffusion can of course be overstated: we are, after all, talking about a largely Euro-American, Protestant, Anglophone people who evidently shared certain cultural traditions, broad experiences as colonial subjects, and abiding norms of civil comportment. Nevertheless, these were scarcely optimal conditions for the invention of a republic of, for, and by the people.

George Washington was nothing if not an optimist, however, and like most Americans he professed and seemed genuinely to believe that "the people" were capable of being, in some sense, one. We need not and must not search for some mysterious ethos or essential character underwriting the grand experiment to ask what Washington thought of his fellow Americans. Better to take our cue from Abbot, an exceptionally astute Washington scholar, who once observed that the Virginian understood in his very being that life was "something a person must make something of." As Washington was himself a master builder, so he must have seen his fellow Americans. Everywhere he looked, all that he had experienced, learned, and assumed about these people indicated that they, too, were builders. Like his friend James Madison, he had every confidence that soon, very soon, "roads will be everywhere shortened, and kept in better order; accommodations for travelers will be multiplied and meliorated [not soon enough!]; and interior navigation on our eastern side will be opened throughout, or nearly throughout the whole extent of the Thirteen states." Hamilton, too, knew that if anything was certain, it was that the "public business must in some way or another go forward." *Homo faber*: man the creator. These were not, manifestly, a people resigned to scraping by; to the extent that he recognized them as "fellow Americans," a phrase Washington employed repeatedly, he saw in them not women and men toiling for subsistence and survival, but a relentless, exasperating, willful people to be feared at times, praised at others, but always respected for the power they held and the authority rightfully claimed as their own.[17]

Here indeed was optimism, and it was not a sentiment universally held. When in 1787 the Virginia squire Mason contemplated the prospects of nationhood, he could only despair. Not only were these Americans so diverse in character and habits, but they were spread out so widely as to doom any pretenses to be a "united" anything. Think about it, Mason warned: "there never was a government over a very extensive country without destroying the liberties of the people." History was absolutely clear on the matter. "Popular governments can only exist in small territories," Mason said, echoing Montesquieu's commonplace. "Is there a single example on the face of the earth to support a contrary opinion?" No, actually, there was not. Everyone knew that much. Thousands of miles drove apart Georgians from the Granite State; from east to west—well, where did they really begin and end? Distance and distribution were only part of the problem, abstractions at best. The new nation's population was not great, but it was not inconsiderable either. And it was growing—and at an extraordinary, indeed unprecedented rate. In its inaugural year the United States claimed roughly four million souls. Of these, about 700,000 were enslaved Africans; some 60,000 were so-called free blacks. Urban centers, such as they were, clustered tightly to the coast and its carrying trade, including, in descending order of population, New York City (33,000), Philadelphia (28,000), Boston (18,000), Charleston (16,000), and Baltimore (13,000). By way of perspective, the entire population of the fifth largest city in the United States could easily fit into a modern basketball arena.[18]

It was not just difference and distance. It was also a question of critical mass or lack of it. Yes, the numbers were rapidly growing, but they were moving, always moving. And why not? The west beckoned, as it always has, but the opportunities for this overwhelmingly rural people to stake their claim out and beyond the seaboard proved irresistible. In the first decade of the new nation's existence, the population of Kentucky shot from about 73,000 in 1790 to 221,000; Tennessee went from approximately 35,000 to a bit over 100,000. In ten years! The political economy driving such change is complex and remains under study. At the very least, however, we are thus reminded that it remained not entirely clear just where this country was going, how it was going to get there, and whether it would ultimately succeed. Trade policies were vexed and often disadvantageous and would remain so for the foreseeable future. Though flanked by Spanish, British, and indigenous peoples, the country could rely on very little in the way of an army and nothing at all on the water. No coherent economic system as yet might make sense of wildly disparate state practices; no common currency and no apparent alternative to the vanquished mercantilism of the past.[19]

All this and more gave plenty of ammunition to the pessimists, and for good reason: America simply was not suited to imagined versions of the European nation-state. It was too different, too big, too diffuse to make good on the dubious promises of large-scale, globally entwined logics of empire. It its pursuit of just such an empire, many Americans seemed willing to barter away the very prize earned through war with its imperial enemy: freedom. Invariably, it would be "the people" who must suffer the depredations of a constitutional system bent on national aggrandizement. Patrick Henry, among many others, had seen this coming. Why? he asked. Why this rush to greatness? "Some way or another we must be a great and mighty empire; we must have an army, and a navy, and a number of things." In this sense, "We the People" was but a fine sounding phrase cloaking an aggressive and ultimately insatiable appetite for growth. The real people, the real Americans, Henry argued, wanted what people always want—jobs, security, and happiness. Now they were being asked, in effect, to relinquish the rights and opportunities afforded by such local concerns to a "powerful and mighty empire." Henry could be affected, blustery, lazy, and stubborn. He could also capture a popular sentiment with great force and insight. He had a point. Who was this "We," and just what did they have to gain from the new order of things?[20]

The question is real, though a summary response is neither possible nor perhaps even desirable. Americans have been attempting with varying degrees of success for over two centuries to reckon the consequences of defining who they are. They have enjoyed more success, arguably, at debating who—or what—they wish to become. The debate has taken some severe turns and has ceased indeed being a debate and devolved into pitched battle, but this has not always been so, not always, and at times has revealed something of the best about the country and its restive, noisy, and aspirant citizens. This characteristic, if not defining, habit of Americans commits its people to deliberations about tomorrow, and tomorrow is always a matter of faith. It is not necessarily religious or even spiritual faith, which in any case has always been uncertain and inconstant in America, but it is an abiding conviction that the future can be made better—can be built—because of or in spite of today. Henry had no such faith, at least in that *annus mirabilis* of 1787. Washington did; he always did, whatever the material realities or the disappointments of the day. One might conclude, with reason, that Henry was the more realistic of the two; perhaps, but faith and realism are not necessarily incommensurable, and in any case one would be hard put to describe the general as anything but clear-eyed about the ways of humankind.

Washington's faith was a product of his realism, born of experience, disciplined by the sword, and guided always by a fundamental belief in the American cause. He sought to help "insure the permanent felicity" of this, his commonwealth. "I think," he wrote to Lafayette in January of 1789, "I see a path, as clear and as direct as a ray of light, which leads to the attainment of that object. Nothing but harmony, honesty, industry and frugality are necessary to make us a great and happy people." Washington's "Dear Marquis" was about to discover for himself how difficult it is to predict in which direction the winds of revolution may blow. However crazy things may get over there, the American promised, "we shall continue in tranquility here. And that population will be progressive so long as there shall continue to be so many easy means for obtaining subsistence, and so ample a field for the exertion of talents and industry." The lines bear some reflection, for though brief and spare, they are deeply suggestive. And though we ought not to read history back into them, it is difficult—impossible?—not do to so.[21]

What might Washington have meant by this "great and happy people"? This population that, under certain given and emerging conditions, seemed destined to realize itself as a people like no other? The question is obviously relevant for one on the way to Federal Hall; at the same time, it can be surprisingly difficult to answer. As he was not a political theorist along the lines of his distinguished colleagues, Washington left no sustained account of his thoughts on "the people." Scholars have sought assiduously to recover the rudiments of a general orientation; the results are suggestive and frequently convincing. Here, it will help to clarify the terms of analysis by taking care of a few preliminary matters. We need first to get straight on the vexed question of "democracy" and its role—if any—in Washington's view of things.

An enormous amount of effort has been expended on establishing democracy's development in early modern and eighteenth-century practice. For our purposes, it is enough to underscore the fact that democracy was a protean, hotly contested, and maddeningly elusive idea. Americans had yet to come to grips with democracy's assumptions and implications, as indeed they still struggle. The word itself shows up often enough in public debates and commentary of the period, nearly always stamped by its Aristotelian inheritance alongside monarchy and aristocracy as available modes of governance. While it is true that democracy came in for plenty of abuse for its "too frequent assemblies of the people, inflammatory harangues, popular rumours, violent proceedings," and "hasty decisions," it was not thus summarily dismissed. When properly conceived and executed, democracy was thought by many to satisfy the imperatives of popular sovereignty; it could be dangerous, but given certain safeguards, it seemed best suited to a freedom-loving people. "Democracy, or republican government," explained a writer in the *Cumberland Gazette*, resides in the people at large," and was therefore "the best in theory; and, where the people are virtuous and well-informed, it is the best in practice."[22]

If "democracy" was to be taken at all seriously, if this was really what Americans were up to, then it had to locate virtue at its very heart. One did not need Aristotle to be reminded that all three forms of political power were susceptible to degeneration. People being people, and power being power, things had a way of going to hell. There was, it seemed to one New Yorker, "a certain malignity in human nature, which fails not to weaken, and in time to destroy the noblest structures its better faculties are capable of raising." This is a fair point and one widely held. "Upon the whole," he nevertheless concludes, "a democracy, fortified by a strong and efficient executive branch, is the most natural and . . . the most beneficial form of government."[23]

We are getting closer to a sense of what democracy might have meant for Washington and his "fellow Americans." All agreed in the principle, at least, of popular sovereignty; most were willing to accept the constitutional form in which that sovereignty was to be given maximum expression. There would be any number of contests over the specifics, but whatever it was called—democracy or republican government—the real point was that the people thus empowered had to act on such reserves of virtue as they possessed. If government was, after all, legitimate only so far as it provided for the happiness of the governed, then the people must, in effect, earn that right through its duty to the common good. This was so, John Adams famously explained, because happiness, "whether in despotism or democracy, whether in slavery or freedom, can never be found without virtue. The best republics will be virtuous, and have been so." And if human nature needed a little push toward these ends, well, thought Adams, that was the glory of America's Constitution. Might not virtue be as much the product as the source of well-conceived government?[24]

Adams was a moralist through and through. No surprise, then, that he would bear down so heavily on the standard of virtue. And, being Adams, his thoughts on this score would undergo fiery mutations as faith in his countrymen came and went. He nonetheless helps us see how foundational this notion of virtue was—understood as a defining obligation—to the prospects of nationhood. Adams also warns us, perhaps, against making too much of the word democracy in the context of the time. We see now that it was a label used promiscuously for vested purposes and with no great explanatory force. The important point for Adams and most of the Founders was that whatever people chose to call it, their system of government absolutely required from the people in whom it was trusted an abiding commitment to its principles and to those elected to put these principles into effect. All this "will require great integrity, patriotism, and prudence," declared the "Federal Republican" in 1788, "to direct those who administer the government, to keep within those bounds of moderation and wisdom, which will render it acceptable and a blessing to the people."[25]

When we ask after Washington's relationship to the American people, then, we must expect less in the way of systematic statements than a set of basic assumptions. At their heart, these tenets undergirded a fairly consistent and long-standing synthesis of commitments, blind spots, habits, and instincts. Washington's sense of "the people" was, like everyone's, an abstraction. It was given substance and force, however, through hard-earned experience. His military education had taught him the dangers of excessive optimism; he had come to realize quite early that men—all men—were inconstant, self-interested, and weak; they could be, as well, principled, generous, and tough as nails. The general's fellow Americans could be, like the militia gathered around Boston in that summer of 1775, "an exceedingly dirty and nasty people." Battle has a way of laying open certain truths about the human animal, and Washington in time grew accustomed to what was plain for all to see. "To expect, among such people, that they are influenced by any other principles than those of Interest," he sighed, "is to look for what never did, and I fear never will happen." The postwar experiment, he confided to John Jay, revealed that "we have, probably, had too good an opinion of human nature in forming our confederation." Americans were in this sense not really different from any other people then or now. "The motives which predominate most in human affairs," he told Madison, were "self-love and self-interest."[26]

Here was not a man, clearly, given to blithe optimism, but neither was he cynical. The difference lay in his ability to discern in fallen man, or certain fallen men, a capacity for growth, for change, and perhaps even for redemption. While it was true that all men were self-interested, it was just as true that they were not only self-interested. Given the right circumstances, resources, and leadership, they might yet bring to fruition a better version of themselves. In this lay the promise of America's experiment in republican government. It was not, in spite of the quite real odds working against the attempt, a cracked-brain venture, or it need not be, because "the people" were thought to possess enough of that one element—virtue—necessary to keep it whole, true, and of consequence in the world. They need only to be given the opportunity and means to effect that all-important transformation from subject to citizen. The Constitution, he believed, provided for just this possibility, and the form of government offered up a way to school the people on which it was grounded in their rights, yes, but their duties as well. There would be exceptions and disappointments, of course, but Washington ultimately was sure that America would not finally disappoint the expectations of her friends. On great occasions, especially, but whenever the public business was required, "all mankind might look to the good disposition," then, concluded Washington, "the good sense of the Americans."[27]

When His Excellency looked out from that rattling carriage, then, he did not so much see something called "the people" as a certain version of it. Was this image, therefore, selective, strategic, exclusionary, tragic, conservative, hierarchical, hypocritical, self-deluding, and doomed? No question. Washington's "fellow citizens" by definition did not include the enslaved, women, indigenous peoples, the abject, and the forgotten. In the years ahead, but soon enough, certain of his most deeply ingrained assumptions about civil order and citizen rights would come under sustained assault. Friends now would all but desert him later as they sought to re-form a yet more perfect union; parties and factional strife were on the way, and foreign and Indian affairs would usher in unforeseen and disruptive forces. Washington was a man of the eighteenth century. He knew it.

But his journey to Federal Hall in the spring of 1789 could not have been better timed: it put on display a living symbol of the virtue that would give to the people both the reason and the means to build and to build again.

JOHN ADAMS AND THE AMBIVALENCE OF POWER

On April 6, 1789, New Hampshire's John Langdon announced before a joint session of Congress that John Adams, Esq., having received the votes of thirty-four electors to Washington's sixty-nine, was now to be considered vice president of the United States of America. Shortly thereafter, arrangements were made to send forth the Boston businessman and future diplomat Sylvanus Bourne to Braintree, there to deliver the news and present Congress's congratulations. The House hurried to appoint its welcoming committee of Fisher Ames (Massachusetts), Nicholas Gilman (New Hampshire), and George Gale (Maryland); the Senate added Tristam Dalton (Massachusetts) and Oliver Ellsworth (Connecticut). As Thomson headed south by horse, Bourne took to the waters next day and arrived at Adams's modest home by late April 9. "Permit me, Sir," read Langdon's message, "to hope that you will soon safely arrive here, to take upon you the discharge of the important duties to which you are so honorably called by the voice of your country." Just exactly what those "important duties" were to be, no one really seemed to know, least of all Adams; the office had been, if not an afterthought, then a by-product of more pressing matters in the summer of 1787. Still, it was something, or might be made something, and the people of Massachusetts were proud of their man who was summoned again to "hazard his tranquility and ease on the boisterous ocean of politicks."[28]

Adams presents us an interesting but no easy challenge. This is true in any general account of the founding and equally so for its inaugural moment. So apparently conflicted, ornery, brilliant, stubborn, loquacious, private, censorious, and expansive was Adams that he is not to be, cannot be, wrestled into any position against his will. This is just as he would have it, of course, but we need nevertheless to inscribe his story into ours, for he, too, was very much a part of the unfolding drama and deserves his moment. To give Adams his due in this context is to acknowledge that if he contained multitudes—he did—then so do we, then and again, and still do. That is to say, in the Adams portrait we discover a markedly distinct version of American character from that in Washington; though different, each informs the composition and gives it complexity and depth—also tension, disappointment, and uncertainty. They shared much—above all, genuine love of country—but where Washington projected equanimity, Adams visibly struggled with others and mostly with himself. Washington embodied authority; he *was* authority. Adams sought it, avoided it, loved it, hated it. One fought a revolution on behalf of freedom and owned hundreds of slaves; the other was deeply conservative and could not abide the benighted system. In the end, as in the beginning, Washington and Adams survived each other because they held in common, for all their differences, an unshakable commitment to what mattered most: the commonwealth.

Thomas Jefferson, no mean judge of character, confessed in 1787 to missing the mark on Adams. This, too, would change, naturally; each found the other endlessly exasperating, compelling, and worth the effort. But after some time together in London and touring the English countryside, the younger man reported back to Madison that he had found Adams "vain, irritable, and a bad calculator of the force and probable effect of the motives which govern men." And yet, Jefferson admitted, "he is profound in his view; and accurate in his judgment except where knowledge of the world is necessary to form a judgment." One notes that last little poke; good humored or not, it points forward to the deep ambivalence that has characterized the Adams historiography. Bernard Bailyn, in his brilliant profile of the man, notes for example that "powerful elements with him beat against his determination to make a name for himself, impeded the easy satisfaction of his ambition, set limits to the possibilities of his success."[29]

Whatever the psychic origin of these forces, they were habitually voiced in the declarative; he was a know-it-all. "He talked too much," thought Stanley Elkins and Erik McKittrick, and "was too opinionated and too censorious." Such crankiness will come at a price; so be it. Adams "rather expected to be unpopular; indeed, he was all but determined to be so, and in large degree he was." Gordon Wood forcefully observed that for all this, there "was never anything disingenuous about Adams," and he reminds us that we are not thinking here of merely being irritable and irritating (although these are not irrelevant). The Adams affect was earned, it was principled, and it could be unflinching, brave, and penetrating. Style and content conspired together to give to Adams a politics at once unmistakably republican and deeply anxious over the prospects of popular will. Thus

Adams, as Wood puts it, "refused to pervert the meaning of language, and he could not disguise, without being untrue to everything he felt within himself, the oligarchic nature of American politics."[30]

And so Benjamin Franklin's famous compliment/put-down—that Adams was "an honest man, often a great one, but sometimes absolutely mad"—has been for the most part seconded by the generations. Franklin was usually right about such things. Then, too, Adams seems to have indulged his doubts with particular relish and perhaps even to have rather enjoyed the exercise it required to wage the battle between the abject and the righteous. He knew full well that his name was being bruited as the presumptive choice for the vice presidency while abroad. Now back at home in the summer of 1788, Adams allows himself this bit of self-pity: "your father," he writes daughter Abigail, "does not stand very high in the esteem, admiration, or respect of his country, or any part of it. In the course of a long absence his character has been lost, and he has got quite out of circulation." All nonsense, as events were soon to make quite clear. But just in case, the defensive ramparts had to go up: if he was to be forgotten in spite of all he had done for the common good, so be it; he would not in any case sacrifice principles for the sake of private ambition. Not that anyone ever suggested as much; who would? It did not matter: "I had rather dig my subsistence out of the earth with my own hands," he declared for no very obvious reason to Abigail, "than be dependent on any favor, public or private." By year's end, he had given the question of service to the new nation a little more thought. Perhaps the people remembered him after all; perhaps they loved him, even. If so, then, "I am willing to serve the public on manly conditions, but not on childish ones; on honorable principles, not mean ones." This kind of self-righteousness, grown habitual, would not serve Adams particularly well in the future, nor had it; he seemed forever to be kicking the prospects of popularity further down the road. His daughter Elizabeth knew as much; she knew that "though a grateful people may yield him a tribute of praise yet all the applause and glory he justly merits may not be given him till some future age."[31]

There is truth in all this. Adams was in fact querulous, judgmental, and quick to offense. Seeking, always, to stand on his dignity, he would falter. Intensely self-conscious of his own shortcomings, he was too quick to point them out in others—a moralist in an age of warriors. But we must be careful here. An excessively selective reading of commentary on the man would lead us to think him slightly unhinged, swinging now toward toxic ego-mania, now toward abjection and self-abasement. Then, too, we might be lulled by his own words as well as those of his critics to think him terribly unpopular, dour, and a gaseous windbag, presenting a kind of necessary but grim reminder of how awfully serious it all was. This would be a regret-table distortion. As Bailyn and others have demonstrated, Adams could be and often was quite funny. Jefferson found him enormously engaging as a companion during their tour of the English countryside. For all his prolixity, this father of a future professor of rhetoric at Harvard could pro-duce brilliant prose; there was a reason Adams was appointed to help draft the Declaration of Independence. And, lest we forget, he was not really as unpopular as he—and others since—was apt to believe. Looked at from another angle, in fact, Adams's career so far had been quite remarkable. Though only fifty-three, he had been acclaimed, appointed, elected, and nudged into local, state, continental, and then international affairs; in a sense, he had never been away from the action since leaving the school-house so many years ago.

Adams, then, was not unbalanced, he was not a relentless prude, and he was not unpopular. He did, after all, secure thirty-four electoral votes, and indeed he had been elected on his return from Europe a delegate to the Continental Congress. Whether he admitted it or not, Adams was, as Tench Coxe wrote to Madison in early 1789, "esteemed by the people . . . a man of pure private Character, and has knowledge and abilities beyond the proper duties of a Vice President which indeed are not very important." Be that as it may, press coverage at the time routinely celebrated the Bay Stater as an "illustrious patriot," "enlightened republican," "our patriotick countryman," and "that distinguished patriot and statesman." If Adams could be exasperating, petty, jealous, officious, self-pitying, and moody, then the same must be said of mere mortals generally; his distinction was to have given both his virtues and vices such enduring expression.[32]

Most Americans, presumably, did not need reminding in the fall of 1789 that "a complete revolution will soon take place in our government." The ratification of the new nation's founding document was by then common knowledge, but the pseudonymous "Federal Republican," like many other commenters, continued to insist publicly that the "powers with which it vests the rulers, are very extensive and multiform—And it will require great integrity, patriotism, and prudence to direct those who administer the government, to keep within those bounds of moderation and wisdom, which will render it acceptable and a blessing to the people." Excepting George Washington himself, his fellow citizens could conceive of no other figure so possessed of "integrity, patriotism, and prudence" as Adams— the squire of Braintree. Again, no one knew what the specifics of his office might entail, but they knew that Adams was a fit representation of their shared interests and aspirations, and they set out accordingly to usher him to Federal Hall in grand style. In this, he—and they—participated in a parallel, if less conspicuous, ritual of affirmation.[33]

Washington was a military man. After receiving his news from Thomson, he left the next day. Adams was not—he took his time and did not leave home until Monday, April 13. Abigail in the meantime had arranged his effects and suited him up properly, as usual. Others had been at work in a more official capacity to make sure the native son was duly feted on his way out of town. Governor John Hancock, who had been in the running for the office himself, thoughtfully ordered a parade of horse and cannonading from the hills and otherwise ensured that the vice president be extended "various honorary notices, both civil and military, which the governor most opportunely displayed, and which our patriotick countryman richly deserves." From the city they descended on Braintree for breakfast on the thirteenth, then it was back to the governor's for lunch. Alighting from his carriage, Adams was "received by the Chief Magistrate with the most affectionate and respectful marks of attention." Hancock, whose pleasure in these kinds of things was perhaps unrivaled in his lifetime, then ordered a thirteen-gun salute from the local artillery company. A fine time was had of it, "and the joyful acclamations of a numerous concourse assembled on the common, testified the high satisfaction which pervaded every bosom on the election of Mr. Adams to so important a station in the national government." How important the station remains a matter of some debate; what matters for our story is the very simple but very important fact that the voters had chosen this man, at this time, and for these reasons to be vice president of the United States of America.[34]

And so he was off, over the flat, lush, and busy stretch that connected two of the nation's great port cities. The vice president-elect was to push on, reported the *Boston Gazette*, "while his numerous friends felicitated themselves, in anticipating the many eminent services he shall hereafter continue to do his county." Festivities, food, horse guards, and huzzahs followed Adams from Braintree to Sudbury, Hartford, New Haven, Kings-bridge, and into New York City. He would not say so directly, of course, but he must have enjoyed it all immensely. And though not as elaborate as Washington's, the pomp seemed to satisfy observers at every step. By Thursday he had reached Hartford, Connecticut. There, Adams was met by an "escort of the principle gentlemen in town, the ringing of Bells, and the attention of the Mayor [Thomas Seymour] and Aldermen of the cor-poration," who thereby announced, "the Federalism of the Citizens, and their high respect for that distinguished patriot and statesman." From these esteemed hosts the guest received a bolt of fine broadcloth, no doubt as a reminder of sorts of the city's textile industry and earnest for future con-siderations. New Haven bestowed on its guest its Freedom of the City; all along the post road Adams was received with "the most flattering atten-tion, the voluntary, sincere, and unrestrained gratulations of an intelligent, virtuous and independent people."[35]

Twenty-five miles from his ultimate destination, Adams and com-pany stopped in John Jay's birth town of Rye, New York, and rested for a few days at the familiar Post Road inn run by the Haviland family. For the first time since leaving Boston, John wrote to Abigail, filling her in on the events of the trip so far. With undisguised pleasure he related the series of warm receptions, the broadcloth from Hartford, and the Freedom of the City from New Haven. At "Horseneck [Connecticut]," he wrote, "we were met by Major Pintard, and Captain Mandeville with a party of Horse from the State of New York, and there is to be much Parade on Monday." True to schedule, the Adams cavalcade made it across the state line by Monday morning of April 20, escorted from Kingsbridge by light horse, military brass, congressmen, and other well-wishers. "From there they followed a procession into the City," reported the *Massachusetts Spy*, "to the house of the Honorable John Jay, Esq; when his arrival was announced by the dis-charge of canon."[36]

John Adams had arrived after a week of travel and a lifetime of service to country, family, and his own vexed ambitions. Even he could not gainsay the pomp and felicities of the trip; he could not help bragging to Abigail that "Governor Clinton[,] The Mayor of New York [James Duane], all the old officers of the Continental Government, and the Clergy, Magis-trates and People, have Seemed to emulate the two houses of Congress, in shewing every respect to me and to my office." Nor, predictably, could he resist observing that no permanent and official quarters had been provided. Just what one would expect of these Americans, thought Adams, who seemed not yet ready "to do any Thing, which will Support the Government in the Eyes of the People or of Foreigners." As it was, he sighed, their "Idea of the 'L'Air imposant' is yet confined to voluntary Escorts, verbal Compliments &c." Such complaints were relatively scarce, however, at least for now. Soon he was welcomed by Jay and other members of the House reception committee.[37]

After a night's rest at the Jay mansion—one would give much to have sat up late with those two characters—the vice president-elect was ushered off in the morning to the Senate chambers on the second floor of the newly renovated Federal Hall. President of the Senate pro tempore Langdon formally received him with a few words. No oath was then conducted, as none yet existed by law; he would take it later in June along with Senate members. But Adams did have a few words of his own to say and turned to the august body seated before him. A veteran of many a deliberative body, the speaker confessed himself more inclined to weigh in than oversee, as his office prescribed. He would struggle with this role, as anyone might have guessed, and he would just as certainly annoy pretty much everyone at one point or another. But Adams was game—he always was—and promised his best. "It shall be my constant endeavor," he declared, "to behave towards every member of this most honorable body with all that consideration, delicacy and decorum which becomes the dignity of his station and character. But, if from inexperience, or inadvertency, anything should ever escape me, inconsistent with propriety" said the new vice president, "I must entreat you, by imputing to its true cause, and not to any want of respect, to pardon and excuse it."[38]

Adams's time in the office would not be altogether a happy one. His critics expected as much, said he usually asked for it. Perhaps they were right; he managed from the outset to either irritate or amuse. Did he ever really enjoy his position or, for that matter, his later term as chief executive? Probably not, although it is usually impossible to tell what exactly satisfied the man and what he found disappointing. These are questions that put us ahead of the story, in any case, which now must recourse to a related but distinctive set of issues about the role of "the people" in Washington's "beloved country." Adams nevertheless helps us deepen our understanding of the inaugural events by reminding us that others, too, of real moment and prospect, were making their way to the nation's capital city. Adams belongs in the account because his assumption of office suggests a more restrained and modest yet important collaboration in the rituals of legitimation through which Americans were constituting themselves.

This dimension of the story is the more telling because of the differences marking our primary protagonists. They were in fact remarkably dissimilar:

Washington:	Adams:
Tall, athletic, graceful	Short, plump, sedate
Soldier	Civilian
Unschooled	Always erudite
Southern provincial	New England cosmopolitan
Restrained, given to taciturnity	See, "talks too much"
Dignity as embodied	Dignity as goal

For all these differences, Washington and Adams shared an even more fundamental set of qualities. These mattered hugely, because they set the tone and standards by which Americans were to judge of their leaders, by which others were to judge the great experiment, and by which indeed Americans were to judge of themselves. Both were men of absolute probity; no one, not their most severe critics, ever second-guessed the essential rectitude that marked and defined their respective characters. Both were by nature, practice, and profession patriotic to the bone. The new nation was for them at once the result and the beginning of something rare and true in the world—a beloved country—to whom they had devoted, it must be said, their lives, fortunes, and sacred honor. And both, through it all, through the defeats and disappointments, retained an abiding faith in the capacity of these people, these Americans, to make good on the promises of republican government. They were, that is to say, men of virtue who, for all their very real shortcomings, blind spots, and human foibles, gave their all for what was most dear.

ONTO THE WATERS

Thursday morning, April 23, 1789. His Excellency was on the way, his arrival "announced by a federal salute from the cannon, and the illustrious hero was received by the grenadiers and light horse under arms." Elizabeth-Town, New Jersey, was a small portside community with little to boast of except location and patriotic ardor. Its citizens intended to make the most of both—even if they did have to import additional worthies. Around 9:00 a.m. the visitors came into view, to be received by townspeople and a specially appointed congressional committee composed of John Langdon, Charles Carroll, William Samuel Johnson, Elias Boudinot, Theodorick Bland, Thomas Tudor Tucker, Egbert Benson, and John Lawrence—a distinguished lot, then, who repaired to Boudinot's house for conversation and last-minute preparations for the fifteen-mile trip over bay waters to the wharves of Manhattan. By noon it was time to be up and out for the final leg of this most extraordinary journey. Washington and company, "attended by a vast concourse of people," now made their way to the Point "after reviewing the troops, who were by this time joined by some respectable companies from Newark and its environs." At the Point they were ceremoniously "conducted on board of the barge prepared for his reception, the beauty of which met his highest approbation."[39]

Americans were builders, as Washington knew so well, so he must have cast an appreciative eye on this interesting example of the craft. One Thomas Randall, a well-known New York civil official and warden of the port, had bent his skills and contacts to ensure that the president-elect would arrive in style. The result was impressive: workers had put the finishing touches on her but two weeks ago, but at forty-five feet at the keel, masted, and equipped with a double row of thirteen oars, she might well have done Randall proud. A Philadelphia observer noted those important touches, including the arrangement to have the barge "manned by the pilots of New-York, who are to be dressed in white frocks and black caps, trimmed and ornamented with fringe." And the coxswain? Mr. Randall, of course. The whole of it was spectacular, as it was designed to be; no one, concluded the Philadelphian, could possibly miss its point. "It is hoped that on this joyful occasion," he slyly noted," the countenance of every friend to his country may bespeak pleasure—and that our enemies, if there are any among us, will not have the audacity to even look upon his sacred person."[40]

Though not far, the trip to Murray's Wharf would take several hours. It was time well spent. Washington's arrival will occupy us in the following chapter, but here we may at least point him on the way: from

Elizabeth-Town Point they cross Newark Bay and make for Kills; passing now Staten Island and north to New York's Upper Bay. Along the way he will be accompanied by boats of every kind, instrumental music, female choruses, ships of state, and the roar of the people. In truth we know frustratingly little of what he thought along the busy route. But we know this, from his own hand: all the ceremonies and good will, Washington recalled in his diary, "filled my mind with sensations as painful (considering the reverse of this scene, which may be the case after all my labors to do good) as they are pleasing." Washington must have known exactly what he was doing and what was being asked of him, by whom, and for what reason. He always knew, and he would not have had it any other way.[41]

CHAPTER 4

His Excellency Arrives in New York

When last we checked in on the president-elect and his retinue, they had cleared the straits and were making for the Upper Harbor. By midafternoon on Thursday, April 23, the lower tip of Manhattan Island hove into view. It had been a leisurely journey on the waters crowded by scores of craft, accompanied by song, salutes, and all manner of signage. The *Galveston*, a Spanish warship, kept the honorary barge company for the last few miles, as did boats carrying assorted members of the new government and its several states, guests, and security personnel. Readers as far away as Savannah learned of the epic arrival of their new president with its pageantry and drama. "The whole scene was highly animated," reported the *Georgia Gazette*, "moving in regular order; the grand Gala formed an object the most interesting imaginable." Eyewitness accounts from the thousands gathered at the Battery uniformly attest to the striking visual impression rendered by the approaching flotilla. As the barge neared, one observer recounted, "a profound Silence prevailed for Fifteen or Twenty Minutes." Now a "unanimous Peal of an immense Multitude, amidst the Discharge of Artillery, burst forth in an instance—the Agitation of the Crowd, and the Expressions of every Face so affected, and overpowered me, that I could not command the Emotions of my Heart."[1]

New York was ready. Congress and city officials a week previously put in writing strict protocols for the reception, including a reminder that the throng of worthy citizens must remember to make way, stand aside, and in general behave themselves. Massed there against the south east cays, townspeople had been waiting since morning for this, "the most solemn and affecting Scene perhaps, that was ever beheld." Thirteen oarsmen now eased the craft up to Murray's Wharf and its wildly festooned stairs. On cue, artillery roared its salute above the noise of the crowd, and George Washington stepped, once more, onto this island of memories. There to meet him were Governor George Clinton, Mayor James Duane, and many others of note. An "amazing concourse of citizens" pressed in close, anxious to catch the sight. "Many persons who were in the crowd," recalled a witness, "were to say, that they should now die contented, nothing being wanted to complete their happiness . . . but the sight of the Saviour of his Country."[2]

As church bells pealed and the crowd eased back, Washington was now escorted by the governor, mayor, assorted officers, and volunteers in uniform in a grand procession up Queen Street to his new house on Cherry. That night he would dine nearby with the Clintons in a city ignited by transparencies of every kind, music, and revelry. Everyone seemed in on the party, and for good reason. A local paper passed on words overheard on the streets that night: "I have beheld [Washington] when he commanded the American army; I saw him at the conclusion of the peace, retiring to his primeval habitation; and now I behold him returning to take the Chair of Presidency. I have not now another wish," concluded the elderly gentleman, "but that he may die as he lived, THE BELOVED OF HIS COUNTRY." We may suspect a bit of editing here, but only the deeply cynical would deny the sentiment or the pathos of age and gratitude thus communicated.[3]

One week until Inauguration Day. The time would be spent with correspondence and endless meetings and deliberations in anticipation of the responsibilities of office. What those responsibilities would be exactly neither he nor anyone really knew, but Washington, as always, would be prepared. Assuming he had any quiet time at all, he may have reflected for a moment on the past several days, on the trip and what must have seemed, to use David Waldstreicher's phrase, the "perpetual fetes" through which he had moved. For all the reports of transported spectators, Washington, too, must have felt himself moved, in his way. Aside from—but not irrelevant to—the quite real satisfactions that come with such mass affirmation, these exhibits of popular enthusiasm stood as incontrovertible evidence that the republican experiment was working or, at least, that it was off to a promising start. This could not be considered a given. Yes, Washington was a celebrity, and no one else would have commanded such ritualized expressions of support. As an essayist for the *Pennsylvania Packet* put it, "Merit must be great, when it can call forth the voluntary honors of a free and enlightened people." Still, he noted, "the attentions shewn on this occasion were not merely honorary, they were the tribute of gratitude, due to a man whose life has been one series of labours for the common good."[4]

We might add as consistent with this line of thought that the recognition of such merit is itself no small achievement. There would be no Washington without a citizenry capable of understanding in just what the "common good" inhered. The Americans of 1789 knew very well what the implications of this moment foretold. It was because of such rituals of collective affirmation and the values they celebrated that Washington's countrymen had a country to contemplate in the first place. "Our political connection with each other," a typically confident New Yorker explained, "becomes daily more intimate and interesting: this will in time assimilate our minds, our habit, our manners, our objects, till we become one great People, cemented by national ideas, national spirit, and national glory." Put another way: it was not only Washington who arrived in April of 1789—America did, too. And together they began to bring something new into the world.[5]

NEW YORK CITY

By late August of 1786 it was time for St. George Tucker and his wife, Frances, to get back home to Williamsburg. The visit north had proved delightful on most every account, but New York City—now that was something. Granted, the water was "execrable," the flies and "muskettoes" a pestilence. Too many of the houses were small and poorly built; the streets were terrible, and (worst of all?) the "butter and Meats are inferior to Phila." For all its evident shortcomings, however, the city seemed to the young Virginia lawyer irresistible. If he could afford it, which he could not, he would call the city home, and he regretted to leave its crowded, crooked, and utterly compelling scenes. "There is something unaccountable in the mind of man," Tucker confided to his diary, "which attaches him involuntarily to certain spots, independent of other Considerations. I feel this attachment to New York. And with the same society would rather live there than any other places I know." Many Americans, before and since, would know exactly how he felt.[6]

But not only Americans—visitors from afar shared the Virginian's delight in "the hurly burly and bustle of a large town," where "you may stand in one place in this City and see as great a variety of faces, figures, and Characters as Hogarth or Le Sage ever drew." By now the City of New-York, as it was frequently referred to, was pulling even with Philadelphia, and if its butter and meats still had a way to go, the town itself would very soon claim preeminence as America's greatest urban center. By European standards, of course, this may not have been so very much to brag about. With thirty thousand souls and counting, the city was substantial, perhaps, but not anywhere close to London, Paris, Lisbon, or other imperial capitals. And yet as Brissot de Warville reported after his own visit of 1788, there was an unmistakable feel to the city that set it apart from all others—including its European big sisters. Like Washington and so many others, Brissot de Warville knew he was witnessing a remarkable phenomenon in America at large and captured locally by New York's relentless will to build and, if necessary, rebuild again. A dozen years ago fire had decimated half the city; two years after that, another fire along the East River had destroyed perhaps sixty structures. The city itself had been occupied to no good effect for virtually the entire war. This was not so long ago. Nonetheless, Brissot de Warville exclaimed, let the doubters but look now on the city. "Whilst everywhere in Europe the villages and towns are falling into ruin, rather than augmenting, new edifices are here arising on all sides." Now, after the depredations of war, after the charred debris had been cleared, New Yorkers "enlarge in every quarter. . . . On all sides, houses are rising, and streets extending: I see nothing but busy workmen building and repairing."[7]

To create in the city is to create before others. It is otherwise on the farm, where the outbuilding may go up without notice, without comment. In the city, never; for it is by definition a space of appearances, where to see is to be, and to be is to see. The urban ecosystem, it is true, requires spaces of privacy as well—spaces of darkness and solitude. But these can only be momentary sites of rest and replenishment, that we may reoccupy the streets once more; to see and be again. This has always been the promise, frequently broken, of the civitas: that here one is most alive. In the city one may flourish as nowhere else because it provides the means to flourish with others—different, exasperating, interesting others. In the city all this is on display, or can be, and if New Yorkers could possibly agree on one thing, it was that the city—this city—was best suited to showing off all that was best and most promising about being an American. "Let those men who doubt the prodigious effects that liberty produces on man," wrote Brissot de Warville, "transport themselves to America. What miracles will they here behold!" He was staying, no surprise, in Manhattan at the time.[8]

New Yorkers will brag, of course; that is part of what it means to be a New Yorker. Aside from irritating nonresidents, this stance has served the more positive ends of showcasing to the world—making public, putting on display—those values deemed quintessentially American. If something very, very important is to happen, then it needs to happen, if not in Philadelphia, then in New York. That is why Washington when last we left him was making his way to a barge that will debark him on the city's strand; why this inaugural's festivities will take place on its streets; why the nation will announce itself to the world from Federal Hall. And it is why we will devote most of a chapter to the city, conceived here as a kind of text, the rhetorical function of which is to give optimal significance to the events of spring 1789. New York may thus be understood as the geopolitical equivalent to what in antiquity was called epideictic address; that is, a form of public expression designed to impart maximum symbolic power on behalf of that which demands our shared acknowledgment. Precisely because New York seemed at once a city—coherent, identifiable, and possessed of character and spirit—and a multitude—diverse, bumptious, grasping, and individualistic—it could serve as the ideal host for the nation's debut on the world stage. Here is the point, better put by a Connecticut writer of the time:

> The city of New-York, furnishes a just Epitome of the inhabitants of no inconsiderable part of the globe. It must be a grateful idea to a liberal mind, to observe such a variety of people collected from different nations; harmonizing in all points that are essential to the happiness and welfare of the whole. The spirit of toleration, that has always characterized the citizens of this State, the various methods taken to render subsistence easy and certain to the honest and industrious, have operated as a powerful means to draw to a center, people diversified in their attachments, prejudices, and manner.[9]

An idealized version of more complex realities, to be sure, but ever since Giovanni da Verrazzano's party sailed past the southern tip of the island in 1524, observers have projected onto Manhattan their most cherished and indeed outlandish aspirations. Its European inhabitants, of course, might and did fall short: "they all drink here," marveled one visitor, "from the moment they are able to lick a spoon," and appeared to have no qualms with hosting "above 500 ladies of pleasure" lodged "contiguous within the consecrated liberties of St. Paul's." And the way New Yorkers talked could (and still does) startle: "cursing and swearing . . . as if they prided themselves both as to the number and invention of them." John Adams, rarely at a loss for words himself, reported on his first trip to the city that New Yorkers "talk very loud, very fast, and altogether. If they ask you a question," he complained to Abigail, "before you can utter three words of your answer, they will break out upon you again—and talk away." On the upside, wrote an early traveler, the island's oysters were "so large than one must cut them into two or three pieces." But New Yorkers were nothing if not interesting, from the Hackensack, Lenape, and other indigenous peoples to the Dutch, Walloons, Africans, free and enslaved, Brazilian Jews, English, and so many others. "The eye of the curious," noted one New Englander in 1789, may now "be gratified by tracing the peculiarities of those who came from different countries . . . and delight in observing the accommodating spirit, and liberal views, that are gaining an ascendency over local feelings and opinions."[10]

The City is tireless and will continue to exhaust the labors of those who would try to capture it in prose, print, and song. Certainly, no such attempt is offered here, but then none is required. If we want to feel the full resonance of the nation's inaugural moment, however, it may be useful to remind ourselves of what it meant for it to take place where it did. Might the oath, the parades, speech, balls, and the capital itself have been situated elsewhere? Yes. But they were not. They were of a time and a place; they took on symbolic force from this fact and can only be rendered meaningful with reference to these situated realities. Here, on the streets of New York City, *here* is where America first showed up.

Before it was a city, before it was New York, it was a trading post operated by the Dutch West Indies Company. Established in 1624 as New Amsterdam, the city staked itself "within two prominent hills, in the midst of which flowed to the sea a very great river which was deep at the mouth."

Others had espied the land, of course: Verrazzano in the early sixteenth century and Henry Hudson in 1609, but it was left to thirty or so families, mostly Walloons, to make a go of it on the island's southern tip. About three hundred souls soon occupied the post, including enslaved Africans who performed most of the actual construction work. Protected in part by a small fort and featuring thirty or so buildings, the outpost was not large, but it was ambitious enough to launch a promising venture in trade, including beaver, mink, and otter pelts from up the river. For a time, at least, relations with native peoples were peaceful, and though the towns-people apparently drank a lot and swore mightily, all seemed relatively quiet among the enterprising Dutch.[11]

But things on the southern end of Manhattan Island never seem to stay quiet for long, and trouble soon arrived. With the 1640s came clashes with native peoples and the inevitable loss of life and property attendant. Then, too, New Amsterdam was above all a business concern, and it was not alto-gether evident that the considerable investments from the old Amsterdam were paying off. The potential was there; lines of commerce were open-ing up beyond Albany to include the coastal trade in addition to the home office. And Peter Stuyvesant, after his own fashion, had worked hard to rationalize and tighten up the town's political and economic infrastruc-ture. By 1660, New Amsterdam could boast a population of nearly 1500 well-governed, neatly housed, religiously tolerant, and ethnically diverse residents. That is to say: it was a sitting duck.

In March of 1788 a local writer boasted of his city that it was "esteemed the most eligible situation for commerce in the United States," command-ing then "the trade of one half of New-Jersey, most of that of Connecticut, and part of that of Massachusetts." By then the City of New-York could claim not only economic pride of place but a social scene like no other— or so its champions bragged. In "point of sociability and hospitality," they declared, the city "is hardly exceeded by any town in the United States." It did seem to have an alarming number of lawyers, and the schools were not what they should be, but all in all, residents might take well-earned pride in their "improvements in taste, elegance of manners and easy unaffected civility and politeness which form the happiness of social intercourse." That so many came from such varied origins, spoke so many languages, and retained distinctive folk ways appeared not to retard but enrich and enliven the town's cultural ethos. For many, it just did not get any better than New York. "Nothing can be more agreeable to one of my frame of Mind than this mode of life," recalled St. George Tucker. The city's short comings were self-evident, but all in all, he concluded, "I would live on the Island of New York in preference to any spot I have seen."[12]

Such paeans to the city are not hard to come by and indeed they seem coded into the very idea of what it means to be a New Yorker. They invariably gloss over the economic misery, racial injustice, disease, and related ills plaguing the modern city then and now. But they do serve to remind us that, while perhaps not really destined to prosper—what is?—the city was from early on an object of interest, greed, hard work, aspiration, and strategic design. Given the imperial dynamics of the period, then, it could have come as little surprise that by the mid-1600s the small Dutch settlement was living on borrowed time. With its splendid deepwater port, temperate climate, easy access to major trading routes, not to say its gigantic oysters, New Amsterdam was simply too promising to remain small, Dutch, or indeed New Amsterdam. The makings were there to all but guarantee a dramatic future, and in fact, as one historian notes, the town even then seemed "a kind of microcosm of the colossus that was to come." All this proved far too tempting, and so the English came, and they conquered with scarcely a fight.[13]

In early 1753, Stuyvesant stumped along Broadway at the head of a parade celebrating his town's municipal independence under the Dutch civil auspices. Neither the people nor their irascible leader could have predicted that within a decade its population of 1,500, its land, and the waters on which the people thrived would be fully reconstituted as English. How all this came about involves more than can be accounted for here, but the story offers as clear an example of imperial logic as might be wished. By midcentury, New Amsterdam had established itself as a nodal point in the Atlantic system of production and shipping; the city shipped to markets from Curaçao to the fatherland, to London and the sugar islands, to West Africa, Boston, and Charleston. Such growth inevitably must challenge English mercantilist policy, and it did. The knotted threads of commerce, law, and custom were at length sliced through in an act of breathtaking presumption when Charles II bestowed on his little brother James a stretch of real estate running from Virginia in the south and north up to the lands of New England. That gift in effect put a very quick end to New Amsterdam. With virtually nothing in the way of military force to resist the English claim, Dutch authorities ceded their rights, Colonel Richard Nichols over-saw the town's relief, and with the Treaty of Breda in 1667, New York was born.

One hundred and twenty-two years later the city would celebrate, not far from Stuyvesant's route, the inauguration of the country's first consti-tutionally elected chief executive. This appointment with the future was not prescribed, whatever the boosters might claim. But it makes sense, or at least it would not surprise those keeping an eye on the twists and turns of the meantime years. Something of the city's career may be suggested by New York's population growth: not as astonishing as it will be, but it is enough to demand notice at about 5,000 in 1700, 13,000 at midcen-tury, and 22,000 by 1770. For much of this period, the city had managed to steer clear of direct involvement with the numerous military commit-ments besetting its regional competitors, notably Boston, Philadelphia, and smaller port centers. New Yorkers were thus relatively free to pursue what they did best, which was buy and sell—and privateer, smuggle, and otherwise hone those great American arts of tax evasion. Competition was keen and mercantilist policy severe; one needed to be innovative to survive, and the city, as ever, could be dangerous. But also, as ever, it was richly textured: a thriving tavern culture competed with a remarkable number of faith practices for a town of its size. In 1687, the Catholic Gov-ernor Thomas Dongan pointed to a few Anglicans and Catholics but also an "abundance of Quakers preachers men and women especially; Sing-ing Quakers, Ranting Quakers; Sabbatarians; Antisabbatarians; some Anabaptists, some Independents; some Jews; in short of all sorts of opin-ions there are some, and the most part of none at all." In the half century since the opening of Trinity Church (1698), New York sited at least nine churches, including Anglican, Dutch Reformed, German Lutheran, Pres-byterian, Huguenot, Quaker meeting, and Jewish temple, Moravian, and Methodist. An impressive list, though not a few retained some doubt as to the influence of these fine institutions on the souls of the island's res-tive inhabitants.[14]

New York was from its inception a commercial enterprise. And this meant that however many churches graced the cityscape, its fate lay ultimately in the grasping hands of London's mercantile elite and their well-heeled political representatives. By certain standards, it had to be admitted, the system did work pretty well, at least for those, as always, in the position to work it well. Peter Kalm, a Swiss visitor at midcentury, marveled at the reach of the city's trade, exporting to London "all the various sorts of skins which they buy of the Indians, sugar, logwood, and other dying woods, rum, mahogany, and many other goods which the produce of the West Indies are. . . . and of late years they have shipped a quantity of iron to England. In return for these, they import from London stuffs, and every other article of English growth or manufacture, together with all sorts of foreign goods."[15]

Within a generation, locals of every bent, party, or station would have ample reason to wonder if New York could survive the storms of revolution into which it was now cast. The city suffered greater physical ruin than any of her sister ports, including Boston, Philadelphia, or Charles Town; it remained occupied by enemy troops for virtually the entire conflict and endured profoundly unsettling demographic shifts well after the treaties had been signed. Refugees fled; armies and navies entered; elites took their business and talents to more peaceful territory. In time the soldiers would leave, and civilians, welcomed and not, would come home again to the island. Wars of liberation are only in part about muskets and flanking the rear; decades of scholarship have demonstrated very clearly that they feed, starve, and replenish the ecosystems from which they are born. In his recent work on the "unruly city" in the late-eighteenth-century Atlantic, the Scottish historian Mike Rapport explains in highly suggestive ways how the urban landscape becomes itself a tableau; in it may be read the ways in which humans will avail themselves of its material and symbolic resources, thereby transforming the very meaning of that "text." This is an important insight, and it will help us capture, perhaps, some of the rhetorical energies that will in course shape the meaning, as well, of the nation's inauguration. In Rapport's words, "The cityscape as a backdrop, as a place where revolution and radicalism inscribed and transmitted their messages, the buildings as sites of political conflict and the reach of political mobilization into communities across metropolises, all of this makes the city itself part of the narrative."[16]

When the time is right, I hope to illustrate how Washington's inaugural address constitutes an ideal vision of republican unity and the values necessary for its survival. If we want to enrich our understanding of that performance, we need then to acknowledge where it was delivered. That much is straightforward: context helps explain text. But we can deepen the account further by dwelling for a moment on Rapport's insight. He may be taken as saying that the city serves not only as host to revolutionary activity, but the city is also and inevitably changed by that activity. No city ever came out of a revolution—successful or not—the same way it went in. If a statement of the obvious may be forgiven, such trauma as they will inflict on the cityscape can never be only physical. Violence of the kind visited on, say, London, Paris, and New York City must be civic and social as well. Violence by definition disorders, and if there will be blood, and there will, so also will there be a kind of shock to the shared assumptions of what it means to live under such conditions. When we ask, then, what it was that Washington's speech constituted, we can look to the charred cityscape of wartime New York for some of the answer. The years between 1775 and war's end in 1783 shook the very meaning of "New York City" every bit as much as what it meant to be an "American." To stand on the balcony of Federal Hall only six years after cessation of hostilities and announce, from a city once nearly decimated, the establishment of the world's first modern republican government—this says a great deal about the creation of the new from the old, the ideal from the real, and birth itself. One chapter in the story of New York, though not long, will help underline this constitutive force of the address; it, too, involves violence, disorder, and renewal. As with so many stories of the sort, it begins with fire.

At 2:00 a.m., September 21, 1776, a chaplain stationed with Colonel John Durkee's regiment in Paulus Hook was startled awake by the attending guard. He and the men were then informed "that New-York was on fire." This was true, up to a point. If it were not for the abating winds, he recalled, "the remainder of this nest of vipers would have been destroyed." In the event, enough of the city was seared to rate the fire as proportionately its worst before or since. Before the long day of the twenty-first was over, one-quarter of its buildings, mostly along the Broadway up to the King's College, lay in ruins. The "nest of vipers" remained safe, at least for now, but large sections of what Hector St. John de Crèvecœur admired for "Dutch neatness, combined with English taste and architecture" had been ravaged. "The Fire raged with inconceivable Violence," reported the royalist *New-York Gazette*. Apparently, it had started in the vicinity of Whitehall Slip on the southern tip of the island; from there it grew north until Trinity Church, "that large, ancient and venerable Edifice was in flames." Down it came, a "vast Pyramid of fire." Women and children perished as well; "their

Shrieks, joined to the roaring of the Flames, the Crash of falling Houses, and the wide spread Ruin which everywhere appeared, formed a Scene of Horror great beyond Description."[17]

The *New-York Gazette* could not resist reporting word that a half-dozen more fires were ignited about town around the same time—no doubt the work of patriot villains. It did seem all a bit too coincidental. Washington's men had been duly chased out of the city just weeks ago; rebel sympathizers were hastening to found Babylons elsewhere. Strange, too, that in addition to the multiple flashpoints, the firefighting equipment should be jammed, the alarm bells were nowhere to be found, and the fires started when they did and just as the winds most favored maximum combustion. All this and more, surely, evinced "beyond the Possibility of Doubt, that this diabolical Affair was the Result of a preconcerted, deliberate Scheme." On this suspicion some rebels were to hang. The author may have been right. Some thought had been given by the departing American forces to torching the city, and Washington famously observed to Hancock that "Providence—or some good honest fellow, has done more for us than we were disposed to do for ourselves." Who did it? We will never know.[18]

We do know that entire stretches of the city lay in smoking embers. Such residents as remained were bereft and many reduced to living in Canvas Town, a makeshift camp of squalor and disease. "The destruction was very great," recounted one New Yorker. It was bad enough living under the reign of an occupying army, "but the Calamity has increased them tenfold. Thousands are hereby reduced to beggary." Ultimately, however, it would take more than the conflagration of 1776 to dispirit the city's beleaguered citizens. In short order they set about rebuilding, improving, not merely enduring, but in fact prospering during the war's duration and after. A brief survey of the years before Washington's inaugural illustrates the point. Between the evacuation of British troops on November of 1783 to 1789, we may note the following: restoration of the local economy and redistribution of loyalist properties; the return to civic festivities, including Evacuation Day, the celebration for Lafayette, and the gigantic parade in support of ratification of the Constitution; the renaming of streets, forts, and buildings, including Columbia (*née* King's College); the founding of philanthropic organizations, including the New York Manumission Society; and the establishment of the Bank of New York. Theaters reopened, streets were paved, and lectures delivered. The Federal Congress took up business in City Hall and Trinity Church underwent restoration. The port began to stir again, to the relief of the new Merchants Coffee House. In 1786 the Friends Seminary welcomed its first class of young scholars, and a year later the African Free School, the city's first, did as well.[19]

There would be trouble: fire, again, in August of 1788 would take out sixty-four structures on the lower east side; the "Doctor's riot" would convulse the town in a spasm of misplaced indignation. Even the most cynical of observers, however, would have to acknowledge that, in spite of war, military occupation, economic depression, and civic unrest, New York seemed unbeatable. Thus a Hessian soldier remarked not a year after the great fire that he found the city "one of the prettiest, pleasantest harbor towns I have ever seen." Being a Hessian soldier, he could scarcely be expected to stop at that: "too bad that this land, which is also very fertile, is inhabited by such people, who from luxury and sensuous pleasure didn't know what to do and so owe their fall to naught but pride." Our mercenary proved himself half right, at least: as it happened, New Yorkers did know what they had; they prized it and put the city on a path that would lead to the nation's capital, and, in short order, to be the preeminent city in the land. New Yorkers would say in the *world*, and they, too, might be right.[20]

FEDERAL HALL

Federal Hall was not particularly ornate, nor was it exceptionally large (fig. 9). A happy synthesis of European and new-world federal tastes, the structure was nevertheless perfectly suited to its time, place, and purpose. "The style is bold, simple and regular," noted one admirer, "the parts few, large and distinct—and we think the whole has an air of grandeur." Situated at the corner of Wall and Nassau Streets, Federal Hall featured three stories, the second of which offered a balcony (12' by 44') facing Wall, arched walkways, and columns along the face. Here was to be the seat of the new government, close on Broad Street and appropriately very much of the city, not far from the busy port, and surrounded by the hurly-burly of citizens, visitors, and other denizens of the early republic. Like the city and its people, the government itself was on the move, and its first home would not last long: within a few years, the capital would decamp to Philadelphia, and before the War of 1812 was over, the proud structure was no more. For the time being, however, it served to house Congress and host

FIGURE 9   *Federal Hall on Wall St. N.Y.—and Washington's Installation 1789*. Lithograph. The Miriam and Ira D. Wallach Division of Art, Prints and Photographs: Print Collection, New York Public Library Digital Collections, 1650646.

the nation's first presidential inauguration. Preparations for the big day had come down to the wire, of course; construction schedules are thus fated. But here, finally, was "a superb edifice, in every way convenient for the grand purposes for which it was designed, and is a rich, and we hope a lasting ornament to the city."[21]

Building in Manhattan is never a simple matter, however. There is, as always, the matter of its physical appearance and location. On these issues, all—or most—seemed to agree that "the convenience and elegance of Federal Hall" were beyond dispute, that it "must afford infinite pleasure to the honorable body for whose reception it was erected." Even the good people of New Jersey had to concede its elegance, which "strikes every spectator with pleasure and surprise, as exceeding their most sanguine expectations." With its first floor assigned to the House of Representatives (approximately 57' by 62'), its second to the Senate (30' by 40'), and the third to such stuff as may be found in most attics, Federal Hall (95' by 145') provided a great deal with economy and grace. Before long it would gather crowds of extraordinary size and purpose on the afternoon of April 30, and here the business of their nation would set America on its course into the future.[22]

The story of Federal Hall and its role in the inaugural ceremonies sat-
isfies because it appears so seamless. As indeed it was—for the most part.
But nothing is entirely so when it comes to this city, and we may learn
something of interest to our own story by briefly treating the background
and strategic dimensions of the capital building. There was nothing inevitable about the choice of Federal Hall; for that matter, there was nothing
inevitable about the choice of New York itself. In addition to its material
appearance in the city, Federal Hall functioned symbolically as a kind
of claim-staking, as if to declare this: here is the capital, here is where it
belongs, and here it will stay! Of this the city was, if ultimately to be disappointed, at least for now quite certain.

And what was there to dislike? Convenient and elegant as it was, Federal Hall would be a daily reminder to members of Congress of why they
ought to stay put and would "inspire them with a predilection for our
capital, insomuch as to induce them to fix upon it as the place of their permanent residence." The city's hopes, though disappointed soon enough,
were not unfounded; much was to be gained from hosting the seat of the
new government, and as the charming mythology surrounding the establishment of the Federal City attests, things could well go this way or that. In
any case, New Yorkers would do their best to convince those who decided
such things that they had the most to offer, and Federal Hall might be a
clincher. Thus one writer (while keeping a straight face, apparently), hoped
to bank the building's impressive offerings to clinch the deal: "We hope
that the respect that has ever been shown by the citizens of New-York to
Congress, and the exertions made to render their situation agreeable, will
so far justify the choice they have been pleased to make, as to prevent any
contention in future on the subject of adjournment."[23]

This combination of idealism, self-interest, hustle, and hard work, with
a wink to certain realities and blunt insistence on others, is scarcely unique
to New Yorkers—though they are rather good at it. The American city, at
once so attractive and repulsive, has functioned generally as a space of affordance; it is, as we have already noted, where the concrete and the abstract
come together in lived experience to reveal who people are and what they
hope to become. When the city works to thus disclose a shared identity,
it is because people act as agents of their own futures—and that means
building, always building. The story of Federal Hall is particularly telling,
accordingly, because it involves not just construction, but reconstruction.

Without pushing the point too far, we may still see in its career something of the American experience; a story, that is, of invention from the given and at hand, where the resources of the past are availed of to create— and re-create—new possibilities. Neither buildings nor nation-states last forever, but those that last longest seem to be characterized by this relentlessly active, transformative capacity to adapt to the new by reimagining what has been bequeathed by tradition. This much is so with respect to the European migration, is it not? To American ways of war, faith, community, science, and nation-building?

Federal Hall may thus be read as a kind of trope, an example of what students of rhetoric call a synecdoche, through which a part may be taken as illustrative of the whole. The point in reflecting on this process, however briefly, is to remind us that where Washington took the oath of office and delivered his inaugural address is not incidental but ingredient to the very content of its message. That message was designed to announce a beginning, but was also fashioned, like Federal Hall, from the plenitude of its own history. "On lofty PILLARS rais'd, whose ample base," as a poet then wrote, "On firm foundations laid, unmov'd shall stand / 'Till happy years unnumbered circles run / The TEMPLE OF CELESTIAL LIBERTY! / Who deigns from Heaven to bless our happy plains."[24]

Should we choose to read the history of the city through its most conspicuous civil ornament, we would begin, appropriately enough, with an abandoned tavern originally of Dutch origins. Here the worthies of New Amsterdam fashioned their *Stadhuis* in the mid-seventeenth century, and here the building conceded itself to the new British colonial government. From its completion in 1700, City Hall supported crown, provincial, and city authorities. Such a concentration rendered it irresistible when trouble arose, serving rather nicely as a gathering point for protests against the Stamp Act in 1765 and the Tea Act almost a decade later. By the summer of 1775, the colonial government's days were numbered, and it sat for a final time in early June. In an act of greater aspiration than foresight, patriot leaders remanded custody of the city to a "Committee of 100." Whatever hopes it improbably sheltered for the effective management of affairs were shattered along with Washington's defense. The British occupation of the city put an end to its civic functions for the duration, but, serviceable as always, City Hall now housed the soldiery in fine if unappreciated style. Evacuation Day on November 25, 1783 returned the structure to those who would have it, and in due course the peripatetic Congress arrived at its doors in 1785. There it would remain until November of 1788.

A fine building it was, and nothing if not durable. But it was no capital building; it had survived much and was well situated. So, something to work with—a fixer-upper for a nation on the make and anxious to impress the neighbors. Once Congress, after the usual wrangling and special-pleading, had finally agreed to seat the new government in New York, the city's Common Council moved to appropriate funds "for the accommodation of the Congress of the United States." For design and supervision of the project, authorities turned to the redoubtable Pierre Charles L'Enfant, former French Major in the Continental Army, architect, and chief designer of the future Federal City on the banks of the Potomac River. Renovations began early in October of 1788 and workers labored with some urgency to get it all done in time and, without success, within budget. The results did not please everyone, but there could be no denying that from the old structure something entirely new and different had been created. The *Massachusetts Monthly* provides a succinct description: "This building is situated at the end of Broad Street, where its front appears to great advantage. The basement story is Tuscan and is pierced with seven openings; four massy pillars in the center support four Doric columns and a pediment. The frieze is ingeniously divided to admit thirteen stars in the metopes; these, with the American Eagle and other insignia in the pediment, and the tablets over the windows, filled with the thirteen arrows and the olive branch united, mark it as a building set apart for national purposes."

In the event, Federal Hall was still not quite completed when Congress was scheduled to meet in early March of the new year. Still, the result was impressive, especially in view of the time crunch within which the renovations were executed (fig. 10). For this, L'Enfant was appropriately feted, having "surmounted many difficulties," wrote the *Columbia Magazine*, and so expertly "accommodated the additions to the old parts, and so judiciously altered what he saw wrong, that he has produced a building uniform and consistent throughout, and has added to great elegance every convenience that could be desired." Finished or not, insisted a Philadelphian, "no building under similar circumstances was ever erected with such rapidity, and with such taste and judgment of construction, as Federal Hall."[25]

FIGURE 10   Hatch and Smillie (engraver), *View of the Old City Hall, Wall St. In Which Washington Was Inaugurated First President of the U.S. Apl. 30, 1789*, 1850. Federal Hall appears in the foreground, with Trinity Church and St. Paul's Chapel in the background. The Miriam and Ira D. Wallach Division of Art, Prints and Photographs: Print Collection, New York Public Library Digital Collections, 1650648.

The architect, as usual, garners the praise when these things turn out well. But the workers knew themselves to be the chief agents of its success, a fact they were keen to remind city officials on occasion. Others knew it as well, for the "exertions of the workmen ought not to pass unnoticed," since it was they "who effected so great a work, in an unfavorable season, in the course of a few months." In truth, Federal Hall as it now stood was the product of many minds and more hands, an emblem of civic resourcefulness, pride, and old-fashioned hustle. It would be hard to summon a more apt testimony to the city's ambitions and the claim it hoped to make on the nation's collective imagination. From its ancient beginnings and turbulent career, the building had reinvented for a new time and a new people.[26]

TRINITY

Hard by Federal Hall on the corner of Wall Street and Broadway stands the venerable Trinity Church, site and symbol of the island's cultural elite.

The two structures still keep each other company, as they did in Washington's day, buried now deep in the canyons of the lower Manhattan financial district. Today it is somehow both startling and pleasing to see these monuments to civic faith stubbornly holding their own—not as relics, to be sure, but as persistent and active sites of shared commitment among the drastically changing fortunes of the city itself. Not long after Washington was sworn into office, a local noted of Trinity that from the "size and height of this noble structure; the simple stile of its architecture; the Gothic arch of its windows, glass of which was set in lead; from the lofty trees which embosomed it, and the graves and monuments of the dead that surrounded it on every side," that from all this and more, he reflected, the church "presented to the passenger a striking object of contemplation, and impressed him with pleasure, corrected by reverence."[27]

Like its civil counterpart in Federal Hall, Trinity's story is very much part of the story of New York City, indeed part of the inauguration and so part of our story as well. This is so in part because Washington was known to attend services there, and immediately after his inauguration address he made a rather conspicuous point of walking up the half-dozen blocks to St. Paul's Chapel to hear Bishop Provoost's sermon on the occasion. More generally, Trinity and its "chapel of ease" on the corner of Broadway and Fulton provide a means to situate the inauguration within a rich history of initiative, adaptation, damage, reconstruction, and sheer persistence. That is to say, it is a familiar story by now, but that is the point. Virtually everything Washington did in public was by definition symbolic; when he chose to sit in St. Paul's that Thursday afternoon of April 30, and when he saw fit to observe the services at the Episcopalian seat, the new president was in effect affirming the power of that history to help guide the newfound people.

For all its centrality to the geographic, spiritual, and cultural life of the city, Trinity was never, in a sense, a given. Few things are—certainly not the City of New-York, or, for that matter, this strange creature called the United States of America. As with town and country, the church was begotten through a combination of nerve and aspiration; it survived by adapting and grew through talent, cussedness, luck, and a great deal of hard work. Thirty-three years after Colonel Nicolls and company relieved Stuyvesant of his island, local Church of England leaders under the good auspices of Governor Benjamin Fletcher managed to secure a charter and establishment rights. Its first sermon was heard in March of 1698, and in one way or another Trinity has never ceased playing its part in the life of the city. This fact is the more telling when we consider that at no point was the church close to being hegemonic; on the contrary, its career throughout the eighteenth century, at least, was marked by rivalry, threats, and outright destruction.

But Trinity prevailed, and it did so not by monopolizing its scene of operations but by working within it to maximum effect. Here it is useful to remind ourselves that while officially established, the church was located within a very diverse and changing landscape of faith, the more so given shifting ethnic and immigration patterns throughout the century. No question, the church did benefit from its preferred status as long as it could claim that distinction: a look through its vestry logs and clergy (Samuel Seabury, Charles Inglis, Thomas Chandler, et al.) during the period reads like a social register, as indeed it rather was. Now, if we pause on the names just above, a certain pattern will soon tell. The Trinity leadership tilted very heavily toward loyalism, with all the entirely predictable problems this would entail; Tory Anglicans and their clergy will leave the city by the thousands, die in it, or sit tight—and very quietly. Trinity Church itself, as we know, will not survive, at least as a physical edifice, burned to the ground under notably suspicious circumstances during the great fire of September 1776, "the burning of it," as a witness reported, "one of the most awful parts of that dreadful spectacle." A bad time for churches generally: four were burned in Massachusetts, two in Connecticut, one burned in Rhode Island, and another in New Jersey. War's end brought no great relief: the church itself was disestablished, which meant no more material support from the Church of England; the Society for Propagation of the Gospel pulled its funding, which meant reliance on volunteers and other forms of local and regional giving; and there were the many other claimants on the faith of New Yorkers, not least of late Deists and others of that vague and liberal tribe of new thinkers. Whither the church now?[28]

Trinity, like the city it served, had suffered grievously during the war. This we know. Less familiar is the story of its rapid reconstruction and resumption of place in the social imagination of the island. "Instead of the church remaining broken and inanimate as a result of the war," notes a leading historian of the institution, Trinity "demonstrated resiliency and vitality," a fact he describes as "nothing short of remarkable." It would take some time, and there was work of a very basic kind to be undertaken at once. The funding pipeline from London had been shut down; locals must open their purses. The clergy had been decimated, and, in the event, Yale, Harvard, Dartmouth, Columbia, and Princeton could be relied on to replace those lost to loyalism and flight. A month after British troops at length evacuated themselves from the premises, plans were already being formalized for the re-creation of the church on its current site. Now, declared Abraham Beach in December of 1783, "let us build our hopes of future posterity, on the firm basis of Religion and Virtue—against a Super-structure raised on this Foundation, the Storm of Adversity may beat in Vain." Five years later, New Yorkers learned that the foundation stone had been ceremoniously laid "To the HONOR of ALMIGHTY GOD, AND the Advancement of the Christian RELIGION." Construction workers are no more prompt building houses for God than for man, and Trinity would not be really completed until Washington was well settled into the presidency. At its dedication in March of 1790, Trinity stood proud at 104 feet by 72 feet, with a steeple rising 200 feet above the cityscape.[29]

And so it was that on the afternoon of April 30, Washington and company strolled past the site, past the masons and carpenters at their trade, up Broadway, and settled into the pews of Trinity's famed St. Paul's Chapel. Founded in 1766 to help ease pressure on Trinity, St. Paul's remains a vital presence within the texture of New York's urban life and rhythms. It seems not an exceptionally attractive structure: boxy and vaguely gothic, though patterned, presumably, after the more successful St. Martin-in-the-Fields. Such misgivings usually drop away on passing the monument to General Richard Montgomery and entering the chapel proper. Here, Washington beheld, as do the faithful and visitors today, the "Glory Altarpiece," described as "possibly the most unusual work ever created for an early American place of worship." Designed by the seemingly very busy L'Enfant, the altarpiece is nothing if not self-confident, an explosion indeed of mythical symbols, iconography, and mottos. One must see it quite to believe it. But there can be no denying the pathos, inside and out. On September 11, 2001, and for days after, St. Paul's served as a crucial resource for first responders, the wounded, and medical professionals. Though on a different scale entirely, the rough Georgian edifice had opened its door to the needful many times before, including to Presbyterians who faced similar rebuilding challenges in the immediate postwar years. The chapel was originally conceived in the mid-eighteenth century as a means to accommodate growing numbers and urban work schedules. "We have resolved," announced Trinity's rector in 1748, "to lay the foundation of a Large Chapel of Ease to Trinity Church Early in the Spring, our Congregation becoming so Numerous that the Church cannot contain them."[30]

The historian Joyce Goodfriend offers us a useful way to think about such sites as Trinity and St. Paul's Chapel. Where we have emphasized the dynamics of urban growth, its diversification, trauma, and relentless straining toward, there yet remains her key insight: these churches—all of them—served an essential social function that cannot be reduced to creedal differences. They operated, Goodfriend writes, "as the nuclei of ethnoreligious communities," which in turn "supplied the institutional networks that brought a measure of coherence to the city's social life during a turbulent era." Few scholars today would describe New Yorkers historically, at least, as terribly pious. None would deny, on the other hand, that its prosperity owes in no small part to the kind of institutional bulwarks embodied in church and chapel. The point verges on truism: still, we must not ascribe Washington's presence in St. Paul's immediately after his inauguration to empty ritual or cynical gesture to the opiated masses. For one thing, the president was incapable of expressing either. More importantly, his attendance represents to dramatic effect his confidence that Americans may be peoples of faith and of republican conviction; that they can have it both ways, and this to the public good. Was George Washington a religious man? An Episcopalian? A Deist? To imagine him sitting in that pew, in that chapel, in view of that altarpiece in New York City hours after taking the oath of office is to understand that the question itself is terribly beside the point.[31]

THE HOUSE ON CHERRY STREET

His Excellency knew only one home, and No. 3 Cherry Street was not it. Now lost to the demands of space on the Lower East Side and the Brooklyn Bridge off Pearl Street, the house had been erected by Walter Franklin in 1770, assumed by his wife, Maria, and passed on by remarriage to the Massachusetts lawyer Samuel Osgood (fig. 11). The new president, after all, had to live somewhere, and it was pleasant enough. Not perfect: a little far from the action at Federal Hall; large but not large enough. But it would

FIGURE 11   *The Presidential Mansion, Franklin Square, 1789.* The Miriam and Ira D. Wallach Division of Art, Prints and Photographs: Picture Collection, New York Public Library Digital Collections, 800062.

do, at least for the time being. Just a few weeks before Washington's inauguration, Congress had resolved "That Mr. Osgood, the proprietor of the house lately occupied by the President of Congress [Cyrus Griffin of Virginia], be requested to put the same, and the furniture thereof, in proper condition for the residence and use by the President of the United States." Workers hastened to put the house into acceptable shape, and, under the watchful eye of Tobias Lear and "spirited exertions," the executive mansion "was put into good order by the arrival of the President." New plate was brought in, mahogany and Chippendale furniture placed just so, the cellar (rather amply) stocked with wine, porter, Champagne, and claret. Visitors thought the house "sumptuously fitted out," and "furnished in the most elegant manner." Most importantly, *Martha approved*: the Osgood House she thought "a very good one and . . . handsomely furnished all new for the General."[32]

The general himself seems not to have paid much attention to the matter. Other than writing ahead to Madison to arrange for private housing, fending off well-meaning but politically unwise invitations, and putting a staff together, Washington treated the house as just that: a place to stay while business got done; camp; headquarters—what Mount Vernon was not and could never be. His real home was a way of being, so to speak, part of his identity and the exquisite moral order giving to that identity its distinctive aspect. There, on the banks of the Chesapeake, he moved to the sempiternal rhythms of time and tide; here, in New York, to the staccato demands of duty and ritual. There, was peace; here, noise and conflict. There, were friends; here, only strangers. But Washington was a soldier, and he knew very well how to make camp, whatever the lay of the field or the battle ahead. This fact gives us permission to reflect for a moment on what the headquarters on Cherry Street might teach us about Washington, his city, and the nation this city helped to reimagine. In the process, we may be led to see that perhaps Mount Vernon and the Osgood House were not so very different after all. Both were haunted by the terrible paradox—the manifold hypocrisies—of slavery, and each purchased its claim to order, function, and republican idealism at a price history would not bear.

The remarkable scholarship on race and slavery in the last few decades has profoundly enriched and reshaped our understanding of the subject on virtually every score. Still, we cannot but be jarred again and again by the seemingly inexplicable dissonance between the discourses of servitude and freedom colliding into each other during our period. Thus in the inaugural month of April 1789, we may read in the *Gazette of the United States* a paean to all that is great about this daring experiment called America. "A native spirit of liberty, and love of freedom," declares the pseudonymous "Americanus," "supported by a sense of common danger, gave union to the councils of America," and at length those who would enslave this land were forced to recognize it "as free, sovereign and independent." We may also learn from advertisement of a desire to purchase "A smart, active NEGRO BOY, from 13 to 14 years of age." Those who can, may "Enquire at the Printing Office, Franklin Head, Hanover Square," not so very far from Federal Hall. Or we might catch this posting: "For Sale: A likely healthy, young NEGRO WENCH, Between fifteen and sixteen years. She has been used to Farming Business. Sold for want of Employ—Enquire at No. 81, Williams-Street." Of these there are many.[33]

How best to inscribe such brute realities into our story of Washington's inauguration is no simple question; certainly, no satisfying attempt here will be made to reconcile, excuse, or otherwise wish away the prob-lem. Then again, we need to acknowledge the voices of dissent that were increasingly being raised—and heard—within the cityscape. The reproach could be and often was withering: "Though you are gliding on in prosper-ity," warned one such voice, "yet, in the hour of death, these things shall rest heavy on your mind, and make your passage to immortality horrid. The ghosts of these innocent blacks, which you have consigned while here on earth to slavery and misfortune, shall await around your expiring soul." Whether Washington heard these voices is doubtful; whether he would have cared is in any case up for debate. The wisest option is perhaps to bear down on some of the known particulars of the moment and seek to capture in some modest way the contexts of race in the spring of this aus-picious year.[34]

Washington and company moved into Osgood House immediately on arrival in the city. In short order, he had assembled about him his clos-est advisors and assistants, including Tobias Lear, William Jackson, and David Humphreys. Martha would arrive a month later, and in the meantime Madison, Hamilton, and numerous others gravitated to the three-story brick structure east of downtown. William Lee, who last we saw off in Philadelphia to get work done on his knees, would eventually make his painful way onward to rejoin the family. Such a household needs a staff, and to assemble and oversee it Washington plucked Samuel Fraunces—he of the Tavern and the general's bittersweet evening in December of 1783. Washington seems to have shared in the general enthusiasm for Fraunce's culinary and management skills. With good reason, apparently: "He tosses up such a number of fine dishes," Lear reported, "that we are distracted in our choice when we set down to table. . . . Oysters and Lobsters make a very conspicuous figure upon the ta[ble] and never go off untouched." The total staff appears to have numbered between a dozen and twenty, including in-house and outbuilding labor. Of these about one-half were enslaved and in time to include Lee; Moll, who served as a nursemaid for the several grandchildren about; Ona Judge, later to light out for freedom in New Hampshire; and Giles, a stable hand and driver.[35]

Some came from home, some were hired in the city; some died, and others lived long and eventful lives; some stayed, and a few fled. As slaves, they now resided in the largest slave-owning state in the north. The histo-rian Shane White, who has submitted the available data to exceptionally keen analysis, notes that at the time of the nation's first inauguration "about one in every five households in the city owned at least one slave." The reader is directed to White's work for further findings, but here we might at least register a few key facts. The total population of blacks in the city at the time comes in at around 3,000, or 10 percent of the total; of these about one-third were free blacks and two-thirds were enslaved. Most of the free black male heads of house were either laborers or artisans; many worked at the docks in such trades as the docks have traditionally required. Interestingly, White finds that the racial composition of the city was quite integrated; deeply etched patterns of segregation would be largely a nineteenth-century development as the city exploded in population, size, economic diversity, and ethnic rivalry. For now, the racial lay of the land was dramatically different from most of Washington's experience. He had lived, fought, and worked among African Americans all his life, of course, but not like this.[36]

The new president could be and was willfully blind to the harsh realities of race, but he was not obtuse. His arrival in the city must have forced on him such scenes of African life and community as to have commanded attention. Among these would have been an active, if not yet fully realized, abolitionist cadre of white philanthropists and their fledgling organizations. Just several years past, a "society for promoting and manumission of slaves, and protecting such of them as have been, or may be, liberated," had published a call to action in the familiar language of the day. "It is our duty," declared the author, "both as free Citizens and Christians, not only to regard with compassion, the injustice done to those among us who are held as slaves; but to endeavor, by lawful ways and means, to enable them to share equally with us, in that civil and religious Liberty, with which an indulgent providence has blessed these States, and to which these our brethren are, by nature, as much entitled to as ourselves." It would take until century's end to begin the slow process of legislating racial servitude out of existence in the city and state, but no one with eyes to see could mistake the trend of public sentiment.[37]

New York's African population, slave and "free," was at the same time busy with its own affairs and its own rituals of affirmation, identity, resistance, and celebration. In this it participated in a rich counterculture that extended throughout much of the northern states, including Negro Election Day festivities, Pinkster, and General Training. In the process, they "inaugurated a discourse of civic inclusion," in the words of Richard

Newman and Roy Finkenbine, "that became the basis for generations of abolitionist and modern civil rights reformers." This "black public sphere" would come to orient its diverse activities around the church and the lodge; the shop and school; the printing office, street, and waterfront. We do not know the extent to which, if any, these forces impacted in a direct way the lives of Washington's staff at No. 3 Cherry. It is certain, however, that amid the interminable visits, the solemn dinners, and staid levees that came to structure the domestic scene of the Osgood House, there could be espied, as through the veil, those who made it all possible. In this sense, again, we are reminded of the complexity of Washington as both man and symbol, who, like the nation he was helping to inaugurate, contained within, but just barely, for now, the powerfully disjunctive energies that would drive Americans for as long as they sought fit to call themselves a people.[38]

CHAPTER 5

Sacred Fire of Liberty

Nine o'clock in the morning, Thursday, April 30, 1789. Broadway is packed. Those not angling for position might be found in nearby churches, where the city's elite had gathered to "implore the blessings of Heaven upon the new government, its favor and protection of the PRESIDENT, and success and acceptance to his administration." Congress had already scripted the day's events, down to order of march, placement of the chairs, and the hundreds of details assuring that all would go off without a hitch. If this was theater—and it was—the thousands of citizen spectators could not have wished for a better stage on which to view themselves becoming Americans.[1]

Not far away, the president-elect waited. Around noon, the officially appointed procession arrived at the house on Cherry Street. It was time. Washington gravely assumed his place in the line, represented in scores of newspapers in the following order:

Col. Lewis,
Attended by two officers.
Capt. Stokes,
With the troop of horse.
Artillery.
Major Van Horne,
Grenadiers, under Capt. Scribs,

Major Bicker,
The Infantry of the Brigade.
Major Chrystie.
Sheriff.
Committee of the senate.

Assistants} PRESIDENT. {Assistants
His Suite

Committee of the Representatives
Hon. Mr. Jay.
Gen. Knox
Chancellor Livingston.
Several gentlemen of distinction.[2]

In short order the procession began its march by way of Queen and Dock Streets to the resplendent Federal Hall. On his arrival there, Washington was escorted in and up to the Senate chambers and formally introduced to members of both Houses and a very select list of guests and administration officials. Outside, the "scene was awful, beyond description." One witness marveled at such public displays of ardor; they were due, he explained, to the "circumstances of his election—the impressions of his past services—the concourse of spectators." All this "conspired to render it one of the most august and interesting spectacles ever exhibited on this globe" (fig. 12). At the designated moment the Honorable Robert Livingston, Chancellor of the State of New York, and George Washington appeared on Senate Gallery fronting Broadway. With his hand on a Christian Bible retrieved for the occasion, Washington then repeated the thirty-five words mandated by Article II, Section 1 of the Constitution of the United States of America (fig. 13): "I do solemnly swear (or affirm) that I will faithfully execute the office of president of the United States, and will to the best of my ability, preserve, protect and defend the Constitution of the United States."[3]

On completion of the oath, Chancellor Livingston turned to the crowd and announced, "Long live George Washington, President of the United States!" Immediately thirteen cannon bellowed in reply, and the crowd roared its approval by chanting the proclamation. And so, reported a

FIGURE 12 Howard Pyle, *Washington's Inauguration*, ca. 1889. Oil on canvas. The Harry and Mary Dalton Collection, 1989.61.2. Collection of the Mint Museum, Charlotte, North Carolina.

FIGURE 13   *Washington Taking the Oath as President, April 30, 1789, on the Site of the Present Treasury Building, Wall Street, New York City.* From *Century Magazine,* April 1889. The Miriam and Ira D. Wallach Division of Art, Prints and Photographs: Picture Collection, New York Public Library Digital Collections, 815048.

Massachusetts paper, "the great and illustrious WASHINGTON, the favorite son of liberty, entered upon the execution of the office of First Magistrate of the United States of America; to which important station he had been unanimously called by the united voice of the people. The ceremony," concluded the author, "was truly grand and pleasing, and every heart seemed anxious to testify the joy it felt on so memorable an event."[4]

George Washington, President, moved now back into Senate chambers for a second order of business. The new Constitution did not, nor does it yet, require that an address of inauguration be delivered. The form itself dates well back into English political history and had been deployed, adapted, and observed more or less intact throughout the colonial experience. The new executive officer of the federal government was not obliged, then, but he obviously thought it important enough to initiate the tradition at this most portentous moment. He was not, as we have more than once observed, by nature, training, or taste much of a public speaker, but he understood very keenly the relationship between symbols and power. Standing now before the assembled representatives and ministers of this new nation, Washington proceeded to give the speech of his life.

"The executive Power shall be vested in a President of the United States of America." Even in a document remarkable for its combination of precision and plasticity, Article II, Section 1 of the United States Constitution does not give us much to go on. Nor do the remaining sections, attending to matters of election, qualification, and other procedural concerns, specify in what, exactly, such "executive Power" may be said to inhere. We do learn that the executive is to serve as commander in chief, that he is to wield powers of pardon, appointment, and treaty making and to otherwise "take Care that the Laws be faithfully executed." This degree of indeterminacy was not, it must be said, for lack of trying: the fifty-five framers gathered in Philadelphia in the summer of 1787 spent a disproportionate amount of time in "tedious and reiterated discussions," Madison recalled, trying to figure out just what the executive was to be and just what the president was to do. The process had been neither smooth nor especially satisfying; "far from everything being settled," Ralph Ketcham notes, "virtually nothing was." The Convention debates over the executive, Jack Rakove suggests, bespeak rather a "tangled record of proposals, tentative decisions, reconsiderations, and reversals from which the presidency finally, belatedly emerged." Historians ever since have agreed that Article II remains one of the most strikingly "cryptic" passages "in all the annals of politics."[5]

The contests and compromises through which the executive office reached its final form remind us of this simple but profound fact: the presidency, like the Constitution more generally, was a product of rhetorical invention. As with all such productions, it bore the marks of antecedent traditions and was funded from a rich supply of common assumptions, principles, and shared aspirations. But the Constitution was in important ways something new in the world, and it was just as surely the result of strategy and selective interest—which is to say, of deliberation among powerful, articulate, and ambitious men. And they were a disputatious lot. "The players of our game are so many, their ideas so different, their prejudices so strong and so various," wrote Benjamin Franklin to Éleuthère Irénée du Pont de Nemours, "that not a move can be made that is not contested." When the "players" of Philadelphia took up the presidency in June of 1787, they accordingly took on themselves questions that had not only offered no ready resolution but in many cases had not even been yet asked.[6]

Nothing was given, nothing decided. All was possible, little probable. And this for one reason: the matter of the presidency—its status, its powers, its limits, and its reach—demanded of its framers that they confront directly the very meaning of republican government. In the process, they rediscovered through the give-and-take, the disagreements, and the disappointments, something fundamental about themselves and their experiment in representative democracy. This realization, hard-won through the years of revolt and confederacy, held that such a people as imagined by the nation builders could not long remain a people without a powerful executive at its center. Here, needless to say, was a tough pill for many to swallow, for had not Americans fought and died precisely in order to relieve themselves of magisterial power? But the constitutional debates and the ratification experience gave evidence that many more now understood that some kind of executive authority was required to counter the centrifugal forces of democracy, of localism, and of individual freedom. Such power unrestrained was tyranny; such liberties were anarchy. The challenge now was to so design the office as to allow for the energetic execution of the laws while acting in a way responsive to the sovereign will of the people. All this was readily enough grasped in the abstract. But what would it look like in action, once the office had been filled and the new nation poised to assume its place among the powers of the earth?

Americans found their answer in the august figure of George Washington. His election, of course, came as a surprise to no one, but this much scarcely settled the matter of what the nation was rightly to expect of its new chief executive. The real test came on April 30, 1789, when Washington undertook the oath of office at Federal Hall in New York City, kissed the Bible, paused, and delivered his—*the*—first presidential inaugural address. I hope to demonstrate in this chapter that we discover therein a staged effort to reconcile these competing claims of power and liberty. Washington manages this resolution by asserting the moral authority necessary to republican government, even as he subordinates his person to the sovereign body of the citizenry. Washington achieves this end, more specifically, by embodying and giving voice to the kind of virtue requisite to securing America's republican aspirations.[7]

The address itself, written with the assistance of James Madison and running to 1,432 words, is brief and largely without ornament. It is, however, an overlooked and woefully underexamined public declaration of what a republican government ought to sound like, what it expects of its people, and of what the people ought to expect of it. By way of proceeding, it will help to identify some of the primary lines of argument advanced against such a presidency, indicate how those objections were met by supporters of the Constitution, and turn then to a close and systematic rendering of the text. This reading is designed to illustrate the rhetorical process through which rival claims on the American political faith are reconciled in a conception of political virtue for which Washington stands as an exemplar.

On June 1, 1787, the Pennsylvania jurist James Wilson rose in the Constitutional Convention to move "that the Executive consist of a single person." Madison duly recorded that the immediate effect was unaccustomed silence. This was understandable. The assembled delegates may have taken a moment to reflect on how things had come to pass; they were now gathered, ready, almost, to deliberate a subject about which many were ambivalent and that some felt was anathema to the republican faith. So deeply rooted were anxieties about centralized power, crypto-monarchism, and abuses and corruption that followed like night the day, that it seemed to some in the cramped room heresy even to approach the subject seriously. The War of Independence had been waged for the express purpose of freeing Americans from one king, and now Congress was being asked to consider an "elective one," a "foetus of monarchy," and thus an unabashed repudiation of the "spirit of '76." The Continental Congress had conspicuously reduced its executive to a near-nullity, and for good reason: what magisterial powers were necessary to the conduct of government were properly located in the states, where they could be held accountable, rotated in and out of office at short intervals, and otherwise made responsive to the will and local interests of the people. True, a few had spoken out, some with great force and clarity, about the need for a stronger, more "energetic" executive at the continental level; but presumption clearly lay with the states, and if any headway was to be made, it had to be made through both a systematic dismantling of arguments on behalf of the status quo and with a positive, convincing plan for its replacement. The story of how this vision was conceived, argued for, and enacted is complex, but it has been told often and well. No attempt here is made to rehearse it, but a few important reminders are offered as a means of ingress into the subject.[8]

When Franklin invoked the image of the Constitutional Convention as staging a large and exceedingly complicated game of chess, he spoke, as usual, to the truth of the matter. On the matter of the presidency, the game played out over the duration of the proceedings with the usual lulls, feints, advances, and retreats typical of the debates at large. So many factors, conditions, and contingencies were unsettled that commitment to one proposal often hinged on the resolution of any number of other decisions. Among these were, notably, issues involving separation of powers and the relationship between the executive, legislative, and judicial branches; the powers, such as they were, to be vested in the presidency; and, of course, seemingly intractable questions surrounding proportionate representation. We need to remember, as well, that the final form of the office was not the result of a fully formed, united front bent from the beginning on pushing through a previously agreed-on model of executive governance. Madison had yet to settle his own views on the presidency even as the Convention got under way, Hancock declared sentiments well beyond the pale of most delegates and was obliged to fall back recurrently, and many others were satisfied to wheedle, concede, and adapt as various options presented themselves. Finally, it is worth reminding ourselves that the final version did not arrive until early September, and then it met with no one's pronounced or total satisfaction. To the extent that full confidence

was placed in the office thus conceived, it was in no small measure owing
to the towering figure of the former commander in chief. As Pierce Butler
later recalled, such executive powers as were finally agreed on would not
"have been so great had not many of the members cast their eyes toward
General Washington as President; and shaped their Ideas of the Powers
to be given to a President, by their opinion of his Virtue."[9]

The American presidency was forged from a convergence of historical, ideological, regional, and procedural forces. These diverse interests
meant that the office itself would bear the strains and tensions of the deliberations from which it issued. We will go a good way toward grasping
the significance of Washington's inaugural address by bearing this fact in
mind. As the first such inaugurator, and because he was George Washington, his speech assumes a disproportionate symbolic resonance. Its
abiding significance rests on the manner in which the speaker seeks to
resolve competing visions of republican government at the very moment
of its birth. These visions may be identified in the arguments advanced
on behalf of a strong executive and in those that protested against that
possibility. Together, the respective appeals of these competing visions
constitute the essential dilemma of republican government: how to sustain
the structural conditions of freedom without anarchy and of order without
tyranny. Washington's inaugural address, we shall see, operates precisely
to transform this dilemma from a paralyzing impasse into a commanding
statement of the American commitment to republican government.[10]

Critics of the proposed Constitution soon enough found themselves
on the losing side of history, and for this they have suffered. But before
remanding these Anti-Federalists to the dust bin of lost causes, we ought
to bear in mind several important facts. Though easily caricatured as shrill,
paranoid, and otherwise blind to the promises borne out of Philadelphia,
they are better understood as a diverse, principled, and often quite articulate body of skeptics who gave voice to some of America's most deep-seated
anxieties over the relationship between centralized power and republican freedom. They may have been "men of little faith," but even Cecelia
Kenyon conceded that the Anti-Federalists were "also first-generation
republicans, still self-consciously so, and aware that their precious form
of government was as yet an experiment and had not proved its capacity
for endurance." Far from being populist cranks and country rubes, they
saw themselves, at least, as holding in trust the revolutionary heritage of

limited government and vigilance against those forces—British or American—that threatened to undo what had been so dearly created. For this reason, Gordon Wood suggests, "the Antifederalists can never be considered undemocratic. They were 'localists,' fearful of distant government, even representational, authority for very significant political and social reasons that in the final analysis must be called democratic." What the Anti-Federalists had to say about the proposed presidency thus not only merits our attention, but we cannot even begin to understand Washington's inaugural address without taking their concerns seriously.[11]

The Anti-Federalist critique of the executive was of a piece and wholly consistent with their case against the Constitution in general. At stake in their position was republicanism itself, and its "greatest enemy," Kenyon stresses, "was man's lust for power, and the only things which could hold this in check, they were convinced, was a carefully written and properly constructed constitution." The document released to the states in late summer of 1787, they believed, clearly failed such a standard; this, precisely because it did not provide adequate checks against the all-too-human propensity for amassing, concentrating, and abusing sovereign authority. This appetite for power was apparently insatiable—ingredient to human nature itself. By centralizing executive authority in the office of a single magistrate, affording to that office the powers vested by the framers, and by granting to it reelection, military command, and other provisions, the Constitution created a presidency perfectly designed to encourage man's worst instincts. "There being nothing to prevent his [the president's] corruption but his virtue," James Monroe observed, "which is precarious, we have not sufficient security." If the Constitution was to be a charter of freedom and not of tyranny, then it had to guarantee against the inevitable. For "such is the nature of man," warned Maryland's acerbic Luther Martin, "that he has a propensity to abuse authority and to tyrannize over the rights of his fellow men; and to whomever power is given, not content with the actual deposit, they will ever strive to obtain an increase." The office on offer was another way of asking for trouble and courting the inevitable. Give a man such power and "his greatest object will be to keep it," wrote the "Federal Farmer," and "this will be the case with nine-tenths of the presidents." True, he notes with an eye toward Mount Vernon, "we may have, for the first president . . . a great and good man, governed by superior motives; but these are not events to be calculated upon in the present state of human nature."[12]

In the end, of course, the Anti-Federalists could not prevail. The Constitution and the executive office it created and vested became law in due time, and we have been living with the consequences ever since. But it would be naïve in the extreme to believe that because the Anti-Federalists "lost," their principles and the arguments giving them voice somehow disappeared from public consciousness. Sentiments so strong do not just go away. Leaders who wish to remain leaders are mindful of the persistence of strongly held convictions, though thwarted by majority vote. Like Washington, they will take these convictions very seriously in deed and in word.

The constellation of talent arrayed on behalf of the energetic executive proved unbeatable. Alexander Hamilton, James Wilson, Gouverneur Morris and a small army of supporters out of doors managed to convince a deeply ambivalent public that such a model of centralized authority was not only possible but essential to the prospects of republican government. Hamilton had long believed the enfeebled executive of the Confederation Congress wholly unfit to the purposes of a strong and growing commonwealth. The chief "defect in our system is want of method and energy in the administration," the result, Hamilton rightly suspected, of "prejudice and the want of a proper executive." Few who had suffered through the war years for lack of such method and energy would disagree, but the problem had persisted and grown in the years since; now more than ever, Hamilton argued, a strong president was needed as ballast to "every sudden breeze of passion, or to every transient impulse which the people may receive from the arts of men who flatter their prejudices to their interests." If nothing else, the decade of the 1780s had confirmed in the negative Hamilton's conviction that "energy in the executive is a leading character in the definition of good government."[13]

As commonplace as that sentiment may now appear, it was by no means a given at the time. In the course of the Constitutional Convention and ratification debates, the question of how much and what kind of power was to be vested in the executive proved exceptionally challenging. Critics, as we have seen, landed hard on the monarchical tendencies thought to inhere in the Federalist model and on Federalism's inevitable dangers of overreach, corruption, and avarice. The sheer number and complexity of the issues were daunting enough: Ought the executive to be unitary or multiform? What were the acceptable means of election? By whom? With what qualifications? How long was he to serve? Might he be reelected, and if so, how often? Could the executive be removed? Could he remove others? What was to be the relationship between the executive and other branches? And which powers were to be delegated to the office, which withheld, and which assumed as prerogative?[14]

These questions and a host of others occupied the Convention for various stretches throughout the summer, and all extended well into the ratification months. Federalist proponents of the strong executive ultimately proved up to the challenges of seeing it through the process; still, their formidable powers of deliberation were severely tested along the way. No complete treatment can be provided here of their efforts, but enough might be said to identify characteristic lines of argument, response, and strategy. The aim, again, is to suggest how these constitutional debates gave voice to rival conceptions of republican government and, specifically, of the role of the president in that government. Only within this context of competing visions can the rhetorical achievement of Washington's address be fully understood.

At the heart of the Anti-Federalist case was an abiding suspicion that a strong presidency was by definition inimical to the people's interests. Committed as they were to a worldview localist in orientation, jealous of individual rights, and insistent on the unfettered pursuit of personal happiness, they could not help but see in the Federalist executive a profound challenge to all that had been fought for and justly earned. If the pro-Constitutionalist spokesmen were to prevail, they had to confront this anxiety head on and convince fellow Americans that the office was not only *not* a threat, but in fact it was the means to their most cherished ends. The presidency, then, had to be construed as the best expression of what was best in the American character. The "history of the rise and progress of liberty amongst this people," as Americanus put it, "has convinced me fully, that it is impossible to subjugate a numerous and free people, spread out over a wide extent of country." And it was for just this reason, he argues, that "nothing can be more chimerical than this idea of the powers of a President finally degenerating into an establishment for life." Far from usurping the power of the people, "The Republican" agreed, "The President of the United States is to be appointed in a manner which is wisely adapted to concentrate the general force of the people. He is an officer appointed by the people," and "he therefore will be the guardian of the liberties of the people."[15]

Americans had successfully constituted themselves into a nation through a long and arduous process of compromise, concession, and no small amount of old-fashioned, back-room dealmaking. But signing off on a document—even one so monumental, so portentous as the Constitution—is not the same thing as making good on its promises, as Americans ever since have come to understand perfectly well. For behind its motive forces remained persistent and unresolved tensions over the proper disposition of power and liberty in a republican government. "An Old State Soldier" captured this tension perfectly: "FREEDOM has its charms, and authority its use—but there are certain points beyond which neither can be stretched without falling into licentiousness, or sinking under oppression."[16] This tension between freedom and authority is as old as government itself. Washington's first inaugural address may with profit be understood as one particularly compelling, surprisingly rich effort to resolve it to optimal effect.

To discern fully the meaning and import of Washington's address is to appreciate the profound transformations worked by and through the constitutional process. At its heart lay a fundamental shift in many Americans' thinking about republican government and its relationship to classically held conceptions of virtue. This much is key: without grasping it, we will miss much that drives the address and commends it to our shared heritage. The terrain here is vast and complex but must be mapped, however briefly, if we are to make sense of the subject. Behind and in front of the arguments over the presidency operated a set of assumptions that, though long-held, were fast giving way under the stresses of nation-building. Chief among these was the traditional role virtue was thought to play in the foundation and fortunes of a republican people. Virtue—the collective commitment to subordinate personal interests to the public good—had since antiquity been taken to be the *sine qua non* of all republican commonwealths. Only virtue so understood and so practiced was strong enough to withstand natural and inevitable excesses of power. Eighteenth-century thinkers from Montesquieu to Adams agreed that without virtue, there could be no future for a freedom-loving people.[17]

But something happened on the way to Philadelphia, something strange and unsettling. Virtue, it seemed, quite nearly dropped out of the discussion, and indeed one looks in vain at the text of the Constitution to find any explicit reference or allusion to the word. The reason, historians have taught us, is that Americans no longer remained altogether convinced that it was a necessary attribute of the citizenry; even, indeed, that if virtue was so important, Americans had not demonstrated much of it in the last decade or so. Either way, the idea seemed for many to belong to another age. "Undoubtedly," as Wood summarizes the case, "virtue in the people had been an essential substitute for the lack of good laws and the indispensable remedy for the traditional defects of most democratic governments. But in America . . . the need for a society of simple, equal, virtuous people no longer seemed so critical." And the reason virtue seemed no longer so critical was that it simply no longer applied to the rapidly emerging, market-driven, aspirational, and freedom-loving energies of modern American society. No one appreciated these new realities as keenly as Hamilton, who dismissed the traditional blandishments about virtue as retrograde: "We might as soon reconcile ourselves to the Spartan community of goods and wives, to their iron coin, their long beards, or their black broth; for it is as ridiculous to seek for models in the simple ages of Greece and Rome, as it would be to go in quest of them among the Hottentots and Laplanders."[18]

To restate the argument thus far: for all their genuine differences over the constitutional status of the presidency, supporters and critics professed fidelity to the republican principle that all power rightly came from the people. The question at issue was whether the Constitution gave to that power its just expression. As it bore on the executive, it seemed to Anti-Federalists that the document did not, inasmuch as it posed too great a distance between the people and so threatened to snap the bonds uniting a virtuous people with their chosen form of government. Conversely, Federalist supporters argued that in fact the Constitution's executive office was ideally constructed precisely because it received from the people its delegation of power and the virtue required to properly execute that power. Because the Federalists ultimately prevailed, they were in a position to put this new way of understanding republican government to the test. The overarching question now was this: what did virtue mean in the new order of things? If through the constitutional process virtue was in effect relocated from a necessary property of American citizenship into the hand of its representatives, then what must become of its traditional role in aligning freedom and authority? Whither virtue? In Washington's first inaugural address we find our answer.

THE FIRST INAUGURAL ADDRESS: AN ANALYSIS OF THE TEXT

No such address had ever been delivered. There was in 1789 no tradition of presidential inaugurals nor were there rituals of nationhood or speeches launching executive administrations. Local, colonial, and state occasions had long featured variations on the theme, but they were so differently conceived and under circumstances so different that little could be availed of to predict just how Washington's performance was to unfold. We do know that Washington, never a fluid or especially elegant speaker, felt keenly the weight of the moment and the gravity of its demands. Fisher Ames, the voluble senator from Massachusetts, recalled that Washington's grave aspect, "almost to sadness; his modesty, actually shaking; his voice deep, a little tremulous, and so low as to call for close attention," produced "emotions of the most affecting kind upon the members." Whatever the speech may have lacked in rhetorical flourish, its impression long remained with those who bore witness that day. The Comte de Montmorin, for one, recalled that "never has a sovereign reigned more completely in the hearts of his subjects than did Washington in those of his fellow-citizens. . . . He has the soul, look and figure of a hero united in him."[19]

The French minister's reference to the unity composing the figure of Washington is telling and may be used as a means to enter our examination of the text proper. As noted earlier, the speech is fairly brief, a little less than 1500 words and arranged into six paragraphs. After an unfortunate turn at the hands of his aide Humphreys, the task of arriving at a suitable draft had been turned over to the more restrained and polished craftsmanship of James Madison. With Washington's collaboration the manuscript achieved its final form and so entered the speaker's coat pocket. Although it has received remarkably little in the way of systematic attention, the address provides in its few pages a rich and enduring statement on the nature of republican government and the role of the presidency within its constitutional structure.[20]

Washington's address is best understood as an answer to this question: what kind of virtue is requisite to the office of the presidency? We have established that the issue is greatly complicated by a fundamental transformation in the way Americans conceived of their own capacities of citizenship, notably their insistence that government is best exercised in protecting individual rights and the pursuit of happiness in an increasingly commercial world. Venerable conceptions of virtue as demanding restraint, sacrifice, and Spartan simplicity no longer applied to the new order of things. The Constitution provided a means to delegate such norms as still obtained through the representative process. In its most basic sense, then, the national charter promised Americans that they could have it both ways—democratic freedom to go about their business unperturbed by despotic government; and authority sufficient to order the workings of society without fear of democratic excess. Virtue was thus transferred into the hands of duly elected leaders, including the president, who in effect represented the people as a whole. Needless to say, such an arrangement presented to the executive an especially severe standard of expectations, and it was these expectations that Washington sought to meet on April 30, 1789. He knew full well that what he said and how he said it would be taken as precedent, both because it was the first such address and because he was the man uttering the words.

Such a speech deserves a careful and systematic reading. To that task we now turn. It will require that we bend toward the text closely and exercise some patience as we follow its unfolding dynamics and attend to its internal economy of meaning. The aim is not so much to gloss the sentences one by one but to discern the way in which the speaker constructs a model of virtue appropriate to the president of the world's first modern republic. Washington's lasting achievement, we will discover, was to create in the image of his own person—his ethos—a standard of virtue strong enough to resolve the rival claims of freedom and authority.

The text is characteristically clear, direct, and formal. Its language is classically late-eighteenth century, syntactically complex to our eyes, perhaps, but wholly in keeping with standards of the time. Uniting as it does the pens of a soldier and a statesman, the speech is conspicuously without excess, easy sentiment, or rodomontade. At the same time, its very parsimony imposes on the reader demands of a kind. Here, it will assist in the work of interpretation to set our coordinates early and so to proceed with some system. The overall work of the inaugural, again, is to model a preferred image of republican virtue; this virtue in turn was to be of sufficient attraction and force as to resolve ideological tensions besetting the new nation. The performative energies of the address are accordingly directed toward enacting and setting on display precisely this sense of virtue—hence the modeling function. To this end, we may identify the internal action of the text as moving from an initial construction of the speaker himself, then to an appeal to divine aid as superintending the American experience, to a strategic rendering of the Constitution, next to a projection of audience agency, and finally to a conclusion in which all these elements come together into a coherent and compelling rationale for republican government. We can use these quite general phases of the address as a means of ingress and direction through to its end, but our insights must take us deeper into the text and toward a more finely grained account of what virtue might look like on the threshold of nationhood.

THE CALL OF DUTY

A week after the inaugural ceremonies, Abigail Adams reported to her husband that the newly installed president "appears to be most sensibly affected with the supreme and over Ruling providence which has called him to Rule over this great people rather than to feel Humble than Elated, and to be overpowered by the Weight and Magnitude of his Trust." Washington had indeed voiced on numerous occasions his anxieties over the assumption of power. True, he had by now perfected the art of publicly declaring such misgivings, but this moment was altogether unique. Aside from managing his affairs at Mount Vernon, the renowned Virginian had been free of formal administrative responsibilities since handing over his sword in the winter of 1783. And though he had every reason to believe that the office would be his, Washington nevertheless seized on the occasion of his address to remind his audience of his own deep and genuine ambivalence. "Among the vicissitudes incident to life," he began, "no event could have filled me with greater anxieties than that of which the notification was transmitted by your order, and received on the fourteenth day of the present month." The use of the word "vicissitudes" alerts us from the beginning of the speaker's personal stake in the prospect: in eighteenth-century contexts, it was frequently deployed to highlight the juxtaposed values of serenity, contemplation, order, and related terms associated with pastoral relief from the world. Here it sets up a series of tensions between the personal and public that will structure the introductory paragraph throughout. The effect is to confront Washington with a decision, and in accounting for why he ultimately chose to leave his beloved grounds on the Potomac, he offers his first lesson in republican virtue:

On the one hand, I was summoned by my Country, whose voice I
can never hear but with veneration and love, from a retreat which
I had chosen with the fondest predilection, and, in my flattering
hopes, with an immutable decision, as the asylum of my declining
years: a retreat which was rendered every day more necessary as well
as more dear to me, by the addition of habit to inclination, and of
frequent interruptions in my health to the gradual waste committed on it by time. On the other hand, the magnitude and difficulty
of the trust to which the voice of my Country called me, being sufficient to awaken in the wisest and most experienced of her citizens, a
distrustful scrutiny into his qualifications, could not but overwhelm
with despondence, one, who, inheriting inferior endowments from
nature and unpracticed in the duties of civil administration, ought
to be peculiarly conscious of his own deficiencies.[21]

Virtually every presidential inaugural in the coming time will feature a
variation on this posture of humility before the office and the call to duty.
We must resist reading backward onto the speech, however, if we are to
appreciate the novelty of Washington's circumstances. No other president would ever come to the office under similar conditions or with such
wide acclaim. By immediately posing a set of tensions between the allure
of private content with the travails of public service, the speaker confronts
himself with a dilemma certain to obtain for all those who would assume
the obligations of republican leadership. The opening passage of the address
stages for his audiences the drama of convictions inevitable and indeed
requisite to the office of the presidency. Thus repose gives way to action,
the pleasures of private life to the demands of public service; ultimately,
the self to the nation. This much is of course the very definition of classical virtue, rendered now not so much an attribute of all citizens as of those
who would presume to exercise the powers of executive authority.[22]

Virtue so conceived was best understood as less a set of principles held
than of motives to action. Under circumstances both historical and immediate, this matter of the appropriate warrant for assuming power proved an
abiding and much vexed question. History and reason had long illustrated
the perils of assuming the good will of aspirants to office; it was indeed
inherent in the nature of power that, once assumed, it tended always to
corrupt—whoever and whatever the professions of its wielders. Very few,

to be sure, suspected Washington of anything but the highest motives, but all knew as well that there could be only one Washington. Others would follow him in office. Was there any guarantee that others would act on similar motives?

The introduction so far may be taken as providing a template for ensuing presidents, a forceful reminder that the office at once demands and threatens the exercise of virtuous command. No other branch of the new government delegated power—however cryptically expressed—into the hands of an individual other than the executive. No other office, consequently, would bear so heavily on the character of its occupant. Washington seems to have appreciated this fact from the very beginning, and he never ceased to worry over its implications. The Constitution may have in a sense relieved the American people of the most burdensome aspects of virtue: by filtering the best of them up and through the representative process, they were freed to pursue such happiness as the country afforded. But no such relief could be afforded the president; on the contrary, he was now expected to hold as in trust that virtue known by all to be America's sacred grant. Given this standard, it is altogether explicable that Washington employs the first-person pronoun no less than nineteen times in the introductory paragraph. He is at pains, because he must be at pains, to make clear to himself, to his audience, and to generations unborn what type of leader the Constitution demands. The answer was *this* type of leader. In the peculiar alchemy of what ancient rhetoricians refer to as the *ingratio*, the image of the speaker's self is so constructed as to grow positively even as it is seemingly diminished by professions of humility.

> In this conflict of emotions, all I dare aver, is, that it has been my faithful study to collect my duty from a just appreciation of every circumstance, by which it might be affected. All I dare hope, is, that, if in executing this task I have been too much swayed by a grateful remembrance of former instances, or by an affectionate sensibility to this transcendent proof, of the confidence of my fellow-citizens; and have thence too little consulted my incapacity as well as disinclination for the weighty and untried cares before me; my error will be palliated by the motives which misled me, and its consequences be judged by my Country, with some share of the partiality in which they originated.

There is nothing coy about this stance, and Washington's audience would have readily recognized the language and the sentiments for what they were: the practiced but no less sincere acknowledgment of the virtuous leader that, having now accepted the powers of office, he yet serves at the pleasure of the public will.

THE CALL OF PROVIDENCE

Virtue in the eighteenth century was taken to be an attribute of the person and thus a definitively moral quality. Humans were understood to be vested with the capacity to operate as agents of the good, indeed obliged to act in ways designed to realize as best they might the designs of a superintending divinity. At its core, then, virtue was an expression of piety that gave public expression to privately embraced convictions. Proponents of the Constitution generally recognized that this quality was somehow integral to the foundations of republican government. Critics likewise attested to its importance by drawing attention to the document's failure in ensuring that the people's virtue was protected or that their leaders' lack of it was sufficiently guarded against—hence the hue and cry over the presidency, its prerogatives, and its inevitable excesses. Here we are tempted to enter the vexed and unresolvable question of the role of religion in the American founding and its constitutional origins. For the purposes of this essay, the temptation will be resisted. At the same time, it is crucial to our understanding of Washington's address that we account for its second paragraph, appealing as it does to the "Invisible Hand which conducts the affairs of men." We will find that, more than a routine gesture to the divine, this phase of the text advances the speaker's ends in important ways and works to secure the overall coherence of its message.[23]

Washington has thus far worked to establish those motives thought proper to justify the assumption of executive power. To the extent that the speaker can be seen as exemplifying such motives, he simultaneously may be taken to embody republican virtue and to model it as a standard for his immediate and future audiences. Such a conception of virtue, however, was not to be circumscribed by so limited a province as the self, or man, or even a George Washington. The new president was not given to conventional rituals of faith—Christian, Deist, or otherwise; the absence of any mention whatsoever of Christ in his voluminous writings is well known. Still, no great effort is required to find in Washington's thought a persistent recognition of divine will at work in the affairs of human-kind—above all in the origins and progress of the American experience. We need look no further than to this second paragraph of the inaugural address to find a masterful summation of precisely this thought. Rhetorically, it works to extend the introduction by shifting attention away from the speaker as such toward a higher standard of virtue than the individual, to sanction the power invested in that individual with providential design, and to set in place what will become soon enough the tenets of American exceptionalism.[24]

Constitutional skeptics—and they were many—who continued to regret the absence of the word "God" in its language, the lack of religious tests or establishment, or a bill of rights may well have found some assurance at this key moment in the text. If so, we may reasonably speculate that this was precisely its point. It would, said Washington,

> be peculiarly improper to omit in this first official Act, my fervent supplications to that Almighty Being who rules over the Universe, who presides in the Councils of Nations, and whose providential aids can supply every human defect, that his benediction may consecrate to the liberties and happiness of the People of the United States, a Government instituted by themselves for these essential purposes: and may enable every instrument employed in its administration to execute with success, the functions allotted to his charge. In tendering this homage to the Great Author of every public and private good I assure myself that it expresses your sentiments not less than my own; nor those of my fellow-citizens at large, less than either. No People can be bound to acknowledge and adore the invisible hand, which conducts the Affairs of men more than the People of the United States.

Washington had spent a fair amount of time, energy, and prose in the weeks leading up to the inauguration assuring religious leaders that his administration would respect their faith practices and freedoms. It would be difficult, given the passage above, to imagine a more ecumenical or more liberal statement of the president's intentions in this regard. More generally, we may observe in its language the work required to identify a disparate people under the auspices of divine authority. The essential benignity of that "Almighty Being" is underscored by what will become a distinctly American self-confidence that God has taken them as his chosen people. More specifically, Washington's appeal to "the Great Author" suggests that such virtue as may be assumed by its leaders is ultimately justifiable only as it expresses and acts on behalf of providential will. If this posture comes perilously close to a discredited version of divine right, listeners and readers were to be reminded that it was not the president's but the people's will thus sanctioned. In this sense, leaders, citizens, and the nation inhere in a unified body, reflected in and through the image of the divine. That the "Invisible Hand" has in fact been at work in bringing about this happy state of affairs is clearly evidenced by history itself:

> Every step, by which they have advanced to the character of an independent nation, seems to have been distinguished by some token of providential agency. And in the important revolution just accomplished in the system of their United Government, the tranquil deliberations and voluntary consent of so many distinct communities, from which the event has resulted, cannot be compared with the means by which most Governments have been established, without some return of pious gratitude along with an humble anticipation of the future blessings which the past seem to presage. These reflections, arising out of the present crisis, have forced themselves too strongly on my mind to be suppressed. You will join with me I trust in thinking, that there are none under the influence of which, the proceedings of a new and free Government can more auspiciously commence.

In the years ahead, such sentiments would feature prominently as a powerful, sometimes dangerous, and sometimes ennobling rationale for American foreign and domestic policy. Again, however, we must resist anachronism here. From John Winthrop's address aboard the *Arbella* in 1630 through the fast sermons, jeremiads, and declarations of the revolutionary era, the appeal to America's God was a fixture of civic life. But now Washington is for the first time providing as president of the United States a moral context for what it means to be a leader of a free people. The Constitution, as its opponents pointed out time and again, offered no such context. Here the speaker insists on it, and in so doing he offers a compelling vision of a people whose liberties are at once granted and ordered by the terms of a divinely sanctioned covenant. In this way, democratic freedoms are disciplined by divine order, and civil authority receives its legitimacy only as it is humbled in the presence of a moral authority greater than itself. Virtue, then, and Washington's virtue in particular, is thus given its full stature as a "token of providential agency."

THE GREAT CONSTITUTIONAL CHARTER

The primal text of American nationhood is of course the Constitution, and to it Washington now turns. In light of his previous emphasis on the moral grounds of republican leadership, Washington here confronts head on the fact that the "great constitutional charter" is conspicuously silent on any sentiments related to matters of virtue. This is, as we have noted, entirely consistent with the transformation in thought characteristic of American politics during the period. The Constitution was constructed as an instrument to better effect the great experiment: if that experiment was to prove successful, it had somehow to shift the burden of virtue from the people to its representatives. At the same time, certain issues continued to haunt the political scene that could not be ignored or easily managed through parchment measures. Chief among these was the problem of faction, seemingly endemic to a people as diversified, numerous, and opportunistic as freedom-loving Americans. The problem was made especially acute because the Constitution was designed not only to withstand but to actually embrace and, ideally, accommodate and maximize political differences. Given Washington's long-standing anxieties over the baleful effects of faction, he may well have wondered what might best be said about the national charter.

The "Great Author" may direct the affairs of America, but he could offer little help in guiding Washington's hand on this day. Seizing his own initiative, the speaker announces first what he will *not* discuss: although the Constitution established the expectation that the executive would recommend measures to Congress, no such attempt will here be made. Washington instead opts to commend the wisdom of its framers and extends "the tribute that is due to the talents, the rectitude, and the patriotism which adorn the characters" who had labored so assiduously in

Philadelphia and after. Such focus on the characters of the framers is telling, and crucial: it reasserts the importance of human agency and civic virtue as prior to the production of such instruments of governance as embodied in the Constitution. And it is on this basis, on the virtue of those who hold that production in trust, that Washington rests his hopes for mediating the restive energies of democracy and the ambitions of power in republican government. If the experiment is to work, that is to say, then it would be not so much because the Constitution guaranteed success, but because those who created it and now occupied its offices were possessed of the virtue requisite to the greater good. "In these qualifications," Washington stated, "I behold the surest pledges, that as on one side, no local prejudices, or attachments; no separate views, nor party animosities, will misdirect the comprehensive and equal eye which ought to watch over this great assemblage of communities and interests: so, on another, that the foundations of our National policy will be laid in the pure and immutable principles of private morality; and the pre-eminence of a free Government, be exemplified by all the attributes which can win the affections of its Citizens, and command the respect of the world."

This is in several ways a striking passage. Read closely, it suggests an idealism—a naïveté?—hardly in keeping with the framers' hard-nosed accommodation to the realities of political life. That even so optimistic a temperament as Washington's could seriously expect to banish "local prejudices, separate views," and "party animosities" strains credulity. But considered again, we note that Washington appeals, with Masonic echoes, to "the comprehensive and equal eye" that will superintend congressional leadership, and with it, to "watch over this great assemblage of communities and interests." The republic will be safeguarded, then, to the extent that it installs those possessed of such character capable of giving to public affairs the stamp of private virtue. In effect, there could be no distinguishing the provenance of virtue understood in this way. Because it was by definition marked by the capacity to hold together in equipoise disparate tendencies, and so render that whole greater than the sum of its parts, virtue conjoined what otherwise must disintegrate through an excess of freedom or of power. If Washington was idealistic, then, it was an idealism based on a faith in virtue as a force strong enough to bring into an ordered whole the ways of humankind and of the divine. "I dwell on this prospect

with every satisfaction which an ardent love for my Country can inspire,"
Washington says,

> since there is no truth more thoroughly established, than that
> there exists in the oeconomy and course of nature, an indissoluble
> union between virtue and happiness, between duty and advan-
> tage, between the genuine maxims of an honest and magnanimous
> policy, and the solid rewards of public prosperity and felicity: Since
> we ought to be no less persuaded that the propitious smiles of
> Heaven, can never be expected on a nation that disregards the eter-
> nal rules of order and right, which Heaven itself has ordained: And
> since the preservation of the sacred fire of liberty, and the destiny
> of the Republican model of Government, are justly considered as
> deeply, perhaps as finally staked, on the experiment entrusted to
> the hands of the American people.

History would in short order disappoint Washington's hopes, though
not all his hopes, or those most cherished. The decade of the 1790s was
to witness the rise of incipient parties, rival and often bitter personality
clashes, and a breakdown in the consensus politics native to the president's
worldview. But this lay in the future, however close at hand. For now, on
this day, in the first of America's first inaugural addresses, Washington
held out the possibility that the "sacred fire of liberty" might be sustained
if the nation's leaders remained mindful that the Constitution was but an
instrument of the "republican model." In the end, the real destiny of the
government it made possible could only be secured by the virtue of those
to whom it was entrusted.

We will have noticed that so far Washington has proposed no policy
and urged no particular plan of action or personal preferences. On the
contrary, he has conspicuously positioned himself in a quite nearly pas-
sive role, pointing out his shortcomings, paying homage to the divine,
and acknowledging the wisdom of others. This posture is extended into
the fourth paragraph, wherein Washington takes up the crucial matter
of constitutional amendment. Functionally it is an extension of the pre-
ceding passage, inasmuch as it gives point and direction to obligations
assumed by those who would exercise "the experiment entrusted to the
hands of the American people." Article V of the Constitution provides for

the all-important process through which alterations to the charter are to be initiated and potentially secured. In view of Anti-Federalist fears over presidential abuse of office and the felt need among many for a bill of rights, Washington's words accordingly assume heightened significance. Article V, we are reminded, cuts directly to the core of what it meant to establish a nation on the grounds of a written charter. It was, in Washington's language, a "model," but a model its framers insisted must be responsive to the will of the sovereign people. For all its novelty and genius, the provision nevertheless promised trouble if left in the wrong hands: if the Constitution was to operate as intended, it must at once secure the order and stability essential to rational government, even as it stretched periodically to accommodate the shifting realities of a growing country.[25]

This challenge is, of course, but a variation on the theme of liberty and order at the heart of the republican experiment. And it is just this theme that superintends the disposition of the inaugural address. Thus far, Washington has labored to make clear that prior to, over, and above any such political contrivance as the Constitution, whatever its genius, must be the active virtue of those to whom it is entrusted. Those who possess and act on its behalf were presumably equipped to find in the play of opposing forces the optimal balance between order and change: to resist the fossilization of the former and the disintegration consequent to the latter. Again, Washington will not seek to impose his own authority in determining how all this is to be accomplished; to do so, indeed, would be to undermine the moral logic so far established. He rather confides to Congress that he will "give way to my entire confidence in your discernment and pursuit of the public good" and assures himself "that whilst you carefully avoid every alteration which might endanger the benefits of an United and effective Government, or which ought to await the future lessons of experience; a reverence for the characteristic rights of freemen, and a regard for the public harmony, will sufficiently influence your deliberations on the question how far the former can be more impregnably fortified, or the latter be safely and advantageously promoted." This much, the speech insists, is and can only be the work not of charters but of men, and not just any men but men of virtue.

The penultimate paragraph may at first glance strike the reader as an interruption in the unfolding economy of the text. In fact, it is altogether consistent and coherent as a way of punctuating the message so far rendered. Promising to keep the matter brief, the president announces that he will "decline as inapplicable to myself any share in the personal emoluments which may be indispensably included in a permanent provision for the executive department." That is to say, Washington will accept no pay during his term of office. As every American surely knew by now—and if they did not, the speaker pointedly reminds them—Washington had forgone direct compensation as commander in chief of the United States Army for the duration of the war. In the event, Congress was to override his wishes and vote the executive a $25,000 per annum salary. But the point was made: by way of dispelling Anti-Federalist concerns over executive dependence or self gain, Washington's refusal of pay could not have but reached its mark. More generally, the gesture underscores the eighteenth-century, distinctly republican principle that office holding ought to be understood as a responsibility assumed rather than an opportunity exploited. The issue, again, was motive: what ought to properly actuate an individual to accept the call of his country? It is a question posed not to Washington alone but to all those now before him, and his answer was this: virtue alone.

We now reach the concluding paragraph. It consists of a single sentence, and though a long one, compresses into its train a tightly compacted summation of the sentiments thus far expressed. Read closely, the address can be seen unfolding through a brief but poignant series of statements on the nature of republican government, the role of the executive within that government, the homage due to the "Almighty Being" for its many dispensations, the status and function of the Constitution and of the obligations of its trustees in securing its ends. Underwriting all these observations has been the insistence that virtue must operate as the ultimate test of all republican government. We have seen Washington so presenting himself as to be seen modeling this principle, both in fulfillment of the constitutional aspirations of the framers and in response to their critics. It remains, then, to reaffirm those convictions to seek benediction, and declare for a final time on this day faith in the coming time:

> Having thus imported to you my sentiments, as they have been awakened by the occasion which brings us together, I shall take my present leave; but not without resorting once more to the benign parent of the human race, in humble supplication that since he has

been pleased to favour the American people, with opportunities for deliberating in perfect tranquility, and dispositions for deciding with unparalleled unanimity on a form of Government, for the security of their Union, and the advancement of their happiness; so his divine blessing may be equally conspicuous in the enlarged views, the temperate consultations, and the wise measures on which the success of this Government must depend.

And with that George Washington, president of the United States of America, sat down. Soon thereafter, he joined members of Congress on a half-mile walk from Federal Hall to St. Paul's Chapel for a special service, and then he retired to his private quarters. The speech was widely reprinted throughout the states and those in attendance who reported on the experience expressed uniform satisfaction at the performance. Fisher Ames wrote to George Minot that he thought its "sentences rather long, and not so simply constructed as Blair would have them, but may not the meaning be readily known? Is not a very considerable degree of beauty and elegance consistent with a small degree of obscurity? I admire the sentiments. The writer seems to have thought and felt when he wrote." Still, Washington's would not achieve the acclaim of Jefferson's first inaugural address, nor either of Lincoln's, or those of Franklin Roosevelt, John Kennedy, or Ronald Reagan. But the sentiments so admired by Ames helped define the moral basis of republican government as such government was coming to be understood at the time. The centuries have distanced us, as they will, from any real access to the immediate conditions of its performance. However remote the man, his words nevertheless continue to invite reflection on their meaning, force, and legacy.[26]

CONCLUSION

In his expert commentary on Washington's inaugural address, Stephen Lucas observes that the performance "was shaped above all by his personal beliefs and by his view of the rhetorical situation as he assumed the presidency." The speaker's aims were in turn given shape by antecedent traditions of office taking, and the address, accordingly, may be seen "as a blend of the old and the new, as a product of personal considerations, situational constraints, and rhetorical customs."[27] Lucas thus reminds us that for all its novelty, America's first presidential inaugural address was fully intelligible as a ritual of power and office. The point is well-taken, but at the same time we are obliged to acknowledge much that *was* singular about both the address and the circumstances to which it gave rise. The presidency and indeed the country itself were but a recent innovation, born of war and peacetime struggles to arrive at the optimal balance of federated power. For the first time in their history, Americans were offered in the image and in the words of their new president what such a government may look and sound like.

Washington's address takes on its full force and meaning as a result of the rival energies at play in postrevolutionary America. The debates attendant to the creation of the Constitution and its ratification channeled these energies into strident though often quite articulate patterns of public argument. As these arguments bore directly on the place and function of the executive office, they gave it shape and purpose, but they also gave voice to persistent conceptions about the relationship between liberty and power. The fulcrum on which this relationship rested was the role virtue was thought to play in the execution of republican government. Anti-Federalist attacks on the proposed presidency bespoke powerful anxieties that the customary ideal of a virtuous citizenry—restrained, simple, selfless, localized, and morally sound—was being hijacked through the constitutional mechanisms of election, representation, and consolidation. Federalist support in turn championed a system that seemed to promise Americans that they could have it all: relief from the obsolete demands of classically conceived virtue and freedom to pursue happiness as the Western world was then beginning to understand it. Such virtue as was still necessary to the integrity of the new political structure was to be assumed by those chosen to operate it. In the words of Hamilton, the "institution of delegated power implies that there is a portion of virtue and honor among mankind, which may be a reasonable foundation of confidence. And experience justifies the theory."[28]

But there remained a most important problem for supporters and critics alike. Experience did *not* justify the theory. History had *not* in fact demonstrated that the political elite could necessarily be trusted to act in ways motivated by the public good—in a word, virtuously. Never mind the benighted story of republics come and gone; if the past decade of Confederation had proved nothing else, it was that a system of delegated power guaranteed nothing. It was thus up to the nation's newly elected leaders, above all its president, to put on display, to make heard and seen, what the Constitution had wrought. Washington's first inaugural address may thus be understood as performing just this function. And to the extent that he could show that liberty and power might be held in productive balance, that such virtue as he possessed was indeed up to the task, he bequeathed to his new country "a reasonable foundation of confidence" in the great experiment that is republican government.

THE DANCE

The city, the country, and its people seemed, for this precious moment at least, as one. From newspapers everywhere, reports told of the day's events with its satisfactions and auspices of a nation borne into history with one voice. "A National spirit distinguishes and adorns the age," they declared, where "the full force and glory of this SPIRIT blazes with meridian lustre in the great national council, where, even local interests are advocated only upon NATIONAL PRINCIPLES, and as they may ultimately advance the happiness and prosperity of the Union." Together the inauguration party proceeded out of Federal Hall now, to Broadway and St. Paul's Chapel. There Bishop Provoost led services before the president and Vice President Adams, members of Congress, administration figures, and select guests. After prayers and a sermon, Washington was at length deposited back at the house on Cherry Street for, one hopes, a few minutes of solitary quiet.[29]

The city, however, would remain very much in the festive spirit. All over lower Manhattan bells pealed, crowds wended the streets, and Colonel Bauman's artillery staged a resounding show of fireworks and salutes. Transparencies illuminated the darkening neighborhoods, elaborate and often ingenious images featuring classical themes and ornate renderings of an emerging national iconography. At the home of Spanish diplomat Don Gardoqui viewers might see an illuminated image of the Graces and "moving pictures." Over at the Comte de Moustier residence, the French representative trimmed the doors and windows with lamps and elegant renderings. "That displayed before the Fort at the bottom of Broadway," noted the *Gazette of the United States*, "did great honor to its inventors and executors, for the ingenuity of the design and goodness of the workmanship; it was finely lighted and advantageously situated. The virtues, FORTITUDE,

JUSTICE, and WISDOM were judiciously applied." After dinner, Washington, Lear, and Humphreys made their way to view the scenes from vantage points afforded by the homes of Livingston and Knox. By ten that night, the President walked home after a very long and memorable day's work.[30]

The predictable rush of administrative, social, and household affairs busied the next few weeks. It would not be long before some kind of strategy was thought necessary to keep it all from swirling out of control. Sundays were off limits; this pleased the pious. The president would accept visitors, though not invitations to drop by. Nor would he return the favor. If you wished to see Washington and had the capital to do so, Tuesdays and Fridays between two and three o'clock were your best bet. In the meantime, Washington might escape the routines of office by catching Sheridan's *School for Scandal* with a few friends or attend the Columbia College commencement exercises at St. Paul's.[31]

The hottest tickets in town were of course reserved for the balls. Variations would follow when Mrs. Washington arrived later in the month, but these grand affairs worked wonders to refresh those worn out by the staid levees and formality of daily business with the president. On Thursday, May 7, the Dancing Assembly over on East Broadway near Wall Street hosted the first such affair. With Livingston, Baron Steuben, Knox, Jay, Hamilton, assorted foreign ministers, and about three hundred others looking on, Washington stepped forward and, taking the hand of Mrs. James Duane, put into motion a gale that would not end until midmorning. A graceful athlete and accomplished dancer, the general would command attention in any case. One cannot help but appreciate the sight of the Knoxes afoot or wonder what the good Baron thought of all this. We do know that Washington was not the only source of fascination, for there was reported "a numerous and brilliant collection of ladies, dressed with consummate taste and elegance." And those outfits were *complicated*. A Colonel Stone described soon after his favorite ensemble:

> a plain celestial blue satin gown, with a white satin petticoat. On the neck was worn a very large Italian gauze handkerchief, with border stripes of satin. The headdress was a *pouf* of gauze, in the form of a globe, the *creneaux* or head-piece of which was composed of white satin, having a double wing, in large plaits, and trimmed with a wreath of artificial roses, falling from the left at the top to

the right at the bottom, in front, and the reverse behind. The hair was dressed all over in detached curls, four of which in two ranks, fell on each side of the neck, and were relieved behind by a floating *chignon*.[32]

Washington, one assumes, enjoyed himself, for a week later they were all back on the dance floor, this time at the home of the Comte de Moustier on Broadway. If anyone knew how to host such a gathering, it was the French minister, who spared nothing in reminding his guests what real elegance looked like. And real dancing: "As a complement to our alliance with France," reported one guest, "there were two sets of Cotillion Dancers in complete uniforms; one set in that of France, and the other in Blue and Buff. The Ladies were dressed in white, with Ribbands, bouquets and garlands of Flowers, answering to the uniforms of the Gentlemen." Elias Boudinot and the rest "retired about ten o'clock, in the height of jollity." It was, he thought, "a most splendid ball indeed."[33]

Rather more grave business would assert itself soon enough. Martha would come soon, and the household must be properly assembled. Appointments must be made, a government funded, and laws made; there was a peace to keep and a country to hold close. Such festivities as we have briefly reviewed here are important, whatever we may think of the apparent excess or exaggerated professions. They function in part as a kind of chorus, not always in perfect tune, for moments of change and presumptive growth. They are made public and thereby enrich the public; they are symbolically resonant and so keep funded the store of rhetorical resources necessary for a loud and talkative people. Above all, they grant occasion for a diverse and contentious people to come together, however briefly and imperfectly, to assist in the work of making republican government meaningful to themselves. This collective act of affirmation, in the words of a Massachusetts orator, "not only confers the greatest honor on the man of their choice that a people can confer, but reflects distinguished honor on themselves, as an evidence that they are feelingly alive to excellence of character, and know how to confer the rewards of virtue."[34]

CHAPTER 6

The First Inauguration in American Memory

THE SEMICENTENNIAL

Tuesday in Manhattan; late morning, April 30, 1839. The seventy-two-year-old former president had finished up breakfast at the City Hotel and made ready for the walk down Broadway to the Middle Dutch Church off Nassau Street. It would prove a long day, but John Quincy Adams had every intention of giving to his views their fullest—and longest—expression. Born before the Boston Massacre, Adams witnessed and eventually participated in an almost unbelievable number of pivotal events in the formation of his country. He came to adolescence during the American Revolution and to adulthood during Confederation and ratification of the Constitution; became the leading diplomatic figure of his generation; served in Congress; composed a highly regarded treatise on rhetoric and oratory for the students at Harvard; and won and lost a presidency. The business of the day, however, was not battle but a celebration of what battle had won for this still-fledgling nation on its fiftieth birthday of constitutional life.

It could be hard to tell whether the speaker was youthful in his age or too old for a man of his years. Something similar might be observed of New York as it set about to host the nation's semicentennial. When Adams was born, the town to his south might claim less than 20,000 souls; on this spring day, the population was crowding toward a third of a million. Not many were still around from the old days, but those who were could justly boast of seeing, if not everything, then one hell of a lot. How perfect, then, how lucky, for the New-York Historical Society to land as its orator of the day history's favorite ex-president, scorned in office, hustled out, still in the mix, and now on his way to the public stage yet again. In this image we may find a means to briefly capture something of the rhetorical culture of this, the first such celebration of Washington's inaugural performance. It can be no more than a glimpse, but perhaps we get a sense of what a city, a people, and a nation sound like when, in spite of all the centrifugal forces—and in 1839 those forces were formidable indeed—they try to remember who they were, *why* they were, and so to steel themselves for who they may yet become.

It all came off without a hitch, New Yorkers being by now rather practiced in the art of civic festivity. "The whole Celebration was creditable to those who originated it," reported a local observer, "and calculated at once to honor and strengthen the tie which binds our twenty-six States into one united and happy people." This last bit was fantasy, of course: in two decades this people would initiate the slaughter of hundreds of thousands of its own. For the moment, in any case, Stuyvesant and company had orchestrated a seamless agenda for the day's festivities. By noon, the city's elite had made their way from the church to the City Hotel where hundreds waited to hear the "scholar, the patriot, the sage." They were not disappointed. "It was delightful to hear the Statesman of four-score years [*sic*]," the press recalled, "describing with the graphic fidelity of an eye-witness and an intimate, the scenes and characters of the revolutionary era—telling of the trials, doubts and sacrifices of the great Apostle and Champion of Liberty." Washington the man may be gone, but his spirit lived, presided over, dubiously, by the hovering image of his mother, Mary. Thus Adams called to mind for present generations "the moral elements of his greatness," and called on them "to emulate the glorious model—while at the same time, the Orator awakened memories in the breasts of men neared his own age, that made their hearts melt within them."[1]

Adams was not by nature a sanguine man. He had seen too much and thought for too long and stood too firmly on his dignity to take much joy in the play of life, much less politics. But he knew a great deal about the birth and growth of his country, probably more than anyone alive; he loved it, and he cherished its prospects. The generation of giants from which Washington—first among equals—had risen to usher in that country had passed or was passing. "They have been gathered to their fathers," Adams noted, and that "posterity for whom they toiled, not less anxiously than for themselves, has arisen to occupy their places, and is rapidly passing away in its turn." And now a new generation "unborn upon the day which you commemorate, forms a vast majority of the assembly who now honor me with their attention." More states, more people, vast tracts under plow: "Never," Adams intoned, "since the first assemblage of men in social union, has there been such a scene of continued prosperity recorded upon the annals of time."[2]

We might with reason chalk this kind of talk up to the dictates of ceremonial address. Certainly Americans then, before, and now seem never to get enough self-congratulation. So much is true, but we might with greater reason recall the circumstances of the speech. Its immediate occasion was the semicentennial. It would require an especially obtuse audience member, however, to ignore who it was on that podium and who, for that matter, was seated on the stage with him: Justice Smith Thompson of the United States Supreme Court, war heroes including Colonel John Trumbull and Generals Winfield Scott and Morgan Lewis, and New Jersey Governor William Pennington. These were personages, retired or active, whose character had been forged, scarred, bruised, and burnished through a very trying stretch of young nationhood. Now we may sharpen the point with a quick reminder of what, in the most general terms, was actually going on in this nation.

Since Adams had taken office in Washington's administration as minister to the Netherlands in 1794, the United States had faced off against its own Native Americans, the French, Barbary pirates, and the British. Its several administrations had expended enormous capital staving off southern secessionist threats and breakaway movements in the west; periodic diseases had ravaged its largest cities; rapid industrialization was wreaking havoc with traditional folkways and communal norms, not to say the money markets; and in the decade of the 1830s alone, deeply troubling urban unrest, rioting, and mob violence over slavery and race relations threatened the very foundations of civil society. That is to say that the fifty-year celebration of Washington's inaugural, far from being an empty ritual of passing self-congratulation, was in fact an absolutely necessary exercise in national reconstitution. Little wonder Adams seemed to so many so serious. He could not, under the circumstances, have been otherwise.

And what of the city itself? How had the decade treated its fair residents? Not so well, actually. True, the usual descriptors, even now becoming a little tired, might still apply: here was Gotham! City of merchants, port of a million sails, the infinitely rich and varied tapestry of humanity, and so on. Visitors from near and far continued to extoll its spirit, "the tremendous commercial activity," in the account of the Spaniard Ramon de la Sagra, "the continual pursuit of industry, the progress of the population, the general affluences and a certain air of well being which prevails among all classes." Even the congenitally disapproving Frances Trollope had to admit that New York was "one of the finest cities I ever saw, and as much superior to every other in the Union (Philadelphia not excepted), as London to Liverpool, or Paris to Rouen."[3]

Those who actually resided there, however, who experienced the decade close at hand, may be forgiven for holding somewhat more complicated views of life in the city. Two notable episodes can help us understand why, and therefore why the celebrations of April 1839 served such important ends. On December 16, 1835, "a most awful conflagration" erupted in the commercial district between the Exchange and Pearl Street, whipped by freezing winds and fueled by densely quartered warehouses. Very quickly the fire was beyond the control of human or technological ingenuity: ice had rendered hoses and ponds worthless, the firefighting crews were utterly overwhelmed, and nothing save Providence itself seemed capable of limiting the damage. The inferno blasted so hot and so high as to be visible in several adjoining states. On it burned, moving north, consuming everything in its path: stores and more warehouses; the Merchants' Exchange and the Tontine Coffee House; up went the statue of Alexander Hamilton; down came the Post Office. Now the fired roared along the East River—indeed, onto the river itself. At length heroic efforts managed to at least contain the damage, but it would be days before the last foundations ceased smoldering. Although remarkably few lives were lost, the damage was truly stunning: between six and seven hundred buildings incinerated and untold businesses destroyed. On December 15, the city hosted twenty-six fire insurance companies. Of those, three survived. For a city whose livelihood depended on water, New York could seem peculiarly subject to contagions like that of 1835. But as it had before and would do again, the people set to work clearing away the charred remains, rebuilding, arguing, cajoling, brawling, looting, and, again, re-creating from the old a better version of itself.[4]

At first, the prospects looked quite good. Locally as well as in the state and nation at large, economic expansion encouraged—demanded—initiative, borrowing, more building, and more trade. Such irrational exuberance, as we might say in our time, would not, could not, last—and it did not. By 1837 a toxic combination of Jacksonian policy, international banking dynamics (notably, the Bank of England's jack of the interest rate), and old-fashioned fear spelled the end of any lingering giddiness as might have afflicted city entrepreneurs. The effects were quick and palpable: in the words of one English visitor in May of 1837, "My appearance at New York was very much like bursting into a friend's house with a merry face when there is a death in it. . . . Suspicion, fear, and misfortune have taken possession of the city." Hard times would settle onto the city and much of the nation for a decade: nearly half the country's banks would fail in part or completely; businesses could not borrow; and the markets staggered and fell. Inevitably, too, came the push back, the riots, crime, scapegoating, as did the anti-Semitism, racism, and xenophobia that so frequently infect the weakened body. Where there was quiet, there was very little else, and now, the diarist Philip Hone noted sadly, "a deadly calm pervades this lately flourishing city." That "deadly calm" could not last, of course, not in New York, but there is no point in trying to convince those who struggled then of this fact. Only they could reckon themselves out of the miseries of the Panic of 1837—and they did, many of them, though certainly not all.[5]

The day's speaker was, after two hours, nearly finished. Thus far his audience had been treated to a deeply satisfying concoction of classic Adams oratory: equal parts Harvard lecture, commencement address, partisan score settling, and New England jeremiad. And they appeared to love every word of it. Inside the church, city elites were given to witness a "soul-chaining composition," a speech so moving that "at times the audience were melted into tears, and at times the church rang with applauses, which were loud and deep at its close." A bit much, these descriptions, at least by the lights of our time; it is nevertheless remarkable how many and how consistent are these reports of Adams's performance. His depiction of Washington's inauguration, wrote one paper, "was graphic, perfect, sublime." Another: "sublimely eloquent and affecting." Why Adams was able, apparently, to strike such deep and resonant chords is perhaps not in the end so very difficult explain, however distant the rhetorical sensibilities then at play. His audience within and without, in the city and in the nation, hungered for what he had to say and needed the nourishment his words could provide. That was the point, after all, of thus enacting once again a ritual of collective self-affirmation, of rehearsing, that is, the national narrative; as if, in this way, the old truths may serve as the foundation stones on which the new may be erected. Adams knew this, surely, and so we let him conclude in his own words:

> Lay up these principles, then, in your hearts, and in your souls— bind them as signs upon your hands, that they may be as frontlets before your eyes—teach them to your children, speaking of them when sitting in your houses, when walking by the way, when lying down and when rising up. . . . So may your children's children at the next return of this day of jubilee, after a century of experience under your national Constitution, celebrate it again the full enjoyment of all the blessings recognized by you in the commemoration of this day, and of all the blessings promised to the children of Israel upon Mount Gerizim, as the reward of obedience to the law of God.

And the children did live to celebrate the day of jubilee. Barely, but they did.[6]

THE CENTENNIAL

America is less a noun than a verb, and ritual is its gerund. Because the nation is always becoming, it is always also coming from and going to. Ritualized acts of collective affirmation of the kind we have been charting give to this process the gift of intelligibility. If such practices work, if they assist in the ongoing task of nation-building, they do so because they allow a people to see and so understand themselves. Rituals make sense. And by making sense of them, in turn, we glimpse some of the manifold forces that conspire to create, maintain, and propel the modern nation-state. Thus far we have observed several such performances, the means through which the country first came to sanctify its coming-into-being in 1789, and then, fifty years on, to confirm its coherence in 1839. We have now an opportunity in the inauguration's centennial year to witness the grandest, most resplendent celebration of all, what Julian Ralph described in *Harper's Weekly* as "the greatest popular display in the history of the republic."[7]

Here and again, Americans may be seen, and heard, speaking themselves anew, and from this we may learn a great deal.

In March of 1883 the voluble Englishman J. E. Peyton set in motion a complex machine that would in six years produce the New York centennial celebration of the nation's inaugural moment. Other cities and states would contribute their share, more or less, but though it was by definition a federal event, and much money would flow from Washington, it fell to New York, inevitably, to host the anniversary festivities. Within a year of takeoff, the New-York Historical Society, Chamber of Commerce, Mayor Abram Hewitt's office, military representatives, and assorted worthies—including Hamilton Fish, Stephen Van Rensselaer, and Elbridge T. Gerry—would combine their considerable time and talent to ensure its success. There would be the expected tussles, snubs, wounded egos, and related silliness attendant to the patrician elite. Still, city leaders—all New Yorkers—were by now quite well-rehearsed in the arts of civic organization and address; no one doubted that. But this time, this time it was special, because in the city it is always special. Not just floats, but statues; not just a parade, but three days of parades, with tens of thousands marching. A martial touch, perhaps? Naturally. But more!—Broadway was to be trod by "the greatest military display since the return of the troops to Washington—the greatest ever made in time of peace in America."[8]

Between Monday, April 29, and Wednesday, May 1, more than a million participants packed lower Manhattan. Locals and fellow Americans, native, immigrant, and foreign; the exalted and the humble; African, Asian, European—so many came. The president of the United States came, and so did two former presidents; civil war veterans came, and so did the laborers, the hustlers, prostitutes, priests, schoolchildren, and the poets. Proud Germans managed to get no less than sixty of their floats down the street, many featuring "living tableaus, in which men and women displayed the vigor, beauty, and poetry of the Teutonic moral qualities and achievements." With scale comes irony, of course. But for all the boosting and noise—indeed because of them—the ritual served its ends; just not in the same way or for the same reasons as fifty years ago. Rituals that are merely backward-looking will soon enough expire. When they prove effective, it is because the past is rendered ingredient to the present, put to work now to cinch tight the ties of civic life. "It is well to honor these milestones in the nation's progress," noted the *Kansas City Times*, "with all the pomp and pageantry and outward observances which ingenuity can devise. They keep alive the fires of patriotism and weld close the bands which unite the states in one nation."[9]

To unite the states in one nation: an outlandish idea, really. Americans, who must, as we have observed more than once, always have it both ways, insist that it can be done and done well. Perhaps it can. The problem, or at least one very big problem, is that the lessons learned from previous struggles in "keeping alive the fires of patriotism" are so readily forgotten, or, if remembered, uneasily applied to drastically shifting historical circumstances. This is to say, it is not at all a given that the constitutional inheritance of 1789 can be repurposed on an as-needed basis so many years later. Ritual as such cannot suffice, but rituals of a kind might, evidence of which may be found aplenty in the events of the centennial. Here we see a very interesting and important development, in which the occasion not only withstands or tolerates a degree of skepticism but plays host to it; indeed, wittingly or not, the occasion welcomes it and becomes defined, in part, by the democratic agon it both celebrates and enacts. That the centennial could play this role was by no means a given either, but that it did cannot have been incidental to the decade of the 1880s.[10]

As far as period tags go, the "Gilded Age" is admittedly quite good. Mark Twain certainly liked it, and historians seem to as well, mostly. As with many such labels, this one has come in for its share of criticism, notably by Rebecca Edwards, who suggests as an alternative something along the lines of the "Long Progressive Era." Not quite Twain, but the option reminds us that at the least we need to be very careful about drawing arbitrary lines, which is probably unavoidable, or reproducing caricatured images of the period, which is. The stretch from Reconstruction's end to century's beginning was marked by excess, exploitation, greed, militarism, commercialism, racism, misogyny, xenophobia, and all manner of related sins. It was also notable, Edwards and others remind us, for serious efforts to reform the civil service; straighten out currency, tariff, and interstate commerce issues; reign in the railroads and trusts; negotiate labor unrest, voters' rights, and workplace safety regulations; and deal responsibly with demands from farmers, women's rights activists, and social work pioneers. The decade of the 1880s saw as well significant advances in environmental policy, educational funding, internal improvements, and attention to veterans' affairs. The age was gilded, yes, but as the historian Charles Calhoun reminds us, its several administrations nevertheless set a "record for peace-time legislative accomplishment unequalled until Theodore Roosevelt's second term."[11]

We are happily, then, beyond thinking of the age as a singularly debased moment against which the Progressive Era is defined. No historical period is resolvable into its excesses of virtue or vice; the point here is to acknowl-edge that the inauguration's centennial participated in both and was at once a product of the Gilded Age and a comment on it. This much, at least, may be said to frame our brief treatment of the celebratory events of spring 1889.

There stands on Wall Street today a statue of George Washington, thir-teen and a half feet and more than three tons of bronzed rectitude. Here the Founder keeps a steady eye on the Street, as perfect a trope as one could wish to capture the tensile energies shaping late nineteenth-century America. "This massive figure," explained *Cosmopolitan*, "is in the heart of an alluring and exciting life of stock speculation," and, fittingly, "adorns the steps of the Sub-Treasury." The creation of John Quincy Adams Ward, it was designed specifically for the centennial and indeed is located quite near the balcony where Washington helped speak the nation into being. Federal Hall was long gone by now, but it continued to serve as a kind of beacon for the many activities driving the anniversary. Here too Washing-ton will stand sentry, and though not fond of crowds, he will guide the millions soon to beset lower Manhattan. His first guest: the sitting presi-dent of the United States.[12]

On the morning of Monday, April 29, President Benjamin and Mrs. Caroline Harrison boarded a car of the Pennsylvania Railroad and, with guests and retinue in place, set off for the nation's original capital city. Harrison had only just been inaugurated himself; having lost the popu-lar vote, he may well have been especially appreciative of the crowds and hoopla attending the journey throughout. Trenton turned out in fine and rousing fashion, and then it was on to Elizabeth-Town for even greater fes-tivity. From there our party, now joined by Vice President Levi Morton, embarked the *Dispatch*, festooned "like some great tropical bird of bril-liant plumage." An estimated 70,000 had taken to the waters, accompanied by ten Navy squadrons, to see the distinguished visitors make their way across the Upper Harbor. "The boom of cannon announced the approach of the President," recalled Julian Ralph, "and just then the sun parted the curtain of clouds that had obscured it, and bathed the white city and the green water in a glorious burst of sunshine, as if nature wanted to commemorate the perfect weather through which Washington was rowed to New York a century ago."[13]

The president and company were greeted on landing by Hamilton Fish, Governor David Hill, and Mayor John Grant, and ushered by carriage immediately to the Equitable Building and its posh Lawyer's Club. After a sumptuous lunch the party was ushered through the growing crowds to City Hall, where Harrison could see and be seen. Then it was dinner at Stuyvesant Fish's mansion and, later that evening, an opulent ball at the Metropolitan Opera House. Here, by all accounts, the champagne flowed and the diamonds sparkled. This was, no doubt about it, a gilded age, and city leaders had every intention of acting accordingly.

Tuesday, April 30, was yet the big day, and seemingly everyone was on the streets. A military parade with a line of march more than five miles wended its way along Broadway toward Central Park. At 9:00 a.m., president, vice president, governor, mayor, justices, Grover Cleveland, Rutherford Hayes, and others "alighted from their carriages and were escorted, amid much applause, to the time honored pews within the beautiful building. It was a thrilling spectacle," reported the *New York Herald*, "this attendance at church escorted by mounted police in squadrons and watched by the eager eyes of a multitude of thousands." Here, "on bended knees," Harrison knelt in Washington's original pew and listened to Bishop Henry Potter reflect on the day's significance. The sermon remains peculiar in the extreme, and though here is not the place to parse the bishop's theology, it so glaringly reflects the tensions of the time as to require a short pause. After the expected benedictions and commonplaces demanded of the occasion—the glory that was Washington, the legacy of freedom and calls to virtue—the speaker took up a jeremiad of sorts to lament the perils of the age, chief among them rank materialism and, most pointedly, the degenerating effects of immigration. Try as we might, Potter insists, we cannot retrieve either Washington or his times, for "the march of a century cannot be halted or reversed, and the enormous change in the situation can neither be disguised nor ignored. Then we were, though not all of us sprung from one nationality, practically one people." Now, the bishop warns, the great influx of "the lowest orders of people from abroad" threatens "to dilute the quality of our natural manhood. . . . Who shall respect a people who do not respect their own blood?"[14]

What the president and others thought of this performance we do not know. It carries on in this vein for a considerable stretch, mixing hagiography and paeans to liberty and virtue with biting social commentary on the evils of racial mixing and "Jacksonian vulgarity." We may chalk all this up to an eccentric personality or to a singularly poor adaptation to audience and occasion. But we are talking, after all, about the preeminent Episcopal authority in the city, speaking before the greatest concentration of political power to gather in one place in a generation. If there is provocation here, and it abounds, it prompts us to keep in mind just how vexed and uncertain this so-called Gilded Age could be—how foreign sometimes can seem its vocabulary of civic virtue, how anxious and confused its moral voices. As with most Americans most of the time, the citizens of 1889 were trying to figure out with varying degrees of success who they were as a people— what it meant to be an American. Attendant to this process is coming to some kind of terms with the past, with such moral claims as it may impose on those to whom it is heir. This much, again, involves the work of ritual: not always or only to consolidate and homogenize shared values but to provide occasions for confusion, dissent, passion, and difference. In this manner, nation-states may be reconstituted through a dialectics of identity and difference, where such rituals as we are observing afford on the one hand a degree of stability and on the other provision for change, growth, and innovation.[15]

Something of this relationship is nicely imagined in the play among officials, parade, and crowd that made up the day's activities. The ministrations at St. Paul's concluded, esteemed guests filed out and into carriages, and then they were delivered to the steps of the Sub-Treasury. At the same time, thousands of military personnel began their rendezvous. Now the crowd "that lines the streets and filled the windows and housetops were unprecedented, even for New York," reported a Richmond paper. "The march was an ovation along the entire route for both the troops and the President. . . . It is estimated that 100,000 persons were able to see the parade from the stands specially built for that purpose." From the steps of the Sub-Treasury, Clarence Bowen, secretary of the organizing committee and chronicler of the centennial, read John Greenleaf Whittier's "Vow of Washington": "For, ever in the awful strife / And dark hours of the nation's life / Through the fierce tumult pierced his warning word! / Their father's voice his erring children heard!"[16]

Whether many heard Bowen is doubtful, but thousands now turned their attention to Chauncey Depew, orator of the day. Even in that self-satisfied day it would have been difficult to find a more perfect distillation of what today is often labeled American exceptionalism. With civil war but a generation ago and storm clouds rising in Europe and Asia, with racial and labor tensions mounting, Depew still insisted that all was well; better than well, in fact, as attested by the apparently relentless aggregation of national wealth. In the century since Washington took the oath near where he spoke, "favoring political conditions have brought the sum of our national wealth to a figure which has surpassed the results of a thousand years for the mother-land herself, otherwise the richest of empires." Americans, the orator proclaimed, create such wealth far out of proportion to their numbers. No wonder, then, that the "sum of our destiny is still rising, and its rays illume vast territories as yet unoccupied and undeveloped, and which are to be the happy homes of millions of people." Gazing over the multitude, Depew could say with supreme confidence, though perhaps with less prescience: "There are no clouds overhead, and no convulsions under our feet."[17]

Clouds and convulsions there certainly were, and they would come again. For the moment, those who could manage it gave a shout and melted into the masses heading for Madison Square. There some 50,000 regulars, militia, National Guard, and cadets of various stripes, led by their state governors, would march before the president and company. "As far as the eye could reach," recounted one observer, "the sidewalks were literally blockaded with people, while windows, doorways and roofs of buildings were a mass of humanity." This would go on for some time, forever it seemed to many, but at length the more illustrious tired, grew hungry, and finally pulled up tables well-laden at the Metropolitan. So grand was the menu that it immediately went public. There is risk here of distracting the reader, but it may be worth a glance at the fare—this for those wishing to make the most of the age's excesses. The fortunate diner was presented with a printed card, from which the following could be had:

To begin:

MENU.
HORS D'ŒUVRES.
Variés.   *Variés.*
POTAGE.
Tortue Verte.
HORS D'ŒUVRE, CHAUD.
Petites Timbales à la Ministérielle.
POISSON.
Saumon du Kennebec, Sauce Hollandaise.
Pommes à l'Anglaise. Salade de Concombres.
RELEVÉ.
Filet de Bœuf Piqué, Sauce Madère.
ENTRÉES.
Ris de Veau à la Périgueux.
Champignons Sautés. Haricots Verts.
Bécassines en Caisse. Flageolets.
Aspics de Foie Gras, Parcele. Sorbet à la Présidence.
RÔTI.
Poulets du Printemps au Cresson. Salade Russe.
Glaces Fantasies.
DESSERT.
Petits Fours. Gateaux Assortis. Pièces montèes.
Mottoes. Fruits. Café. Liqueurs.
VINS.

The drink list and its intended effect are easily imagined.[18]

Joined now by their wives, the president and a truly impressive array of figures, including William T. Sherman, the Widow Grant, Cleveland, Hayes, and Melville Fuller, Chief Justice, pushed back their chairs and readied themselves for the expected round of toasts. To George Washington! Our People! Soon it was the recently deposed Cleveland's turn, who as a native son "was greeted in the most tumultuous fashion, many of the men on the floor rising from their chairs and cheering, while the occupants of the boxes leaned forward and waved their handkerchiefs." The former president took as his theme this notion of "our people," but what he had to say proved more than a toast, was in fact a strikingly frank

statement on the dangers of provincialism, class arrogance, and dispari-
ties of wealth. In effect, what Cleveland, of all people, offered was a direct
counter to the blandishments floated by Depew earlier in the day. Standing now amidst the rococo trappings of the Metropolitan, he warned his
well-fed and pleasantly intoxicated audience of the dangers borne by "material advancement" and "the turmoil of business and activity," especially
as they strain against "love of country and that simple faith in virtue and
enlightenment, which constituted the hope and trust of our fathers."[19]

An obscure address by an unheralded president: true, but for that
reason what Cleveland had to say, at this moment, in this place, functions
as a powerful corrective on several fronts. He puts the lie to caricatured
versions of the age as unrelentingly avaricious, and he quite explicitly
mobilizes ritual—the occasion, the toast, the dinner, etc.—to reassert and
empower values essential for the common good. We will let his words,
accordingly, conclude this busy day: "Ill-natured complaints of popular
incompetency and self-righteous assertion of superiority over the body
of the people, are impotent and useless. . . . The rich merchant or capitalist
in the center of wealth and enterprise hardly has a glimpse of the country
blacksmith at his forge or the farmer in his field. . . . This centennial time,
which stirs our pride by leading us to the contemplation of our tremendous strides in wealth and greatness, also recalls to our minds the virtues
and the unselfish devotion to principle of those who saw the first days of
the Republic."[20]

Those who could bestir themselves after the evening's "monster
open-air concert in Madison Square" crowded into the streets Wednesday morning for the third and final day of festivities. This was to be the
people's day, May 1, featuring labor organizations, industrial guilds, and all
manner of associated groups organized into a massive parade beginning
on Fifth Avenue and winding up on Canal Street. Harrison was joined by
General Sherman and other veterans, including several dating to the War
of 1812, who together with various dignitaries relished "the greatest official, popular, and successful series of displays which the American people
ever witnessed, or in which they ever took part." By late afternoon fatigue
had set in, however; now the president retreated to prepare for the ride
home, and many would-be marchers fell out to otherwise enjoy the city's
manifold pleasures. These included, no doubt, the satisfaction of knowing
that their three-day party was being reported on across the country. From

Salt Lake City, the *Woman's Exponent* applauded the event for recogniz-
ing "these heroic men whom God inspired to establish religious liberty
and freedom upon this goodly land, America." Further west, readers were
assured that such rituals as transpired in New York served to enshrine "the
civil and constitutional history of this great country," a shared past that
will "certainly be held in the same light and be similarly appreciated by
the hundreds of millions of patriotic Americans that are to come." Even
the *Phrenological Journal* set aside its usual preoccupations to commend
the occasion and its "singular expression of patriotic feeling." New Yorkers—indeed Americans everywhere—had demonstrated "that in spite of
the commercial spirit that has been supposed to control everything else
in and about the metropolis," there was yet "an undercurrent of national
sentiment that needs only a great occasion, or the memorial of a great
occasion, for its development into overwhelming activity."[21]

No one of note would argue. The 1889 centennial had in fact been a
smashing success, and this for all the right reasons. At a time when partisan strife was, even for American politics, particularly severe, as social
unrest threatened to disperse institutional loyalties, and the unholy mix-
ture of money and appetite strained basic decencies, the celebration was
just what the country needed. This much seems reasonable to say, but it
is scarcely all that might or should be said. In truth many thoughtful individuals, including those actually participating in the festivities, voiced
grave reservations about the undertones self-satisfaction, commercialism, and greed that yet made themselves heard. We have heard Cleveland
on this matter; there were many, many more. The point here is to remind
ourselves that these countervailing notes were in no trivial sense afforded
an audience precisely because of the celebration. Ritual can flatten out,
silence, contain, and otherwise limit dissent, but not always. In the event
of the inauguration's centennial, it simultaneously functioned to reaffirm
shared commitments and to provide a hearing for those in a position to
make themselves heard. This is not everything, but it is something, and
something important at that.

W. H. Auden once wrote that it was the role of the wise to teach doubt,
that we may learn how to believe. As with people, so with peoples: Americans have always been skeptical, perhaps most loudly when things seem to
be going their way. The centennial was a ritualized act of collective faith—
faith that the virtues of the Founders might still obtain and faith that though

time had changed, it could not disestablish the American polity. For such faith, which is the citizen's faith, doubt must be expressed, confronted, indeed given its own stage on the parade grounds. Its basis now, as Cleveland warned, was a certain crassness that comes with material gain, but more importantly, that crassness could be nothing more than the external sign of something more dangerous or more deadening to the democratic spirit.[22]

The symptoms might manifest in several ways—in the arts, for example, when the late decades of the century seemed oddly small. "We shall perhaps have a sufficient number of pigmies," ran a typical lament, "but of giants not any." Why? "The spirit of the ages: that is to say, in the commercial spirit, in the ascendency of Mammon." Harvard's Charles Eliot Norton saw it in the halls of learning. The old virtues were evidently on the wane, no longer served to shape such character as Washington exemplified. "Wealth has become the chief modern form of power," Eliot warned, "and, usurping the dominion of the old ideals over the imagination, it is sought, not only as a means to other ends, but as itself an end." Bishop Potter saw it in the pews, "the infinite swagger of our American speech and manners, mistaking bigness for greatness." Lowell saw it, too, and indeed admired "our energy, our enterprise, our inventiveness, our multiplicity of resource." Still: "Prosperous we may be in other ways, contented with more specious success, but that nation is a mere horde supplying figures to the census, which does not acknowledge a true prosperity and a richer contentment in the things of the mind."[23]

Every age is at once lapsing and emerging. We fix such moments as command our attention by giving them a name, mindful, one hopes, that it is but a name. Some moments nevertheless do seem more self-conscious than others, when in the American experience at least citizens may be heard coming to the realization that they really are living in history. The nation's 1889 centennial appears to be one such moment. We need not project back on it more than is already there; it is enough to register the growing complexity of what it meant to live in such an age when woeful social evils compete with a profound need to recover, celebrate, and thus sustain those values capable of dealing with just those problems. And all this in the midst of an unprecedented explosion of commercial expansion, finance capitalism, partisanship, and the anxieties attendant to life in the 1880s. The centennial rituals of late April and early May are thus to be seen as resources for the collective self, summoned at moments when that self is felt to be most at stake and at risk.

"We have no myths or legends, like other nations, upon which are founded the usages now prevalent. These were all established and set down for certain one hundred years ago," mused Ausburn Towner at the time, "and from them there has never been any important deviation. What our forefathers then did, we do." On reflection, it would be difficult to arrive at a more wrong-headed assessment of the practices of citizenship we have seen thus far. Americans before they were Americans were already deeply committed to their myths and legends and have never felt much compunction about bending them to their most exigent, present needs. That is the point and purpose of such ritualized narratives. We have noted, too, that these rehearsals of collective identity very seldom—if ever—impose any kind of hegemonic control over what gets said and how.[24]

This American habit, of simultaneously celebrating and lambasting itself, can be satisfyingly captured in the city way, but New Yorkers just speak more loudly and certainly display the restive energies typical of their fellow citizens generally. The Americans of 1889 knew what they were doing and meant what they said; they knew, too, as a writer from Saint Louis put it, that the events surrounding Washington's inauguration "have a deep, solemn and spiritual significance, and the spectacle of a great commercial and industrial people pausing in their multifarious pursuits to realize belief by an act of collective worship will be profoundly impressive and significant." Even such spectacles as that of 1889, the greatest of them all, must end, and next morning it is back into the daily accident. But it all seemed worth it, and for good reason: "This great country took a much needed breathing spell yesterday," wrote a Wisconsinite, "while it took stock of its belongings and wondered what another century would bring forth."[25] As well it might.

THRESHOLDS OF DESTRUCTION AND REBIRTH: 1939

And you that shall cross from shore to shore years hence are more to me, and more in my meditations, than you might suppose.

—WALT WHITMAN

No American beheld the coming time with such equanimity, but even Whitman might have flinched in the year of 1939, if he could have comprehended the world at all; no one else did. The one hundred and fiftieth anniversary of the country's inauguration arrived at a time of unprecedented anxiety over the prospects of democracy at home and abroad, when protracted economic crises had joined, not at all coincidentally, with harrowing developments on the continent. What the future—the very near future—held was anyone's guess, but all thinking people, everywhere, knew that a reckoning of some kind was due. And that New York City should host in that spring of all springs a World's Fair, that its theme proclaimed "The World of Tomorrow," offered up such ironies as required no poet's slant. A century and a half ago the nation's first president felt no particular reason to mention world affairs in his first address to the people. Washington had not forgotten; it just did not seem at the moment to matter that much. Now, only eight years after taking office, Franklin Roosevelt was obliged to note in his annual message to Congress that "world events of thunderous import have moved with lightning speed." Indeed they had: "All about us rage undeclared wars—military and economic. All about us grow more deadly armaments—military and economic. All about us are threats of new aggression—military and economic." For nearly a decade now Americans had steadfastly "clung to the hope that the innate decency of mankind would protect the unprepared who showed their innate trust in mankind. Today we are all wiser—and sadder."[26]

How wise Americans were at the moment was a question yet to be determined. That they had much about which to be sad was self-evident. For too many the promises of the New Deal, so boldly declared, so self-confident, seemed now betrayed by unrelenting problems with employment, growth, labor unrest, rank partisanship, and talk, just talk. Republicans had only recently made significant inroads through the last election cycles, and to their agenda they had every intention of strengthening resistance to Roosevelt's overweening ambitions. Chief among their aims was pushing, hard, on an isolationist line with which they had been associated closely for a generation. Even now—*especially now*—Republican leaders aimed to beat back any further "Lend-Lease" proposals and other such misguided concessions to international pressures. At the same time, those pressures simply must not be ignored, or so Roosevelt and his many supporters believed, indeed must be confronted now and with absolute strength of purpose. "The troubles of the world," insisted the president in January of 1839, had to be met "with a unity born of the fact that for generations those who have come to our shores, representing many kindreds and tongues, have been welded by common opportunity into a united patriotism. If another form of government can present a united front in its attack on a democracy, the attack must and will be met by a united democracy. Such a democracy can and must exist in the United States."[27]

A "united democracy"—here is a phrase worth contemplating. What can this mean? Is it not a contradiction in terms? One need not be a James Madison to acknowledge that even in the best of times it is only an ideal; very frequently, as history more than once shows, a very complicated, sometimes dangerous one at that. Then and now, we might well chalk up Roosevelt's "united democracy" to his penchant for airy platitudes. And perhaps we would be right in doing so. But probably not, because Roosevelt was possessed of an extraordinary, indeed preternatural ability to anticipate the winds, political and otherwise, and now he must have understood in the most primal sense that the stakes of the American experiment had been raised to unprecedented levels. On the other hand, one need not have been a Roosevelt either to sense the atmospheric currents and in which direction they were tending. Put another way, we can reflect on the fact that the sesquicentennial and World's Fair took place in late April–early May of 1939. In the last four months alone,

- Otto Hahn proved the possibility of nuclear fission;
- Spanish Nationalists seized Barcelona and moved on Catalonia;
- Hitler prioritized the Kriegsmarine;
- Czechoslovakia was gone;
- Franco seized power;
- Hitler initiated plans for the invasion of Poland;
- Italy invaded Albania; and
- Hitler declared an end to the Anglo-German Naval Agreement.

America, Roosevelt insisted, "had a rendezvous with destiny." Destiny beckoned. "To us much is given; more is expected. This generation," he intoned, "will nobly save or meanly lose the last best hope of earth." If then there was a supreme and tragic irony in playing host to the World's Fair and the sesquicentennial in this of all years, it was yet explicable within the logic of Americans' sense of themselves and of their identity, shared aspirations, and obligations to the world itself. At this moment as in no other, its people needed a ritualized affirmation of their collective ethos, of who they were and might become. To these ends, the celebration of Washington's inaugural address could serve no better, no higher purpose.[28]

The city was, as might be expected, anxious to get the party started. And for all the very real portents of crises on the near horizon, optimists were not hard to find, chief among them the nation's president and the indomitable mayor Fiorello LaGuardia. The general idea was to simultaneously host the World's Fair and to commemorate Washington's inaugural in one grand spectacle. In this, all parties could agree, the city met and superseded expectations. Preparations had been under way for a year now, from commissioning a three-cent stamp bearing an image of the 1789 oath to arranging for the visit of ninety-seven ships from the U.S. fleet, "the greatest concentration of naval strength ever assembled on the North Atlantic seaboard," commanded by Admiral Claude C. Block. There would be, invariably, endless logistical problems and challenges of a more general sort: New Yorkers were perfectly aware, as always, that the world was watching, and more than a few seized the opportunity for such publicity as the occasion might afford. Complaints over price gouging and exploitative rents abounded; labor issues found voice; the Greater New York Coordinating Committee for Employment would picket the Fair offices at the Empire State Building "until such time as Negroes are given employment in all categories."[29]

New York's habitual self-awareness was not delusional. The world was in fact watching—strategically, curiously, and with self-interest, fear, and genuine amity. Roosevelt and his circle had been laboring to get Great Britain's royalty to pay a visit; they would eventually make it over but timed it to avoid the crush of humanity that would press on Flushing Meadows and lower Manhattan. Still, the former mother country made ample provision for its pavilions, including several hundred works of art and, in its "colonial" exhibits, relics depicting "the life and work of the people of the British Empire, grouped in six main sections—East Africa, West Africa, Malaya and the Far East, West Indies, Mediterranean, and Indian Ocean." Italy was to pay a visit, presumably to the delight of its many sons and daughters in the city. If so, they would be disappointed: Mussolini thought twice and kept his delegates home. Representatives and heads of state would come from over the globe, including Denmark's Crown Prince Frederick and Princess Ingrid. Japan seemed preoccupied but managed with surrealistic timing to convey its best wishes via radio. Washington's inauguration and the Fair, proclaimed Premier Hiranuma, served well as guideposts "for building the World of tomorrow, to inspire hope, courage and ideals in the minds and hearts of all people and to promote international cooperation in a spirit of tolerance and good will, with a view to bringing later happiness and prosperity to mankind."[30] Enough said, perhaps.

Closer to home, the fictions were rather more real and certainly more creative. On April 9 the *Times* reported that "George Washington," acted by New York artist Denys Wortman, together with "Charles Thomson" and "David Humphreys," would set off from Mount Vernon "in an eighteenth-century coach with as much or more fanfare than when he came to take the oath as first President of the United States." The paper tracked the original route for its readers, providing a convenient map and efficient little history lessons as the party made the week-long trek toward the foot of Wall Street. To see them off in proper fashion, the sitting president ventured out to Mount Vernon on the morning of April 14. From its front steps Franklin Roosevelt, who knew something about the cares of office, reflected on the events of 1789. Then, he recalled, "the summons to the Presidency had come [to Washington] in a time of real crisis and deep emergency. The dangers that beset the young nation were as real as though the very independence Washington had won for it had been threatened once more by foreign foes. . . . So it came about that once more he put from him the life he loved so well and took upon himself the Presidency."[31]

By noon on April 16, four white horses and a restored Van Rensselaer coach pulled away from Mount Vernon and began the 233-mile journey to Manhattan. The trip was sponsored by Daughters of the American Revolution, which had recently earned lasting damage to its reputation for the Marian Anderson fiasco; its counterpart Sons of the American Revolution; various state and city agencies; Society of the Cincinnati; and other private concerns. With such support, managers of the festivities were able to ensure much lively press along the way, including an exact reproduction of the barge that would ferry the esteemed guests across the harbor from Elizabeth-Town. "An impressive harbor display has been planned," readers learned, "with booming guns, resounding bands and bellowing whistlers." In this manner, fittingly, the "world of yesterday will meet in dramatic pageantry the world of tomorrow." "Washington" and company duly arrived amidst it all at the designated time and place and were met by

"Henry Knox" and "George Clinton" and ushered at length to City Hall, where the inaugural address and oath-taking were reenacted. After lunch at the Metropolitan, it was off for a tour of Radio City Music Hall. "A big change since I was here last," the first president was heard to comment.[32]

It was to be the first of many ritual gestures to the founding in the next several days. Friday morning found the crew on the steps of the Sub-Treasury building, current site of the long-gone Federal Hall; then it was on to venerable St. Paul's, Reverend Frederick Fleming, Rector of Trinity presiding. Roosevelt and LaGuardia were there to meet the travelers; there were more speeches, more toasts, receptions, and sermons from virtually every center of faith on the island. Enormous crowds gathered, as they had before, to acknowledge in public, together, as Americans, the iconic instantiation of their better selves. In all, wrote one observer, "an impressive pageant that brought from thousands of applauding spectators new and hearty proof that Washington still lives in the hearts of his countrymen." That Roosevelt chose this day, Sunday, April 30, 1939, to open a World's Fair dedicated to the "world of tomorrow" was accordingly and entirely to the point. He would need Washington in the hearts of his countrymen; for though an optimist, Roosevelt, like Washington, was a deeply serious, deeply realistic leader. "In a scene of republican simplicity and surrounded by the great men of his time," the president recalled, "the oath was administered to him by the Chancellor of the State of New York, Robert R. Livingston. And so we, in New York, have a very personal connection with that thirtieth of April, one hundred and fifty years ago."[33]

Such connections as Roosevelt imagined would in short order be tested severely, and some would snap. Before the year was out, Poland would fall; the Manhattan Project would be under way and the Neutrality Act embellished beyond recognition. In retrospect, it is easy enough to see in the events of April a charming though desperately quaint effort to relive a past never so distant. Ritual of this kind invites just such skepticism. It is fair: bewigged actors being rowed across the waters to lower Manhattan and overweight old men in leggings ought not to be taken entirely seriously. But they need to be taken seriously enough, enough that is to help explain why Americans have always insisted on rehearsing through words and gestures that moment when they came into being. Not every people so insist, not every tribe, faith, or nation-state. But Americans, for good and ill, seem always to have relied on such rituals of collective affirmation to remind them of what it means to be American.

As if, otherwise, they might forget. And so they seek, in their way, to remember that they may face the uncertain with what they hold true and dear. John Dewey got it just right in this very year, his eightieth: "There was in existence," he wrote in "Creative Democracy: The Task Before Us," "a group of men who were capable of readapting older institutions and ideas to meet the situation provided by new physical conditions—a group of men extraordinarily gifted in political inventiveness." At the center of this group was George Washington, who in 1939 could not, must not be forgotten.[34]

THE FUTURE OF MEMORY: 1989

On January 20, 1989, George Herbert Walker Bush removed his hand from the Bible to face a world very much on the edge. Before year's end, the Berlin Wall would come down, the Warsaw Pact would be dissolved, and the Soviet Union would be well on its way to utter and well-deserved ruin. Tiananmen Square, stained red, would become forever associated with state brutality and human courage; Nicolae Ceauşescu deposed, Hirohito dead, and Andrei Sakharov dead. And Francis Fukuyama would publish in the *National Interest* an essay proclaiming "The End of History." It would be a busy year.[35] Unburdened by what he could not now know, the new president turned to the task at hand. Bush was not much of an orator, to put it charitably, but he had firm enough sense of the occasion, and he was nothing if not sincere. "I've just repeated word for word the oath taken by George Washington 200 years ago, and the Bible on which I placed my hand is the Bible on which he placed his. It is right," Bush explained, "that the memory of Washington be with us today not only because this is our bicentennial inauguration but because Washington remains the Father of our Country. And he would, I think, be gladdened by this day; for today is the concrete expression of a stunning fact: our continuity, these 200 years, since our government began."[36]

Bush was right: it was and is a stunning fact, this continuity. Certainly, "the Founder of our Country" would have been pleasantly surprised to learn that, after all, the republic for which he stood remained pretty much intact. These things are not given. The forty-first president labored to impress this fact on his audience, in his way, though no one could plausibly think this a particularly eloquent effort to do so. Elizabeth Drew noted that, "with the passage of time, the speech grew thinner and thinner, to the point where there is almost nothing memorable about it at all." She was correct, mainly, but we have reason to go back to the address for certain lines of thought that have been unfortunately forgotten; reason, that is, because though so much obviously separated the first and forty-first presidents, certain commitments remained strong enough to again demand their expression at a time of ritualized transition into an uncertain and formidable future. "I take as my guide the hope of a saint," Bush declared, "in crucial things, unity; in important things, diversity; in all things, generosity." We strain now, in the first decades of the twenty-first century, to recall a time when "compassionate conservatism" might have actually meant something genuine, when a Republican president might say to all: "No matter what your circumstances or where you are, you are part of this day, you are part of the life of our great nation."[37]

The new president, too, spoke of the ties that bind, and so have we. We have observed as well that these ties, these values perpetually associated with Washington, are cinched and strengthened through ritualized acts of self-affirmation. This is the work of inaugural addresses, generally, and of such celebrations designed to call to mind again not only the founding but the moral obligation to make good on its promises. But we know, too, that remembrance and forgetting are very closely related, that indeed one is not possible without the other. The story of America's bicentennial anniversary of Washington's inauguration can tell us much about this relationship, its perils, and its prospects. For though George H. W. Bush chose to remind us of Washington's precedent—indeed attended in person its celebration in New York—we must confront the fact that the day's festivities rather paled in comparison to its antecedents. How to explain this?

The question is difficult. In attempting an answer, we are obliged to return to the basic terms of our general theme, our "through line," and acknowledge its potential limits. Put bluntly, we have asked ritual to assume significant explanatory weight throughout this study, to show us how and why people come together as they do and what kinds of rhetorical resources they mobilize on behalf of a collective expression of solidarity. A stronger version of this thesis holds that such rituals, far from being noise in the system, are integral to it; they give structure, affordance, and direction to a people forever self-conscious about their status as Americans and as actors in the world. Such performances can be almost willfully blind to historical and existing realities and offer up images of coherence and unity at times when both are in fact at risk. But they persist, and that is the point. We need them. We need celebrations of Washington's inauguration because a people who cannot remember themselves will cease to be a people.

But nothing lasts, not nations and not the rituals that sustain them. Not forever. Can we detect in a nation's flagging enthusiasm for its founding signs of the inevitable? What does a nation look like when in the process of forgetting? Are such questions, really, a bit overwrought? Perhaps; we shall see. In the meantime, we at least reflect for a moment on the work of ritual and its limits and proceed then to a more familiar account of the bicentennial events.

If rituals are not forever—certainly not rituals of nationhood—then why do they fade, perhaps die? History seems relatively clear on the matter, if only because the record possesses so many examples of a similar cast. The will to maintain rituals may be crushed by those who see in them evidence of corruption, perfidy, evil, or the enemy: the iconoclast will smash the relic, pull down the monument, or blast the Buddhist statuary from the mountainsides. Then, too, the exigency that gives rise to a commemorative practice may fade to oblivion; who now celebrates Guy Fawkes Day? Stalin's birthday? VJ Day? What would be the point, exactly? On another front, these rituals may find themselves so crowded on the calendar that they must fight for attention and against what we might call ritual fatigue. In the years surrounding and including 1989, Americans celebrated passage of the Constitution, Bush's inauguration, and Washington's, in addition to all the traditional days of civic and religious recognition. "Seldom has a year been so filled with celebrations and commemorations of the past," wrote a columnist for the *Seattle Post-Intelligencer*, "seldom have people been so preoccupied with recollections of events that helped shape their lives." A surfeit of memory, then, can paradoxically weaken the content and force of any one such ritual. We may readily admit, too, that while rituals may come and go, the will does not; rituals just express themselves in different ways to different ends.[38]

All of the above concerns are entirely plausible responses to the question of why rituals fade. But however convincing at a certain level of generalization, none really confront the most important, most pressing possibility: what if the assumption of unity that must predicate the very act of collective ritual is no longer tenable? American national identity has always relied on ritual precisely because of its many differences; what if those differences, the very condition of its existence, become so great as to render such rituals passé, kitsch, irrelevant, or, in a word, forgettable? Over and against this possibility, ritual presents itself as the antidote to the dangers of amnesia, political and otherwise. When it works, it works because humans must remember. In Arendt's rendering, this capacity is indeed definitively human, "pitting its strength against the inherent futility of everything that is subject to change; it collects and re-collects what otherwise would be doomed to ruin and oblivion." [39] In the end, perhaps, all we can say, all we can hope for, is that she is right; for she had seen as clearly as anyone what happens when citizens forget what it means to live and flourish in polity.

To balance the account: New Yorkers, as always, were game for hosting yet another "flag-flapping salute to the first inaugural." On Friday, April 28, President Bush declared the thirtieth "a day to celebrate the bicentennial of the inauguration of George Washington, and I join Congress in inviting houses of worship to celebrate this anniversary by ringing bells or undertaking other appropriate activities." Not an eloquent proclamation or even particularly enthusiastic, but enough perhaps to stamp the occasion with some authority, but only some—much was familiar, a little worn in the retelling it seems now. But much was impressive: the fireworks, the twenty-one-gun salute, the festooned ships in the harbor. The wind and rain did not help, however, "and the ceremonies honoring George Washington's inauguration as first President of the United States in New York City 200 hundred years ago," reported the *Times*, "did not bring to the shoreline the millions who had thronged there for previous bicentennial celebrations." On the other hand, thousands did come out to witness the events of the day, and there was after all plenty to see. This time up for the role of Washington was fifty-nine-year-old Philadelphian William Sommerfield, who, along with his Humphreys and Thomson, made their way from Mount Vernon for the eight-day journey to Federal Hall National Memorial. Their itinerary was rather more crowded than any heretofore, including numerous appearances at civic centers, churches, schools, and town squares. [40]

The party arrived in Elizabeth-Town by noon Sunday, April 23, embarked, and a few hours later were welcomed at the South Street Seaport.

That gave organizers a week to prepare and execute a characteristically elaborate day, including parades, martial music, exhibits, and bathing the Empire State Building in red, white, and blue lighting. On Saturday the twenty-ninth, the carriers USS *Forrestal* and USS *Ticonderoga* led a fleet of seventy-five ships on the harbor along with "a gaggle of hooting, honking, flag-flapping civilians in its wake." Sunday morning called to St. Paul's again some three hundred of the city and national elite, including President Bush, Chief Justice Burger, Governor Cuomo, Mayor Koch, Senators Moynihan and D'Amato, and Helen Hayes, parade marshal. There was no sermon. After the services, the crowd made its way to the Federal Hall National Memorial; here it joined a sitting president in viewing an actor playing the first president taking the oath of office. Virtually no reference was made to the first Congress. Of Washington's inaugural address—nothing.[41]

Those close enough had to be satisfied with a brief speech by President Bush, speaking behind bulletproof shields, in front of television cameras, and over the shouts of protest from AIDS activists. "For all the turmoil and transformation of the last 200 years," said Bush, "there is a great constancy to this office and this Republic. So much of the vision of that first great President is reflected in the paths pursued by modern Presidents. . . . It was Washington's vision, his balance, his integrity, that made the presidency possible. . . . Today we reaffirm ethics, honor, and strength in government." All in all, thought William Safire, it was "a good speech, suitably solemn and unifying, coherent and appropriately brief." Thus our standards for eloquence in the electronic age are not very high, to be sure, but camera-ready. And indeed the whole affair did prove itself well contained and so well broadcast. Television and radio picked up the day's events along with print media; viewers wanting more or unable to attend the actual ceremonies might enjoy the Public Broadcasting Service's "George Washington: The Forging of a Nation," hosted by Bill Moyers, starring Barry Bostwick and Patty Duke and based on James Flexner's award-winning volume.[42]

Not everyone, in any case, was happy with the production. No one ever is, and certainly not in New York. The reasons matter, not least those voiced by one Air Force Reservist on the scene. Struggling to get a glimpse of the speakers, he complained that the whole affair was "an elitist celebration. The people are being held back from the festivities. I saw a print from the inauguration from 200 hundred years ago; there were people sitting on the rooftops and out in the streets cheering. It's a statement about the world we live in that we can't see it up close." For that, he and the many others gathered about the old site of Federal Hall would need to join the parade, now led by Ms. Hayes on its confetti-strewn path up Broadway to Washington Square Park. It all went off without a hitch—thanks in part to the presence of over four thousand of the city's finest and tightly controlled lines of march. A contingent of CPAs twirled briefcases and a women's kazoo band made itself heard; children danced, and bagpipes wailed, as they will. That evening thunderous fireworks announced the conclusion of the 1989 bicentennial of America's first inauguration. And inside, a thousand guests at $2,500 a head danced in the ball room of the Waldorf-Astoria hotel. Their cause: to fund a museum at Federal Hall.[43]

And then it was all over. Soon enough the world would start crowding in on the streets and lives of the city and beyond, and the bicentennial quickly became a memory. But not much of a memory: in truth, the events of that day proved ephemeral and out-classed by comparison to their predecessors fifty, one hundred, one hundred and fifty, and two hundred years ago. National media coverage was strikingly limited: few major newspapers bothered to accord them more than a column or two; none offered anything at all in the way of serious reflection or commentary. Had Americans grown tired of it all? The question does not admit of an answer, really, but it is worth a moment's reflection to ask after the future of a memory so ingredient to America's sense of itself.

It is complicated. Today we struggle to make sense of this slave-owning military figure, the oldest, deadest, whitest male, in Joseph Ellis's reckoning. Historians have longed enjoyed describing the ways in which the Founder has been rendered by their colleagues; this is good sport. We have "successfully congealed him into marble," lamented Bernard Mayo, "a national deity, august and severe." Saul Padover: "If there is such a thing as a crime of herocide, Washington was its victim. To his countrymen he became an embalmed image, a figure of wood, a mindless icon." Karal Ann Marling: "He is, perhaps, a cultural cliché. But, since nobody knows exactly what he is good for anymore, he can also be confusing, tedious, even annoying." Albert Furtwangler: "Much of the monumental Washington is monumental in the way that funerary sculpture is: larger and stiffer and blanker than life and much more expensive." If this is so, then we can hardly be surprised that the first president's inauguration, much less its keynote address, should be remanded at length to the dust heap of history. On the other hand, it surely bears mentioning that the decade of the 1980s benefited from a number of very fine, indeed quite remarkable works of scholarship on Washington, and we continue to learn from a new generation of gifted writers on the founding. Academic history departments may not feature much in the way of courses specializing in the subject, but popular appetites remain hungry for the next volume, the next meeting of the roundtable. *Hamilton!*[44]

A half century ago, the British historian Marcus Cunliffe concluded his study of Washington with these lines: "The man is the monument, the monument is America. *Si monumentum requiris, circumspice.*"[45] Memory is a peculiar thing and can for often quite good reasons make itself scarce. But if we wish to summon the past as a touchstone for the coming time, we need only look about for Washington's steady example. It is here, among and for us.

Epilogue

The inauguration of April 30, 1789, was not Washington's alone. It announced both the end and the beginning of a process of self-government that continues to challenge, exasperate, disappoint, and, sometimes, ennoble. It was in truth a revolution. Like any such turning point in human affairs, the invention of the modern republican state—its meaning and prospects—remains the object of contest, anxiety, cynical appropriation, and genuine pride. That is the effect of real revolutions. America has always been "America," a creation of human hearts and minds, arms, words, and the deepest aspirations. In this sense, the founding remains fair game for hypocrites, sinners, saints, and the rest of us seeking to make sense of ourselves, our shared legacies, our possibilities. The meaning of "America" has not, cannot, and will not ever be fixed. This is as it should be.

What was the founding about? An absurd question, perhaps, but it will not go away. We have floated different answers of greater and lesser degrees of plausibility. The inauguration and all it represented may be viewed as the signal moment when ideas of a certain and bracing kind were ushered into the modern world: *American ideas*, like no other! To be championed, taught to the young, exported, leveraged, fetishized, commodified, monetized, and idolized. Others have stressed, by contrast, a more "realistic" interpretation, focusing on the material conditions underwriting the founding, not least slavery, and the Atlantic economy and imperial relations on which it was bottomed. Every generation comes to the question anew, and each will have its way. For better or worse, I have sought in this brief volume not to enter in any systematic fashion into the historiographic debates that continue to enrich and expand our understanding of that long-ago time and place when the world seemed to many—though not all—new again. Here seems an appropriate place, nevertheless, to offer a few summary observations on what we might have learned from the story of the nation's first presidential inauguration. I will try not to rehash or belabor points already made but to build on them as warrants for certain broad generalizations.

All revolutions—military, political, religious, social, or economic—are ultimately matters of faith. However one comes at the American founding, as old Whig, Neo-Whig, Progressive, or otherwise, one cannot but be struck by the sheer nerve exhibited by its many agents. They were brave, outrageously so, and they had no real evidence to suggest that such courage would ever be vindicated by their sacrifices. I think this posture is a matter of faith, though not in any confessional sense. I mean to stress, rather, the will to concerted action on behalf of ideals, both in spite of and because of all the quite real impediments to their realization. The question being posed has been asked many times before, but a quick reminder should not hurt: what are we talking about except faith when a disparate people, perched on the far edge of the Atlantic, aim to liberate themselves, through armed conflict, from the greatest colonial power on earth? Did they really believe they could pull this off? Yes, they did. And they believed they could do so with no standing army, no navy, no colonial superstructure of their own and among a good many doubters, loyalists, and slackers. They believed, too, that once having started a war, they could sustain it and feed and provision its soldiers.

Human beings have shown themselves to be quite adept at starting wars, rather less so at ending them, and not very good at all in winning the peace. The inaugural celebrations we have examined tell us that here, in addition, early Americans evinced an extraordinary faith in their capacity to both win the war and invent a system of government worthy of the sacrifices it required. They laid down face cards and beat the odds of history.

What can we say about the sources of such faith? Again, a question at once impossible to answer convincingly, but necessary to ask. Europeans, of course, settled British North America in a fit of religious zeal, and if that zeal waned, erupted, and knotted itself into complex and competing motives, we must never discount it as a force in the shaping of early nationhood. Today the Christian origin of America remains a contested, often frustrating, but always available resource for those with a stake in the question. I do not find it especially interesting.

Within the more circumscribed ambit of the inauguration, however, the function of faith, though not in its narrow or sectarian sense, is very interesting and essential to the analysis. Something of the pragmatics of faith may be seen in Washington's own deployment of its powers. He routinely urged his men during the war to attend chapel services, and we recall his appeal to Providence during the several addresses delivered along the route from Mount Vernon to Federal Hall. We have seen it in the inaugural speech itself and will see it again in the Farewell Address. Here is a fine representation from the final gesture to the new nation: "Let us with caution indulge the supposition, that morality can be maintained without religion. Whatever may be conceded to the influence of refined education on minds of peculiar structure, reason and experience both forbid us to expect, that national morality can prevail in exclusion of religious principle. It is substantially true, that virtue or morality is a necessary spring of popular government."[1]

But what, we may still ask, can explain the source of that "necessary spring" in the first place? Faith traditions were of course very much in play at virtually every level of military and civic engagement throughout the period, but the Revolution was not waged on behalf of a given creed. Nor are we referring to that desperate, often reckless faith born of dearth and abjection that marked other revolutions of the age; nor indeed of the kind of faith driving the great Haitian Revolution that erupted in just a few years after Washington took office. This is hardly surprising: white Americans, after all, could be counted among the freest, most literate, least taxed, and economically advantaged people on earth. Such faith as demonstrated by the early nation builders was not then a positive assertion in the face of negative power. Something else was at work.

The faith of the Founders was rather found within. They believed in themselves. Is the ascription trite? Not if we reflect on the stakes involved and on the implications of failure and the bleak historical record of such dreams as they pursued. Self-confidence of the kind necessary to the moment could not be simply blind, illusory faith; in spite of that record, the colonists had shown themselves to be fairly adept, overall, at limited forms of self-government. No one could claim total and unyielding faith.

Too many skeptics remained for that kind of naïveté; indeed, most of the Founders could give way on occasion to bouts of pessimism and self-doubt. What the early republicans had to possess, rather, was just enough faith to pull it all off—and they did.

I would suggest here that such faith was the product not of some mystical endowment or Anglo-Saxon genetic inheritance. It was discovered, rather, and put to work *through the process itself.* Through the experience of making war and of inventing peace, Americans confronted their limits; through the embarrassments, doubts, anger, and fear they learned to fail, and through indefatigable labor, good luck, and a bruised but abiding commitment to the common good they taught themselves to succeed. And still they persisted. Here Max Edling's fine analysis of the constitutional ratification is instructive: the key to its success and legacy, he shows, lay in the process itself. The debate "over ratification was significant," Edling argues, "to the adoption of the Constitution because public debate was a necessary step in the decision-making process leading to ratification. It was a necessary step because adoption would not have been legitimate without the possibility of public debate."[2] That is a very sharp insight, and it holds more generally for the founding itself. Its leaders learned through the process, and that process taught them to believe.

One way to get at the point is to recall what the early nationals did *not* do. Above all, the revolutionary generation did not, in Arendt's famous formulation, eat their own children. No reign of terror set in, no pogroms, purges, or purification. This is not to understate the very real hardships experienced by loyalists and their families, but in comparison to other revolutionary moments, even this harsh reality pales. The successful ratification of the Constitution did not, as so often happens, install a permanent class of recalcitrant outsiders bent on the restoration of lost powers. Remarkably, Anti-Federalists did in fact adjust rapidly to the new order of things; they became indeed champions of constitutionalism before the end of Washington's first administration. They were not "men of little faith" after all; like most Americans, they believed in the essential integrity of themselves and what they had wrought.

April 30, 1789, was a product of this faith and a re-instantiation of it. To harness its power, Americans did not have to consult the gods, Aristotle, Cicero, John Locke, the commonwealth men, Montesquieu, or David Hume. They did, of course, but in a much more immediate and compelling sense they had only to acknowledge and learn from what they had accomplished in just the past few decades. Consider this: a twenty-five year old at the time of the inauguration would have lived through these events: the Stamp Act, Townshend duties, and Port Act investing Boston and New York; the Boston Massacre, Tea Party, and Intolerable Acts; the advent of the Continental Congress and the Battles of Lexington and Concord; the Declaration of Independence; War; Yorktown, Newburgh, Peace, and Evacuation Day; sitting of the Confederation Congress, Constitution and attending debates; Ratification; first federal elections; and the first inauguration of the first president of the United States of America. If, like most Americans, she kept her eyes open and thought about the world coming into being, reflecting on its struggles and rewards, she would have learned a great deal indeed; she would come to believe that Americans could actually make a go of this thing called republican government.

Among the tenets born of this experience, three seem of particular relevance to our story. Americans proved themselves to have faith that (1) their government really was *their* government; (2) dissent, debate, and public argument were ingredient to political life; and (3) they were capable of selecting a leadership worthy of the republican promise.

The War of Independence was fought on behalf of the promise that power properly rested in sovereignty of the people. The Constitution delivered on this promise by giving such power its necessary structure, force, and perdurance. The inauguration of George Washington affirmed and celebrated this promise as a gift to all American citizens. I hope to have made clear that such rituals of affirmation as we have witnessed cannot be reduced to a form of hegemonic containment, nor were they simply vestiges of old-world acclamations of the king's body. The speeches, parades, huzzahs, salutes, music, dance, and revelry were in fact popular expressions of the hard-won conviction that this was to be their government, their power, their source of strength, pride, and political identity. "Such rituals," David Waldstreicher has powerfully demonstrated, "might have aspired to a unity beyond political division, but, because of their origins and the political needs of various groups, they did not and could not merely reflect ideological consensus. Instead," he concludes, these rituals "engendered both nationalism and political action."[3]

The people knew very well what they had gained through the process and knew, too, that from those to whom much is given much is expected.

From this fountain, this America, wrote a Marylander, "that hospitality, gratitude, and generosity flow, with all the pleasing charities which adorn human nature." The new government, their government, secured to them a space wherein they might flourish as distinctively American citizens. "For where have these virtues their theatre, where is the scene of action, or how can they exert themselves," asked the writer, "but in society? When charity rises into public spirit, and partial affection is extended into general benevolence, then it is that man shines in the brightest lustre, and the truest image of his divine Creator." The rituals of shared identity we have seen give evidence that Americans intended to stage themselves as first citizens of the modern age: generous, benevolent, active; a people of faith.[4]

Americans argue a lot, often quite loudly and at great length. This has been a source of great annoyance at home and more so abroad. It has always been thus, it seems; certainly, one cannot help but be struck how terribly voluble were the colonists and their republican heirs. Was ever a revolution in world history so much debated in chambers, print media, on stumps, podia, altars, in the streets, taverns, shops, and parlors before a shot was fired? Here we are reminded of the great advances ushered in by the work of Bernard Bailyn, Gordon Wood, Pauline Maier, Mary Beth Norton, Jack Rakove, Joyce Appleby, and Peter Onuf, among others: for the first time in the historiography, really, they asked us to take seriously what people were saying, how they said it, and why. Rhetoric matters.

Noisy people, then, and we have heard plenty of them on the road to Federal Hall. But we know, too, that it was not just noise—not when the gravest matters were being worked out prior to war, and not during the ratification debates or in inaugurating the new government. Americans believed, as we might expect, that such disputation was essential to the very lifeblood of the republican body. We are today perhaps grown complacent on this matter; we ought not to be. There is no such thing as a quiet democracy, republican or otherwise. The first generation of American nationals understood this; they believed fervently, for the moment at least, that any power from whatever source threatening to shut down public debate was by definition intolerable. This standard, too, presupposes an enormous faith that such debates are in fact constitutive and not destructive of genuine polity—and they had such faith.

On the eve of Washington's arrival in New York City, one local writer paused before the spectacle about to unfold to reflect on the nation coming into being. His formulation is so precisely apt that I will offer it here without further comment and move on. "Debate and Dissention," the author declares, "not only flow from civil liberty, but contribute to preserve it." There will be excess and hurt feelings, of course, but "time and experiences will correct those extremes of temper, which have been excited by special causes. It must have its own course and work its own remedy. The love and the practice of dispute, strike out light upon the various, relative to government. It habituates men to reflection. . . . But while the spirit of liberty exists, controversy is unavoidable."[5]

One issue early republicans did not argue about was their choice for president. No one then or now would doubt the wisdom—the faith—necessary to put into the executive office the one figure on whom all Americans could agree. Again, the truism invites us to pause for a moment to consider the implications. Washington was as close to an absolute as Americans have ever dared conceive. Is this a good thing? Not on its face: republics genuinely committed to popular sovereignty and the contingencies of public deliberation must contemplate such a prospect with deep misgivings. Critics of the Constitution were quite right in saying so; without mentioning Washington specifically, they articulated a powerful and compelling case against the centralization of executive power. That anxiety persists, as well it should. Supporters in effect sought to allay such concerns with two responses, one more convincing than the other. No need to worry, they argued: we can trust His Excellency not to abuse the office. True, but he would not live forever.

The more lasting provision against such a threat was to be found in the Constitution and its distribution of prerogatives. This vastly consequential provision suggests in turn that the system itself could be a fit object of faith; that is to say, Americans might have it both ways. They could believe in the rule of law to supersede the claims of any given officer on the will of the people, and they could insist that their chief executive be possessed of real character. Ultimately, however, they understood that the prospects of republican government depended on themselves—on the people from whom all power found its legitimate source. Again, a matter of faith in their own character. The Constitution was a marvelous thing, they knew, and "Wisdom may devise—experience and patriotism may enforce its dictates," but in the end, wrote a Bay Stater, "the great body of the people must give the tone to the administration of the new system—*And they will do it.*"[6]

The inauguration, with its attendant rituals, I suggest, was one very important way in which "the great body of the people" helped create the conditions of its own possibility. They were capable of doing so because they had faith in themselves and their leadership. Such faith could only be vindicated by the success of what, together, they brought into and offered the world. Beyond this they could not know—that their words would be taken up by the dispossessed of generations unborn or that America would in time come very, very close to collapsing in on itself. They could not know that it would recover and emerge into a superpower of unimaginable strength, beset by epic challenges from within and without. But faith does not require knowledge of this kind: it demands only an abiding commitment to the ideals so memorably addressed by Washington on behalf of his country, and ours.

NOTES

ABBREVIATIONS

PGW Conf   *The Papers of George Washington: Confederation Series*

PGW Pres   *The Papers of George Washington: Presidential Series*

PGW RevWar   *The Papers of George Washington: Revolutionary War Series*

WGW   *The Writings of George Washington*

CHAPTER 1

1. For a standard account of Washington's preparations, see James Thomas Flexner, *George Washington and the New Nation: 1783–1793* (Boston: Little, Brown, 1969), 5–170.

2. John Zimmerman, "Charles Thomson, 'the Sam Adams of Philadelphia,'" *Mississippi Valley Historical Review* 45 (1958): 464–80.

3. Charles Thomson, quoted in *The Papers of George Washington: Presidential Series*, vol. 2, *April–June 1789*, ed. W. W. Abbot (Charlottesville: University Press of Virginia, 1987), 55. This series will appear hereafter as *PGW Pres*.

4. Ibid., 54–55.

5. John Langdon to George Washington, April 6, 1789, in *PGW Pres*, 2:29.

6. George Washington to Lafayette, February 1, 1784 in *The Writings of George Washington from the Original Manuscript Sources, 1745–1799*, vol. 27, *June 11, 1783–November 28, 1784*, ed. John C. Fitzpatrick (Washington, DC: United States Government Printing Office, 1931), 317–18. *The Writings of George Washington* will appear hereafter as *WGW*.

7. George Washington to Henry Knox, April 1, 1789 in *PGW Pres*, 2:2.

8. George Washington to George Clinton, December 28, 1783, in *WGW*, 27:288; George Washington to Chevalier de Chastellux in *WGW*, 27:314–15.

9. George Washington to "Learned Professions of Philadelphia," December 13, 1783, in *WGW*, 27:269.

10. Jacques-Pierre Brissot de Warville, *New Travels in the United States of America: Performed in 1788* (Dublin: P. Byrne, A. Gueber, 1792), 155; David Humphreys in *American Museum*, January 1792, 40; George Washington to Mary Washington, February 15, 1787, in *WGW*, 29:160; George Washington to Lafayette, May 10, 1786, in *The Papers of George Washington: Confederation Series*, vol. 4, *April 1786–January 1787*, ed. W. W. Abbot and Dorothy Twohig (Charlottesville: University Press of Virginia, 1995), 40. This series will appear hereafter as *PGW Conf*.

11. Robert F. Dalzell Jr. and Lee Baldwin Dalzell, "Interpreting George Washington's Mount Vernon," in *George Washington Reconsidered*, ed. Don Higginbotham (Charlottesville: University Press of Virginia, 2001), 95; *Massachusetts Centinel*, April 21, 1798, 37; Jessica Kross, "Mansions, Men, Women, and the Creation of Multiple Publics in Eighteenth-Century British North America," *Journal of Social History* 33, no. 2 (1999): 387; for a comprehensive treatment of Mount Vernon, see Robert F. Dalzell Jr. and Lee Baldwin Dalzell, *George Washington's Mount Vernon: At Home in Revolutionary America* (New York: Oxford University Press, 1988).

12. John Hunter, "An Account of a Visit Made to Washington at Mount Vernon, by an English Gentleman, in 1785," *Pennsylvania Magazine of History and Biography* 17 (1893): 79.

13. David Humphreys, "Mount Vernon, an Ode," *Connecticut Courant*, June 20, 1785, 5.

14. Kross, "Mansions, Men, Women," 385.

15. For the relationship between Washington's military and political thought, see

especially Glenn A. Phelps, *George Washington and American Constitutionalism* (Lawrence: University Press of Kansas, 1993), 23–61.

16. For the standard account of Washington's assumption of leadership, see James Thomas Flexner, *George Washington in the American Revolution* (Boston: Little, Brown, 1967), 9–43.

17. George Washington to Martha Washington, June 18, 1775, in *The Papers of George Washington: Revolutionary War Series*, vol. 1, *June–September 1775*, ed. W. W. Abbot (Charlottesville: University Press of Virginia, 1985), 3. This series will appear hereafter as *PGW RevWar*.

18. "Address from the New York Provincial Congress," in *PGW RevWar*, 1:40; *PGW RevWar*, 1: 41. See, on this issue, Maurer Maurer, "Military Justice under George Washington," *Military Affairs* 28, no. 1 (1964): 8–16.

19. "Address from the Massachusetts Provincial Congress, July 3, 1775," in *PGW RevWar*, 1:53.

20. Ibid.; "Address to the Massachusetts Provincial Congress, July 4, 1775," in *PGW RevWar*, 1:60. For representative examples of Washington's efforts to keep order in camp, see "General Orders," July 4, 1775, in *PGW RevWar*, 1:54–56.

21. "General Orders," July 14, 1775, in *PGW RevWar*, 1:114.

22. "General Orders," July 5, 1775, in *PGW RevWar*, 1:63.

23. Don Higginbotham, *George Washington and the American Military Tradition* (Athens: University of Georgia Press, 1985), 67.

24. George Washington to Richard Henry Lee, August 29, 1775, in *PGW RevWar*, 1:372.

25. Washington's arrival in Boston is treated especially well in Fred W. Anderson, "The Hinge of Revolution: George Washington Confronts a People's Army, July 3, 1775," *Massachusetts Historical Review* 1 (1999): 20–48; for his stay and departure, see Flexner, *George Washington in the American Revolution*, 58–97, and Don Higginbotham, *The War of American Independence: Military Attitudes, Policies, and Practices, 1783–1789* (New York: Macmillan, 1971). See also John Shy, *A People Numerous and Armed: Reflections on the Military Struggle for American Independence*

(Ann Arbor: University of Michigan Press, 1990).

26. Richard Beeman, *Plain, Honest Men: The Making of the United States Constitution* (New York: Random House, 2001), 48–49, gives a standard account of the episode.

27. Edmund Morgan, "George Washington: The Aloof American," in Higginbotham, *George Washington Reconsidered*, 287–308; William Maclay, *The Diary of William Maclay and Other Notes on Senate Debates*, ed. Kenneth R. Bowling and Helen E. Veit (Baltimore: John Hopkins University Press, 1988); Abigail Adams to Mary Smith, July 12, 1789, in Margaret A. Hogan, C. James Taylor, Jessie May Rodrique, Hobson Woodward, Gregg L. Lint, and Mary T. Claffey, eds., *The Adams Papers: Adams Family Correspondence, March 1787–December 1789*, vol. 8 (Cambridge, MA: Harvard University Press, 2007), 388; Timothy Pickering, quoted in Ron Chernow, *Washington: A Life* (New York: Penguin Press, 2010), 195.

28. For a useful and comprehensive treatment of Washington's relationships with his men, see Robert M. S. McDonald, ed., *Sons of the Father: George Washington and His Protégés* (Charlottesville: University of Virginia Press, 2013).

29. George Washington to Nathanael Greene, September 25, 1780, in *WGW*, 20:84–85.

30. George Washington to Nathanael Greene, December 13, 1780, in *WGW*, 20:469.

31. Hannah Arendt, *The Human Condition*, 2nd ed. (Chicago: University of Chicago Press, 1998), 51–52.

CHAPTER 2

1. George Washington to John Augustine Washington, June 15, 1783, in *WGW*, 27:13.

2. The best account of the trip is unquestionably to be found in the correspondence and attending scholarly treatment in *PGW Pres*, 2. I rely heavily, and gratefully indeed, on this work.

3. George Washington to Richard Conway, March 4, 1789, in *PGW Pres*, 1:368.

4. George Washington to George Steptoe Washington, March 23, 1789, in *WGW*, 30:247.

5. George Washington to Henry Knox, January 29, 1789, in *WGW*, 30:280.

6. George Washington to William Hartshorne, April 1, 1789, in *PGW Pres*, 2:1; George Washington to James McHenry, April 1, 1789, in *PGW Pres*, 2:3.

7. George Washington to George Clinton, March 25, 1789, in *WGW*, 30:251; George Washington to James Madison, March 25, 1789, in *WGW*, 30:255.

8. George Washington to Samuel Vaughn, March 21, 1789, in *WGW*, 30:238.

9. Arendt, *Human Condition*, 7–8.

10. Washington to Samuel Vaughn, in *WGW*, 30:238.

11. George Washington to Samuel Hanson, in *WGW*, 30:177.

12. Jared Sparks, ed., *Life of George Washington* (London: Henry Colburn, 1839), 2:227.

13. Dennis Ramsay, in *PGW Pres*, 2:61.

14. *Pennsylvania Packet*, April 30, 1789, 2; Dennis Ramsay in *PGW Pres*, 2:61.

15. George Washington to the Mayor Corporation and Citizens of Alexandria in *PGW Pres*, 2:59–60.

16. *Maryland Journal*, March 31, 1789, 3.

17. See *PGW Pres*, 2:62–65.

18. United States Presidents and James D. Richardson, *A Compilation of the Messages and Papers of the Presidents, 1789–1897* (Washington, DC: Published by authority of Congress, 1900), 45.

19. *PGW Pres*, 2:63.

20. Ibid., 62–65.

21. Ibid., 63.

22. Aristotle, *On Rhetoric: A Theory of Civic Discourse*, trans. George Kennedy, 2nd ed. (New York: Oxford University Press, 2006); Andrew S. Trees, *The Founding Fathers and the Politics of Character* (Princeton: Princeton University Press, 2004); Gordon Wood, *The Creation of the American Republic, 1776–1789* (Chapel Hill: University of North Carolina Press, 1969).

23. George Washington, "To the Citizens of Baltimore," in *PGW Pres*, 2:62.

24. Ibid.

25. *Massachusetts Spy*, May 14, 1789, 3; *Pennsylvania Packet*, March 12, 1789, 2.

26. Quoted in Walter A. Powell, *A History of Delaware* (Boston: Christopher Publishing House, 1928), 189.

27. See *PGW Pres*, 2:78.

28. George Washington, "To the Officials of Wilmington, Delaware," in *PGW Pres*, 2:77.

29. Ibid., 81.

30. *Independent Chronicle* [Boston], May 8, 1789, 3.

31. *New York Journal*, April 30, 1789, 3.

32. *Federal Gazette*, April 22, 1789, 2.

33. *New York Daily Gazette*, April 30, 1789, 422.

34. *Federal Gazette*, April 22, 1789, 2; William S. Baker, "Washington after the Revolution," *Pennsylvania Magazine of History and Biography* 19, no. 4 (1895): 331–32.

35. *Columbia Magazine*, May 1789, 282; *Independent Gazetteer*, April 21, 1789, 3.

36. Billy G. Smith and Paul Sivitz, "Idenitifying and Mapping Ethnicity in Philadelphia in the Early Republic," *Pennsylvania Magazine of History and Biography* 140, no. 403 (2016): 393–411.

37. *Pennsylvania Mercury*, April 21, 1789, 1; *Columbia Magazine*, July 1788, 391; Excellent treatment of the big day may be found in Laura Rigal, "'Raising the Roof': Authors, Spectators and Artisans in the Grand Federal Procession of 1788," *Theatre Journal* 48, no. 3 (1996): 253–77; Jurgen Heideking, "The Federal Processions of 1788 and the Origins of American Civil Religion," *Soundings: An Interdisciplinacy Journal* 37, nos. 3/4 (1994): 367–87; David Waldstreicher, *In the Midst of Perpetual Fetes: The Making of American Nationalism, 1776–1820* (Chapel Hill: University of North Carolina Press, 1997).

38. Albrecht Koschnik, "Political Conflict and Public Contest: Rituals of National Celebration in Philadelphia, 1788–1815," *Pennsylvania Magazine of History and Biography* 18, no. 3 (1994): 248.

39. *New York Journal*, April 29, 1789, 2; *Independent Gazetteer*, April 21, 1789, 3.

40. The order of toasts is reported in the *New York Daily Gazette*, April 27, 1789, 410.

41. On the Society generally, see especially Minor Myers Jr., *Liberty Without Anarchy: A*

History of the Society of the Cincinnati (Charlottesville: University Press of Virginia, 1983); Markus Hünemörder, *The Society of the Cincinnati: Conspiracy and Distrust in Early America* (New York: Berghahn Books, 2006).

42. See *PGW Pres*, 2:82.

43. George Washington, "To the Pennsylvania Society of the Cincinatti," in *PGW Pres*, 2:80–81.

44. Ibid., 85–86; Ibid., 84.

45. George Washington, "The Mayor, Recorder, Aldermen, and Common Council of Philadelphia," in *PGW Pres*, 2:83.

46. Ibid., 87. George Washington, "To the President and Faculty of the University of Pennsylvania," in *PGW Pres*, 2:86.

47. See *PGW Pres*, 2:106; George Washington, "To the Pennsylvania Legislature," in *PGW Pres*, 2:105.

CHAPTER 3

1. George Washington to Thomas Mifflin, April 21, 1789, in *PGW Pres*, 2:101.

2. *Pennsylvania Mercury*, May 2, 1789, 1; *New York Journal*, May 6, 1789, 2–3; The Trenton reception was widely reported and remains a set piece in the Washington historiography. A useful account may be found in Kenneth Silverman, *A Cultural History of the American Revolution* (New York: Columbia University Press, 1987), 598–601.

3. *Pennsylvania Mercury*, May 2, 1781; *PGW Pres*, 2:109.

4. *New Jersey Journal*, May 6, 1789, 3; *Columbian Magazine* 3 (1789): 288–90.

5. See *PGW Pres*, 2:110; *Pennsylvania Packet*, May 2, 1789, 1.

6. For a general overview of the theme, see David L. Holmes, *The Faiths of the Founding Fathers* (New York: Oxford University Press, 2006); Frank Lambert, *The Founding Fathers and the Place of Religion in America* (Princeton: Princeton University Press, 2003); and William Lee Miller, *The First Liberty: America's Foundation in Religious Liberty* (Washington, DC: Georgetown University Press, 2003).

7. On Washington and religion, see especially Paul F. Boller, "George Washington and Religious Liberty," *William and Mary*

Quarterly 17, no. 4 (1960): 486–506; Vincent Phillip Muñoz, "George Washington and Religious Liberty," *Review of Politics* 65, no. 1 (2003): 11–33; John C. Fitzpatrick, "George Washington and Religion," *Catholic Historical Review* 15, no. 1 (1929): 23–42; James H. Hutson, *Religion and the New Republic: Faith in the Founding of America* (Lanham, MD: Rowman and Littlefield, 2000).

8. On Washington and Deism, see Holmes, *Faiths of the Founding Fathers*, 65–71.

9. See *PGW Pres*, 2:60; 62; 77; 83; 85; 110.

10. Madison, quoted in Holmes, *Faiths of the Founding Fathers*, 71.

11. See *PGW Pres*, 2:181; 412; 21; 25.

12. On Washington and the Enlightenment, see Caroline Winterer, *American Enlightenments* (New Haven: Yale University Press, 2016), 211–25.

13. Muñoz, "George Washington and Religious Liberty," 25.

14. George Washington to the Hebrew Congregation in Newport, Rhode Island, August 18, 1790, in *PGW Pres*, 6:285.

15. George Washington to the German Lutherans of Philadelphia, in *PGW Pres*, 2:180; George Washington to the Bishops of the Methodist Episcopal Church in *PGW Pres*, 2:411–12; George Washington to the General Assembly of the Presbyterian Church in *PGW Pres*, 2:420.

16. George Washington to the United Baptist Churches of Virginia, in *PGW Pres*, 2:424; *PGW Pres*, 2:420.

17. W. W. Abbot, "An Uncommon Awareness of Self: The Papers of George Washington," in Higginbotham, *George Washington Reconsidered*, 277; James Madison, Federalist No. 14, and Alexander Hamilton, Federalist No. 22, in *The Federalist*, ed. Jacob E. Cooke (New York: Meridian Books, 1961), 87 and 141, respectively.

18. George Mason, quoted in Bernard Bailyn, *Faces of Revolution: Personalities and Themes in the Struggle for American Independence* (New York: Vintage, 1992), 245.

19. For the demography of the early republic, see Michael R. Haines and Richard H. Steckel, eds., *A Population History of North America* (Cambridge: Cambridge University Press, 2000); Herbert S. Klein, *A Population History*

of the United States (Cambridge: Cambridge University Press, 2012), 37–106.

20. Patrick Henry, "Patrick Henry Speech Before Virginia Ratifying Convention," in *The Complete Anti-Federalist*, ed. Herbert J. Storing (Chicago: Chicago University Press, 1981), 289.

21. George Washington to Lafayette, January 1, 1789, in *WGW*, 30:186–87.

22. *Cumberland Gazette*, April 6, 1787, 1.

23. *New York Packet*, June 15, 1787, 2.

24. John Adams, quoted in *The Founders on God and Government*, ed. Daniel L. Dreisbach, Mark D. Hall, and Jeffry H. Morrison (New York: Rowman and Littlefield, 2004), 32.

25. *New York Journal*, November 22, 1788, 3.

26. George Washington to Lund Washington, August 20, 1775, in *PGW RevWar*, 1:336; George Washington to John Jay, August 15, 1786, in *PGW Conf*, 4:212–13; George Washington to Madison, quoted in Abbot, "Uncommon Awareness of Self," 208.

27. George Washington to Lafayette, January 29, 1789, in *WGW*, 30:186.

28. Margaret A. Hogan, *The Adams Papers: Adams Family Correspondence, March 1787–December 1789*, 331; *American Mercury*, April 20, 1789, 3.

29. Thomas Jefferson to James Madison, January 30, 1787, in *Thomas Jefferson: Writings*, ed. Merrill D. Peterson (New York: Library of America, 1984), 884; Bailyn, *Faces of Revolution*, 7.

30. Stanley Elkins and Eric McKitrick, *The Age of Federalism: The Early American Republic, 1788–1800* (New York: Oxford University Press, 1993), 532; Wood, *Creation of the American Republic*, 569.

31. Thomas Jefferson to James Madison, July 29, 1789, in Julian Boyd, ed., *The Papers of Thomas Jefferson* (Princeton: Princeton University Press, 1958): 15: 223; John Adams to Abigail Adams Smith, June 16, 1788, in Hogan, *Adams Papers*, 279; John Adams to Abigail Adams Smith, November 11, 1788, in Hogan, *Adams Papers*, 305; Elizabeth Smith Shaw to Abigail Adams, June 22, 1788, in Hogan, *Adams Papers*, 275–76.

32. The best full-length study of Adams's personality is unquestionably Joseph J. Ellis, *Passionate Sage: The Character and Legacy of John Adams* (New York: W. W. Norton, 2001);

Tench Coxe to James Madison, January 27, 178, 9 in *The Papers of James Madison: March 7, 1788–March 1, 1789, Congressional Series*, ed. William T. Hutchinson et al., vol. 11, 1st ser. (Charlottesville: University of Virginia Press, 1977), 432; *American Mercury*, April 20, 1789, 3.

33. "A Federal Republican," in *Documentary History of the First Federal Congress of the United States of America, March 4, 1789–March 3, 1791*, ed. Linda Grant DePauw, vol. 3 (Baltimore: John Hopkins University Press, 1977), 213.

34. *American Mercury*, April 20, 1787, 3.

35. *Boston Gazette*, April 20, 1789, 1; *American Mercury*, April 20, 1789, 3; Hogan, *Adams Papers*, 333.

36. John Adams to Abigail Adams, in Hogan, *Adams Papers*, 333; *Massachusetts Spy*, April 30, 1789, 1.

37. John Adams to Abigail Adams, April 22, 1789, in Hogan, *Adams Papers*, 336.

38. John Adams, "Vice President's Address," *Massachusetts Spy*, April 30, 1789, 1.

39. *New Jersey Journal*, April 29, 1789, 2.

40. *Freeman's Journal*, April 7, 1789, 3.

41. George Washington, quoted in Flexner, *George Washington and the New Nation*, 181.

CHAPTER 4

1. *Georgia Gazette*, May 14, 1789, 1; *Maryland Journal*, May 5, 1789, 1.

2. *Maryland Journal*, May 15, 1789, 1; *Georgia Gazette*, May 14, 1789, 1.

3. *New York Daily Gazette*, April 25, 1789, 406.

4. Waldstreicher, *In the Midst of Perpetual Fetes*; *Pennsylvania Packet*, May 2, 1789, 2.

5. *Gazette of the United States*, April 2, 1789, 11.

6. St. George Tucker, quoted in Bettina Manzo, "A Virginian in New York: The Diary of St. George Tucker, July–August, 1786," *New York History* 67, no. 2 (1986): 196.

7. Ibid., 186; Jacques-Pierre Brissot de Warville, *New Travels in the United States of America: Performed in 1788* (Dublin: P. Byrne, A. Gueber, 1792), 160–61.

8. Brissot de Warville, *New Travels*, 160.

9. "A Philosophic Scrap," *New-Haven Gazette, and the Connecticut Magazine*, May 21, 1789, 7.

10. Quoted in Still, *Mirror for Gotham*: Nicasius de Sille, 10; Patrick M'Robert, 35; John Miller, 24; John Adams, 27; de Sille, 10.

11. Giovanni da Verrazzano, quoted in Still, *Mirror for Gotham*, 3.

12. "General Description of the City of New York," *American Magazine, Containing a Miscellaneous Collection of Original and Other Valuable Essays*, March 1788, 221; Tucker, quoted in Manzo, "A Virginian in New York," 196.

13. Oliver E. Allen, *New York, New York: A History of the World's Most Exhilarating and Challenging City* (New York: Atheneum, 1990), 12.

14. Thomas Dongan, "Governor Dongan's Report on the State of the Province, Etc.," quoted in Thomas E. Carney, "A Tradition to Live By: New York Religious History, 1624–1740," *New York History* 85, no. 4 (2004): 301–30.

15. Peter Kalm, quoted in Still, *Mirror for Gotham*, 33.

16. Mike Rapport, *The Unruly City: Paris, London, and New York in the Age of Revolution* (New York: Basic Books, 2017), xvii.

17. Quoted in Thomas Jones, *History of New York During the Revolutionary War: And of the Leading Events in the Other Colonies at That Period*, vol. 1 (New York: New-York Historical Society, 1879), 615; Jean de Crèvecœur, quoted in Still, *Mirror for Gotham*, 16; "New-York, Sept. 30," *New-York Gazette, and the Weekly Mercury*, September 30, 1776, 2.

18. "New-York," *New-York Gazette*, 2; George Washington to Lund Washington, October 6, 1776, in *PGW RevWar*, 6:495.

19. Quoted in "Letter from New York, September 23," in *The Remembrancer, or Impartial Repository of Public Events*, ed. J. Almon and T. Pownall, vol. 3 (London, 1775), 8.

20. Quoted in Still, *Mirror for Gotham*, 52.

21. *Salem Mercury*, March 24, 1789, 1; *Independent Chronicle*, March 19, 1789, 4.

22. *Pennsylvania Packet*, March 20, 1789, 2; *New Jersey Journal*, March 11, 1789, 2.

23. *Pennsylvania Packet*, March 20, 1789, 2; *New Jersey Journal*, October 29, 1788, 3.

24. "The Birth of Columbia," *Massachusetts Centinel*, December 5, 1788, 93.

25. *New York Journal*, March 5, 1789, 1; *Massachusetts Magazine*, June 1789, 331; *Columbia Magazine*, August 1789, 3; *Pennsylvania Packet*, March 30, 1789, 2.

26. *Columbia Magazine*, August 1789, 3; *New Jersey Journal*, March 11, 1789, 2.

27. "Account of Trinity Church in the City of New-York," *New-York Magazine*, January 1790, 3; ibid.

28. Ibid.

29. Fredrick V. Mills, "The Protestant Episcopal Churches in the United States 1783–1789: Suspending Animation or Remarkable Recovery?" *Historical Magazine of the Protestant Episcopal Church* 46, no. 2 (1977): 156, 61; Abraham Beach, quoted in Richard W. Pointer, "Religious Life in New York During the Revolutionary War," *New York History* 66, no. 4 (1985): 373; *Daily Advertisement*, August 23, 1788, 2.

30. Henry Barclay, quoted in Joyce D. Goodfriend, "The Social Dimensions of Congregational Life in Colonial New York City," *William and Mary Quarterly* 46, no. 2 (1989): 271; Michael Paul Driskel, "By the Light of Providence: The Glory Altarpiece at St. Paul's Chapel, New York City," *Art Bulletin* 89, no. 4 (2007): 715.

31. Goodfriend, "Social Dimensions of Congregational Life," 278.

32. "Resolve of the House of Representatives of the United States Respecting Mr. Osgood's Preparing His House for the Reception of the President of the United States, April 15, 1789," in James D. Richardson, *A Compilation of the Messages and Papers of the Presidents, 1789–1897*, vol. 1 ([Washington, DC]: Published by authority of Congress, 1898), 45; quoted in Douglas Southall Freeman, *George Washington: A Biography* (New York: Scribner's, 1954), 6; quoted in Damie Stillman, "Six Houses for the President," *Pennsylvania Magazine of History and Biography* 129, no. 4 (2005): 413; Martha Washington, "Letter to Fanny Bassett Washington, June 8, 1789," in *"Worthy Partner": The Papers of Martha Washington*, ed. Joseph E.

Fields (Westwood, CT: Greenwood Press, 1994), 215.

33. "A Sketch of the Political State of America," *Gazette of the United States,* April 22, 1789, 13; "Advertisement," *New York Daily Gazette,* May 1, 1789, 427; "Advertisement," *New York Daily Gazette,* 428.

34. "On Slavery," *New York Daily Gazette,* March 3, 1789, 222.

35. Tobias Lear to George Augustine Washington, May 3, 1789, in *PGW Pres,* 2:248.

36. Shane White, *Somewhat More Independent: The End of Slavery in New York City, 1770–1810* (Athens: University of Georgia Press, 1991), 5.

37. Samuel Hopkins, "A Dialogue Concerning the Slavery of the Africans," in *Proceedings of the New York Society for Promoting the Manumission of Slaves* (New York: Judah P. Spooner, 1776), 1.

38. Richard S. Newman and Roy E. Finkenbine, "Black Founders in the New Republic: Introduction," *William and Mary Quarterly* 64, no. 1 (2007): 88.

CHAPTER 5

1. *New York Weekly Museum,* May 2, 1789, 2.

2. *New York Journal,* May 7, 1789, 1.

3. *Massachusetts Magazine,* May 1789, 327.

4. Ibid.

5. James Morton Smith, ed., *The Republic of Letters: The Correspondence Between Thomas Jefferson and James Madison, 1776–1826* (New York: W. W. Norton, 1995), 497; Ralph Ketcham, *Presidents Above Party: The First American Presidency, 1789–1829* (Chapel Hill: University of North Carolina Press, 1987), 8; Jack Rakove, *Original Meanings: Politics and Ideas in the Making of the Constitution* (New York: Vintage, 1996), 244; Emmet John Hughes, *The Living Presidency: Resources and Dilemmas of the American Presidential Office* (New York: Penguin, 1974), 40.

6. Benjamin Franklin, *The Writings of Benjamin Franklin,* ed. Albert Henry Smith (New York: Haskell House, 1970), 9:659.

7. Standard treatments of the inaugural events and festivities may be found in Freeman, *George Washington: A Biography,*

6:167–98; Flexner, *George Washington and the New Nation,* 325–48; The only serious treatment of Washington's address to date is Stephen E. Lucas, "Genre Criticism and Historical Context: The Case of George Washington's First Inaugural Address," *Southern Speech Communication Journal* 51 (1986): 354–70. Although I have opted not to stress the text's generic features, my reading of the speech is indebted to Lucas's perceptive analysis.

8. James Wilson and Edmund Randolph in *The Records of the Federal Convention of 1787,* ed. Max Farrand (New Haven: Yale University Press, 1966), 1:64 and 1:65, respectively; the following treatment is indebted to Rakove, *Original Meanings: Politics and Ideas,* 244–87; Jack N. Rakove, "Thinking Like a Constitution," *Journal of the Early Republic* 24 (2004): 1–26; Lance Banning, "Republican Ideology and the Triumph of the Constitution, 1789–1793," *William and Mary Quarterly* 31 (1974): 167–88; Isaac Kramnick, "'The Great National Discussion': The Discourse of Politics in 1787," *William and Mary Quarterly* 45 (1988): 3–32.

9. Pierce Butler, in Farrand, *Records of the Federal Convention of 1787,* 3:301.

10. The best treatment of Washington's political thought generally is found in Phelps, *George Washington and American Constitutionalism;* see also Harold W. Bradley, "The Political Thinking of George Washington," *Journal of Southern History* 2 (1945): 467–86; Arthur N. Holcolmbe, "The Role of Washington in the Framing of the Constitution," *Huntington Library Quarterly* 19 (1956): 317–44; Robert F. Jones, "George Washington and the Politics of the Presidency," *Presidential Studies Quarterly* 19 (1980): 28–35; Richard Loss, "The Political Thought of President George Washington," *Presidential Studies Quarterly* 19, no. 3 (1989): 471–90; Simon P. Newman, "Principles or Men? George Washington and the Political Culture of National Leadership, 1776–1801," *Journal of the Early Republic* 12 (1992): 472–507; Barry Schwartz, "George Washington and the Whig Conception of Heroic Leadership," *American Sociological Review* 48 (1983): 18–33; John Ray, "George Washington's Pre-Presidential Statesmanship,

1783–1789," *Presidential Studies Quarterly* 27 (1997): 207–20.

11. Cecelia Kenyon, "'Men of Little Faith': The Anti-Federalists on the Nature of Representative Government," *William and Mary Quarterly* 12 (1955): 22; Wood, *Creation of the American Republic,* 520; the best treatment of the Anti-Federalist campaign is Pauline Maier, *Ratification: The People Debate the Constitution, 1787–1788* (New York: Simon & Schuster, 2010); see also Richard E. Ellis, "The Persistence of Anti-Federalism After 1789," in *Beyond Confederation: Origins of the Constitution and American National Identity,* ed. Richard Beeman, Stephen Botein, and Edward C. Carter II (Chapel Hill: University of North Carolina Press, 1987), 295–314.

12. Kenyon, "'Men of Little Faith,'" 22; James Monroe in *The Debates in the Several State Constitutions,* ed. Jonathan Elliot (Philadelphia: J. B. Lippincott, 1907), 3:489; "Federal Farmer," in Storing, *Complete Anti-Federalist,* 2:312.

13. Alexander Hamilton in *The Papers of Alexander Hamilton,* ed. Harold Syrett (New York: Columbia University Press, 1962), 2:400; Alexander Hamilton, Federalist No. 7, in Cooke, *The Federalist,* 471.

14. For a useful treatment of issues at debate over the functions and powers of the executive office see Morton J. Frisch, "Executive Power and Republican Government—1787," *Presidential Studies Quarterly* 17 (1987): 281–91; Broadus Mitchell, "Alexander Hamilton, Executive Power, and the New Nation," *Presidential Studies Quarterly* 17 (1987): 329–43; Rakove, *Original Meanings,* 256–87; Jeffrey Leigh Sedgwick, "James Madison and the Problem of Executive Character," *Polity* 21 (1988): 5–23; Charles C. Thach Jr., *The Creation of the Presidency, 1775–1789: A Study in Constitutional History* (Indianapolis: Liberty Fund, 1923, 1969); Akhil Reed Amar, *America's Constitution: A Biography* (New York: Random House, 2010), 175–201.

15. "Americanus," in *The Debate on the Constitution: Federalist and Antifederalist Speeches, Articles, and Letters During the Struggle over Ratification,* ed. Bernard Bailyn, 2 vols. (New York: The Library of America, 1993), 1:464; "The Republican," in Bailyn, *Debate on the Constitution,* 1:715.

16. Bailyn, *Debate on the Constitution,* 2:33.

17. On virtue, see Wood, *Creation of the American Republic,* 68–69, 95–96, 415–20.

18. Hamilton in Syrett, *Papers of Alexander Hamilton,* 103.

19. Fisher Ames, in *Works of Fisher Ames,* ed. W. B. Allen (Indianapolis: Liberty Classics, 1983), 1:568; Comte de Montmorin, quoted in Freeman, *George Washington: A Biography,* 195. Although the circumstances of Washington's inaugural address were in many respects unique, its composition was nevertheless shaped by discernible antecedents of the genre. Lucas makes a convincing case that the address "appears to have been modulated by a set of generic constraints derived from the rhetoric of office-taking, from the inaugural speeches of Virginia's colonial governors, and, perhaps, from the accession speeches of eighteenth-century British monarchs" (Lucas, "Genre Criticism and Historical Context," 369); Washington's deployment of rhetorical conventions is treated more broadly in "George Washington and the Rhetoric of Presidential Leadership," in *The Presidency and Rhetorical Leadership,* ed. Leroy G. Dorsey (College Station: Texas A&M University Press, 2001), 42–72.

20. For a useful review of the drafting process, see *WGW,* 30:296–97.

21. All quotations cited seriatim from George Washington, "Inaugural Address," in *WGW,* 30:291–96.

22. For treatments stressing the rhetorical dimensions of inaugural addresses generally see especially Karlyn Kohrs Campbell and Kathleen Hall Jamieson, "Inaugurating the Presidency," *Presidential Studies Quarterly* 15 (1985): 394–411 and *Presidents Creating the Presidency: Deeds Done in Words* (Chicago: University of Chicago Press, 2008), 29–56; Edward W. Chester, "Beyond the Rhetoric: A New Look at Presidential Inaugural Addresses," *Presidential Studies Quarterly* 10 (1980): 571–82; Michael J. Lax, ed., *The Inaugural Addresses of the Presidents of the United States, 1789–1985* (Atlantic City, NJ: American Inheritance Press, 1985).

23. For the history of the "invisible hand" and its providential resonance see Peter Harrison, "Adam Smith and the History of the

Invisible Hand," *Journal of the History of Ideas* 72 (2011): 29–49.

24. Studies examining Washington in relationship to religion include Paul F. Boller, *George Washington and Religion* (Dallas: Southern Methodist University Press, 1963); Holmes, *Faiths of the Founding Fathers*, 59–72; Peter R. Henriques, "The Final Struggle Between George Washington and the Grim King: Washington's Attitude Toward Death and an Afterlife," *Virginia Magazine of History and Biography* 107 (1999): 73–97; Robert P. Hay, "George Washington: American Moses," *American Quarterly* 21 (1969): 780–91; Mary V. Thompson, *In the Hands of Good Providence: Religion in the Life of George Washington* (Charlottesville: University of Virginia Press, 2008).

25. The origins and career of the amendment clause are examined in John R. Vile, "American Views of the Constitutional Amending Process: An Intellectual History of Article V," *American Journal of Legal History* 35 (1991): 44–69.

26. Fisher Ames in Allen, *Works of Fisher Ames*, 1:583.

27. Lucas, "Genre Criticism and Historical Context," 369.

28. Alexander Hamilton, Federalist No. 76, in Cooke, *Federalist*, 514.

29. *Gazette of the United States*, May 6, 1789, 27.

30. *Gazette of the United States*, May 2, 1789, 21.

31. Rufus W. Griswold, *The Republican Court, or American Society in the Days of Washington* (New York: D. Appleton, 1895), 145.

32. Ibid., 155.

33. Ibid., 158.

34. *United States Chronicle* [Providence, Rhode Island], June 3, 1790, 1.

CHAPTER 6

1. *New Yorker*, April 28, 1839, 110.

2. John Quincy Adams, *The Jubilee of the Constitution: A Discourse Delivered at the Request of the New-York Historical Society, in the City of New York, on Tuesday, the 30th of April,* *1839; Being the Fiftieth Anniversary of the Inauguration of George Washington as President of the United States on Thursday, the 30th of April, 1789* (New York: Samuel Colman VIII Astor House, 1839).

3. Ramon de la Sagra, quoted in Still, *Mirror for Gotham*, 119; Frances Trollope, quoted in Still, *Mirror for Gotham*, 117.

4. "Still Further of the Great Conflagration," *New York Herald*, December 21, 1835, 2.

5. Frederick Marryat, quoted in Still, *Mirror for Gotham*, 120; Philip Hone, quoted in Edwin G. Burrows and Mike Wallace, *Gotham: A History of New York City to 1898* (Oxford: Oxford University Press, 1999), 614.

6. "The Inauguration of Washington," *Centinel of Freedom*, May 7, 1839, 1; "The Celebration," *Commercial Advertiser*, May 1, 1839, 2; "Oration of J. Q. Adams," *Sun*, May 4, 1839, 4; Adams, *Jubilee of the Constitution*, 119–20.

7. Julian Ralph, "The Centennial Celebration," *Harper's Weekly*, May 11, 1889, 375.

8. Ibid.

9. Ibid.; "To-Day's Celebrations," *Kansas City Times*, April 4, 1889, 4.

10. "To-Day's Celebrations," 4.

11. Rebecca Edwards, "Politics, Social Movements, and the Periodization of U.S. History," *Journal of the Gilded Age and Progressive Era* 8, no. 4 (2009): 463–73; Charles W. Calhoun, "Reimagining the 'Lost Men' of the Gilded Age: Perspectives on the Late Nineteenth Century Presidents," *Journal of the Gilded Age and Progressive Era* 1, no. 3 (2002): 225–57.

12. Charles E. Dowe, "The Inauguration of the First President," *Cosmopolitan: A Monthly Illustrated Magazine*, April 1889, 533.

13. Ralph, "Centennial Celebration," 375.

14. "On Bended Knees: President Harrison in Washington's Pew at St. Paul's Chapel," *New York Herald*, May 1, 1889, 1; Bishop Henry Potter, quoted in "On Bended Knees," 1.

15. Potter, quoted in "On Bended Knees," 1.

16. "A Hundred Years Since the First Inauguration," *Richmond Daily Telegram*, April 3, 1889, 1; "Vow of Washington," as recorded in "The Washington Centennial," *Critic: A Weekly Review of Literature and the Arts*, May 1889, 225.

17. Chauncey M. Depew, quoted in "Oration," *Independent . . . Devoted to the Consideration of Politics, Social and Economic Tendencies, History, Literature, and the Arts*, May 2, 1889, 1.

18. Menu as recorded in Ralph, "Centennial Celebration," 379.

19. "Mr. Cleveland's Address," *New York Times*, May 1, 1889, 2; Stephen Grover Cleveland, quoted in "Mr. Cleveland's Address."

20. Cleveland, quoted in "Mr. Cleveland's Address," 2.

21. Ralph, "Centennial Celebration," 380; "Washington's Inauguration," *Woman's Exponent*, May 15, 1889, 188; Isaac Smucker, "A Great Event of a Century Ago: Washington's Inauguration and Inaugural," *Magazine of Western History*, May 1889, 522; "The Washington Centennial," *Phrenological Journal of Science and Health* 88, no. 5 (1889): 239.

22. W. H. Auden, "Atlantis," in *Selected Poems: Expanded Edition*, ed. Edward Mendelson (New York: Vintage International, 2007), 126.

23. Charles Eliot Norton, "The Intellectual Life of America," *New Princeton Review* 6 (1888): 315; Potter, quoted in "On Bended Knees," 1; Lowell, quoted in "The Big Banquet: The Centennial Dinner Last Night," *Daily Nebraska State Journal*, May 1, 1889, 2.

24. Ausburn Towner, "Our First President's Inauguration," *Frank Leslie's Popular Monthly* 27, no. 4 (1889): 386.

25. "A Nation's Prayer," *St. Louis Republic*, April 4, 1889, 4; "The Past and the Present," *Milwaukee Daily*, May 1, 1889, 1.

26. Franklin D. Roosevelt, "Annual Message to Congress, January 4, 1939," in *The Public Papers and Addresses of Franklin D. Roosevelt, 1939 Volume, War and Neutrality (Book 1)* (Ann Arbor: University of Michigan Library, 2005), http://name.umdl.umich.edu/4926579.1939.001, 1, 4.

27. Ibid., 5.

28. Ibid., 12.

29. "Welcome to Fleet Is Mapped by City," *New York Times*, April 3, 1939, 3.

30. "New York Fair Opens to-Day," *Sunday Times*, April 30, 1939, 1; Premier Hiranuma, quoted in "Japan's Good-Will Broadcast to Fair," *New York Times*, April 3, 1939, 3.

31. "Washington's Trip to Start April 16," *New York Times*, April 9, 1939, G5; Franklin D. Roosevelt, quoted in Felix Belair Jr., "Roosevelt Extols Washington of 1789," *New York Times*, April 15, 1939, 9.

32. "D. A. R. Bans Marian Anderson," *Black Worker* 5, no. 4 (1939): 1; "'First President' Takes Coach Today," *New York Times*, April 16, 1939, 16; Denys Wortman, quoted in "'Washington' Here, a Bit Coach-Weary," *New York Times*, April 25, 1939, 1.

33. "Washington's Inaugural Is Re-Enacted at the Fair: Inaugural Scene of 1789 Is Enacted," *New York Times*, May 1, 1939, 8; Franklin D. Roosevelt, quoted in "The President of the United States Opens the World's Greatest World's Fair," *New York Times*, May 1, 1939, 5.

34. John Dewey, "Creative Democracy: The Task Before Us," in *John Dewey: The Later Works, 1924–1953*, ed. J. Boydston (Carbondale: Southern Illinois University Press, 1976), 225.

35. Francis Fukuyama, "The End of History?" *National Interest* 16 (1989): 3–18.

36. George H. W. Bush, "Inaugural Address," January 20, 1989, The American Presidency Project, https://www.presidency.ucsb.edu/documents/inaugural-address.

37. Elizabeth Drew, "Letter from Washington," *New Yorker*, February 27, 1989, 78; Bush, "Inaugural Address."

38. Robert Thompson, "The Lessons of Yesterday Can Shape a Better Tomorrow," *Seattle Post-Intelligencer*, July 31, 1989, A7.

39. Hannah Arendt, *The Life of the Mind: The Groundbreaking Investigation on How We Think* (New York: Houghton Mifflin Harcourt, 1978), 1:12.

40. George H. W. Bush, "Proclamation 5963—Bicentennial Celebration of the Inauguration of George Washington," April 28, 1989, American Presidency Project, https://www.presidency.ucsb.edu/documents/proclamation-5963-bicentennial-celebration-the-inauguration-george-washington; Dennis Hevesi, "A Flag-Flapping Salute to the First Inaugural," *New York Times*, April 30, 1989, 1.

41. Hevesi, "Flag-Flapping Salute," 1.

42. George H. W. Bush, "Remarks at the Bicentennial Celebration of George

Washington's Inauguration in New York," April 30, 1989, American Presidency Project, https://www.presidency.ucsb.edu/documents/remarks-the-bicentennial-celebration-george-washingtons-inauguration-new-york-new-york; William Safire, "On Language: Marking Bush's Inaugural," *New York Times*, February 5, 1989, SM10; William A. Graham, "George Washington: The Forging of a Nation" (Arlington, VA: PBS, 1986).

43. Fred Beachum, quoted in James Barron, "A Day Celebrates 200 Presidential Years," *New York Times*, May 1, 1989, A1.

44. Bernard Mayo, "George Washington," *Georgia Review* 13, no. 2 (1959): 139; Saul K. Padover, "George Washington: Portrait of a True Conservative," *Social Research* 22, no. 2 (1955): 199–222; Karal Ann Marling, *George Washington Slept Here: Colonial Revivals and American Culture, 1876–1986* (Cambridge, MA: Harvard University Press, 1988), 376; Albert Furtwangler, "George Washington Fading Away," *American Literary History* 2, no. 2 (1990): 318–27.

45. Marcus Cunliffe, *George Washington: Man and Monument* (Boston: Little, Brown, 1958), 213.

EPILOGUE

1. Washington, "Farewell Address," 229.

2. Max M. Edling, *A Revolution in Favor of Government: Origins of the United States Constitution and the Making of the American State* (New York: Oxford University Press, 2003), 15.

3. Waldstreicher, *In the Midst of Perpetual Fetes*, 8.

4. *Maryland Journal*, "Essay on Patriotism," April 3, 1789, 1.

5. *Gazette of the United States*, April 22, 1789, 12.

6. *Gazette of the United States*, April 29, 1789, 17.

BIBLIOGRAPHY

Abbot, W. W. "An Uncommon Awareness of Self: The Papers of George Washington." In *George Washington Reconsidered*, edited by Don Higginbotham, 275–86. Charlottesville: University Press of Virginia, 2001.

———, ed. *The Papers of George Washington: Presidential Series*. Vol. 1, *September 1788–March 1789*. Charlottesville: University Press of Virginia, 1987.

———, ed. *The Papers of George Washington: Presidential Series*. Vol. 2, *April–June 1789*. Charlottesville: University Press of Virginia, 1987.

———, ed. *The Papers of George Washington: Revolutionary War Series*. Vol. 1, *June–September 1775*. Charlottesville: University Press of Virginia, 1985.

Abbot, W. W., and Dorothy Twohig, eds. *The Papers of George Washington: Confederation Series*. Vol. 4. *April 1786–January 1787*. Charlottesville: University Press of Virginia, 1995.

Adams, John Quincy. *The Jubilee of the Constitution: A Discourse Delivered at the Request of the New York Historical Society, in the City of New York, on Tuesday, the 30th of April, 1839; Being the Fiftieth Anniversary of the Inauguration of George Washington as President of the United States on Thursday, the 30th of April, 1789*. New York: Samuel Colman VIII Astor House, 1839.

Alden, James. *George Washington: A Biography*. Baton Rouge: Louisiana State University Press, 1996.

Allen, Oliver E. *New York, New York: A History of the World's Most Exhilarating and Challenging City*. New York: Atheneum, 1990.

Allen, W. B., ed. *Works of Fisher Ames*. Vol. 1. Indianapolis: Liberty Classics, 1983.

Almon, J., and T. Pownall, eds. *The Remembrancer, or Impartial Repository of Public Events*. Vol. 3. London, 1775.

Amar, Akhil Reed. *America's Constitution: A Biography*. New York: Random House, 2010.

Anderson, Fred W. "The Hinge of Revolution: George Washington Confronts a People's Army, July 3, 1775." *Massachusetts Historical Review* 1 (1999): 20–48.

Appleby, Joyce. *Inheriting the Revolution: The First Generation of Americans*. Cambridge, MA: Harvard University Press, 2001.

Arendt, Hannah. *The Human Condition*. 2nd ed. Chicago: University of Chicago Press, 1998.

———. *The Life of the Mind: The Groundbreaking Investigation on How We Think*. Vol. 1. New York: Houghton Mifflin Harcourt, 1978.

Aristotle. *On Rhetoric: A Theory of Civic Discourse*. Translated by George Kennedy. 2nd ed. New York: Oxford University Press, 2006.

Auden, W. H. "Atlantis." In *Selected Poems: Expanded Edition*, edited by Edward Mendelson, 125–27. New York: Vintage International, 2007.

Bailyn, Bernard, ed. *The Debate on the Constitution: Federalist and Antifederalist Speeches, Articles, and Letters During the Struggle over Ratification*. 2 vols. New York: The Library of America 1993.

———. *Faces of Revolution: Personalities and Themes in the Struggle for American Independence*. New York: Vintage, 1992.

Baker, William S. "Washington after the Revolution." *Pennsylvania Magazine of History and Biography* 19, no. 4 (1895): 331–32.

Banning, Lance. "Republican Ideology and the Triumph of the Constitution,

1789–1793." *William and Mary Quarterly* 31 (1974): 167–88.

Barron, James. "A Day Celebrates 200 Presidential Years." *New York Times,* May 1, 1989.

Bartoloni-Tuazon, Kathleen. *For Fear of an Elective King: George Washington and the Presidential Title Controversy of 1789.* Ithaca, NY: Cornell University Press, 2014.

Beeman, Richard. *Plain, Honest Men: The Making of the United States Constitution.* New York: Random House, 2001.

Belair, Felix, Jr. "Roosevelt Extols Washington of 1789." *New York Times,* April 15, 1939, 9.

Boller, Paul F. *George Washington and Religion.* Dallas: Southern Methodist University Press, 1963.

———. "George Washington and Religious Liberty." *William and Mary Quarterly* 17, no. 4 (1960): 488–506.

Boyd, Julian, ed. *The Papers of Thomas Jefferson.* Princeton: Princeton University Press, 1958.

Bradley, Harold W. "The Political Thinking of George Washington." *Journal of Southern History* 11, no. 4 (November 1945): 469–86.

Brissot de Warville, Jacques-Pierre. *New Travels in the United States of America: Performed in 1788.* Dublin: P. Byrne, A. Gueber, 1792.

Brumwell, Stephen. *George Washington: Gentleman Warrior.* New York: Quercus, 2013.

Burrows, Edwin G., and Mike Wallace. *Gotham: A History of New York City to 1898.* Oxford: Oxford University Press, 1999.

Bush, George H. W. "Inaugural Address." January 20, 1989. The American Presidency Project. https://www .presidency.ucsb.edu/documents /inaugural-address.

———. "Proclamation 5963—Bicentennial Celebration of the Inauguration of George Washington." April 28, 1989. The American Presidency Project. https://www.presidency.ucsb.edu /documents/proclamation-5963

-bicentennial-celebration-the -inauguration-george-washington.

———. "Remarks at the Bicentennial Celebration of George Washington's Inauguration in New York, New York." April 30, 1989. The American Presidency Project. https://www .presidency.ucsb.edu/documents /remarks-the-bicentennial-celebration -george-washingtons -inauguration -new-york-new-york.

Calhoun, Charles W. "Reimagining the 'Lost Men' of the Gilded Age: Perspectives on the Late Nineteenth Century Presidents." *Journal of the Gilded Age and Progressive Era* 1, no. 3 (2002): 225–57.

Campbell, Karlyn Kohrs, and Kathleen Hall Jamieson. "Inaugurating the Presidency." *Presidential Studies Quarterly* 15 (1985): 394–411.

———. *Presidents Creating the Presidency: Deeds Done in Words.* Chicago: University of Chicago Press, 2008.

Carney, Thomas E. "A Tradition to Live By: New York Religious History, 1624–1740." *New York History* 85, no. 4 (2004): 301–30.

Chernow, Ron. *Washington: A Life.* New York: Penguin Press, 2010.

Chester, Edward W. "Beyond the Rhetoric: A New Look at Presidential Inaugural Addresses." *Presidential Studies Quarterly* 10 (1980): 571–82.

Cooke, Jacob E., ed. *The Federalist.* New York: Meridian Books, 1961.

Cunliffe, Marcus. *George Washington: Man and Monument.* Boston: Little, Brown, 1958.

Dalzell, Robert F., Jr., and Lee Baldwin Dalzell. *George Washington's Mount Vernon: At Home in Revolutionary America.* New York: Oxford University Press, 1988.

———. "Interpreting George Washington's Mount Vernon." In *George Washington Reconsidered,* edited by Don Higginbotham, 94–113. Charlottesville: University Press of Virginia, 2001.

DePauw, Linda Grant, ed. *Documentary History of the First Federal Congress of the United States of America, March 4,*

1789–March 3, 1791. Vol. 3. Baltimore: Johns Hopkins University Press, 1977.

Dewey, John. "Creative Democracy: The Task before Us." In *John Dewey: The Later Works, 1924–1953*, edited by J. Boydston, 224–30. Carbondale: Southern Illinois University Press, 1976.

Dorsey, Leroy G., ed. *The Presidency and Rhetorical Leadership*. College Station: Texas A&M University Press, 2002.

Dowe, Charles E. "The Inauguration of the First President." *Cosmopolitan: A Monthly Illustrated Magazine*, April 1889, 533.

Dreisbach, Daniel L., Mark D. Hall, and Jeffry H. Morrison, eds. *The Founders on God and Government*. New York: Rowman and Littlefield, 2004.

Drew, Elizabeth. "Letter from Washington." *New Yorker*, February 27, 1989, 78.

Driskel, Michael Paul. "By the Light of Providence: The Glory Altarpiece at St. Paul's Chapel, New York City." *Art Bulletin* 89, no. 4 (2007): 715–37.

Ecclesiastical Records, State of New York. Vol. 2. Albany, NY: J. B. Lyon, 1901.

Edling, Max M. *A Revolution in Favor of Government: Origins of the United States Constitution and the Making of the American State*. New York: Oxford University Press, 2003.

Edwards, Rebecca. "Politics, Social Movements, and the Periodization of U.S. History." *Journal of the Gilded Age and Progressive Era* 8, no. 4 (2009): 461–73.

Elkins, Stanley, and Eric McKitrick. *The Age of Federalism: The Early American Republic, 1788–1800*. New York: Oxford University Press, 1993.

Elliot, Jonathan, ed. *The Debates in the Several State Constitutions*. Philadelphia: J. B. Lippincott, 1907.

Ellis, Joseph J. *Passionate Sage: The Character and Legacy of John Adams*. New York: W. W. Norton, 2001.

Ellis, Richard E. "The Persistence of Antifederalism After 1789." In *Beyond Confederation: Origins of the Constitution and American National Identity*, edited by Richard Beeman,

Stephen Botein, and Edward C. Carter II, 295–314. Chapel Hill: University of North Carolina Press, 1987.

Farrand, Max, ed. *Records of the Federal Convention of 1787*. 3 vols. New Haven: Yale University Press, 1966.

Fields, Joseph E., ed. *"Worthy Partner": The Papers of Martha Washington*. Westwood, CT: Greenwood Press, 1994.

Fitzpatrick, John C. "George Washington and Religion." *Catholic Historical Review* 15, no. 1 (1929): 23–42.

———, ed. *The Writings of George Washington from the Original Manuscripts, 1745–1799*. 39 vols. Washington, DC: United States Government Printing Office, 1931–44.

Flexner, James Thomas. *George Washington and the New Nation (1783–1793)*. Boston: Little, Brown, 1969.

———. *George Washington in the American Revolution*. Boston: Little, Brown, 1967.

Franklin, Benjamin. *The Writings of Benjamin Franklin*. Edited by Albert Henry Smith. New York: Haskell House, 1970.

Freeman, Douglas Southall. *George Washington: A Biography*. 7 vols. New York: Charles Scribner's Sons, 1954.

Frisch, Morton J. "Executive Power and Republican Government—1787." *Presidential Studies Quarterly* 17 (1987): 281–91.

Fukuyama, Francis. "The End of History?" *National Interest* 16 (1989): 3–18.

Furtwangler, Albert. "George Washington Fading Away." *American Literary History* 2, no. 2 (1990): 318–27.

Goodfriend, Joyce D. "The Social Dimensions of Congregational Life in Colonial New York City." *William and Mary Quarterly* 46, no. 2 (1989): 252–78.

Graham, William A. "George Washington: The Forging of a Nation." Arlington, VA: PBS, 1986.

Griswold, Rufus W. *The Republican Court, or American Society in the Days of Washington*. New York: D. Appleton, 1895.

Gustafson, Sandra M. *Eloquence is Power: Oratory and Performance in Early*

America. Chapel Hill: University of North Carolina Press, 2000.

Haines, Michael R., and Richard H. Steckel, eds. *A Population History of North America*. Cambridge: Cambridge University Press, 2000.

Harrison, Peter. "Adam Smith and the History of the Invisible Hand." *Journal of the History of Ideas* 72 (2011): 29–49.

Hay, Robert P. "George Washington: American Moses." *American Quarterly* 21 (1969): 780–91.

Heideking, Jurgen. "The Federal Processions of 1788 and the Origins of American Civil Religion." *Soundings: An Interdisciplinary Journal* 37, no. 3/4 (1994): 367–87.

Henriques, Peter R. "The Final Struggle Between George Washington and the Grim King: Washington's Attitude Toward Death and an Afterlife." *Virginia Magazine of History and Biography* 107 (1999): 73–97.

Henry, Patrick. "Patrick Henry Speech Before Virginia Ratifying Convention." In *The Complete Anti-Federalist*, edited by Herbert J. Storing, 289. Chicago: University of Chicago Press, 1981.

Hevesi, Dennis. "A Flag-Flapping Salute to the First Inaugural." *New York Times*, April 30, 1989, 1, 42.

Higginbotham, Don. *George Washington and the American Military Tradition*. Athens: University of Georgia Press, 1985.

———. *The War of American Independence: Military Attitudes, Policies, and Practices, 1783–1789*. New York: Macmillan, 1971.

Hogan, Margaret A., C. James Taylor, Jessie May Rodrique, Hobson Woodward, Gregg L. Lint, and Mary T. Claffey, eds. *The Adams Papers: Adams Family Correspondence, March 1787–December 1789*. Vol. 8. Cambridge, MA: Harvard University Press, 2007.

Holcombe, Arthur N. "The Role of Washington in the Framing of the Constitution." *Huntington Library Quarterly* 19 (1956): 317–34.

Holmes, David L. *The Faiths of the Founding Fathers*. New York: Oxford University Press, 2006.

Hopkins, Samuel. "A Dialogue Concerning the Slavery of the Africans." In *Proceedings of the New York Society for Promoting the Manumission of Slaves*. New York: Judah P. Spooner, 1776.

Hughes, Emmet John. *The Living Presidency: Resources and Dilemmas of the American Presidential Office*. New York: Penguin, 1974.

Humphreys, David. "American Museum, January, 1792." In Jacques-Pierre Brissot de Warville, *New Travels in the United States of America: Performed in 1788*, 405. Dublin: P. Bryne, A. Gueber, 1792.

Hünemörder, Markus. *The Society of the Cincinnati: Conspiracy and Distrust in Early America*. New York: Berghahn Books, 2006.

Hunter, John. "An Account of a Visit Made to Washington at Mount Vernon, by an English Gentleman, in 1785." *Pennsylvania Magazine of History and Biography* 17 (1893): 76–82.

Hutchinson, William T. et al., eds. *The Papers of James Madison: March 7, 1788–March 1, 1789, Congressional Series*. Vol. 11, 1st ser. Charlottesville: University Press of Virginia, 1977.

Hutson, James H. *Religion and the New Republic: Faith in the Founding of America*. Lanham, MD: Rowman and Littlefield, 2000.

Jones, Robert F. "George Washington and the Politics of the Presidency." *Presidential Studies Quarterly* 19 (1980): 28–35.

Jones, Thomas. *History of New York During the Revolutionary War: And of the Leading Events in the Other Colonies at That Period*. Vol. 1. New York: New York Historical Society, 1879.

Kenyon, Cecelia. "'Men of Little Faith': The Anti-Federalists on the Nature of Representative Government." *William and Mary Quarterly* 12 (1955): 3–43.

Ketcham, Ralph. *Presidents Above Party: The First American Presidency, 1789–1829*.

Chapel Hill: University of North Carolina Press, 1987.

Klein, Herbert S. *A Population History of the United States*. Cambridge: Cambridge University Press, 2012.

Koschnik, Albrecht. "Political Conflict and Public Contest: Rituals of National Celebration in Philadelphia, 1788–1815." *Pennsylvania Magazine of History and Biography* 118, no. 3 (July 1994): 248.

Kramnick, Isaac. "'The Great National Discussion': The Discourse of Politics in 1787." *William and Mary Quarterly* 45 (1988): 3–32.

Kross, Jessica. "Mansions, Men, Women, and the Creation of Multiple Publics in Eighteenth-Century British North America." *Journal of Social History* 33, no. 2 (1999): 385–408.

Lambert, Frank. *The Founding Fathers and the Place of Religion in America*. Princeton: Princeton University Press, 2003.

Lax, Michael J., ed. *The Inaugural Addresses of the Presidents of the United States, 1789–1985*. Atlantic City, NJ: American Inheritance Press, 1985.

Longmore, Paul. *The Invention of George Washington*. Charlottesville: University Press of Virginia, 1999.

Loss, Richard. "The Political Thought of George Washington." *Presidential Studies Quarterly* 19 (1989): 471–90.

Lucas, Stephen E. "Genre Criticism and Historical Context: The Case of George Washington's First Inaugural Address." *Southern Speech Communication Journal* 51 (1986): 354–70.

———. "George Washington and the Rhetoric of Presidential Leadership." In *The Presidency and Rhetorical Leadership*, edited by Leroy G. Dorsey, 42–72. College Station: Texas A&M University Press, 2001.

Maclay, William. *The Diary of William Maclay and Other Notes on Senate Debates*. Edited by Kenneth R. Bowling and Helen E. Veit. Baltimore: Johns Hopkins University Press, 1988.

Maier, Pauline. *Ratification: The People Debate the Constitution, 1787–1788*. New York: Simon & Schuster, 2010.

Manzo, Bettina. "A Virginian in New York: The Diary of St. George Tucker, July–August, 1786." *New York History* 67, no. 2 (1986): 177–97.

Marling, Karal Ann. *George Washington Slept Here: Colonial Revivals and American Culture, 1876–1986*. Cambridge, MA: Harvard University Press, 1988.

Mastromarino, Mark A., ed. *The Papers of George Washington: Presidential Series*. Vol. 6, *July–November 1790*. Charlottesville: University Press of Virginia, 1996.

Maurer, Maurer. "Military Justice under George Washington." *Military Affairs* 28, no. 1 (1964): 8–16.

Mayo, Bernard. "George Washington." *Georgia Review* 13, no. 2 (1959): 135–50.

McDonald, Robert M. S., ed. *Sons of the Father: George Washington and His Protégés*. Charlottesville: University of Virginia Press, 2013.

Miller, William Lee. *The First Liberty: America's Foundation in Religious Liberty*. Washington, DC: Georgetown University Press, 2003.

Mills, Fredrick V. "The Protestant Episcopal Churches in the United States 1783–1789: Suspending Animation or Remarkable Recovery?" *Historical Magazine of the Protestant Episcopal Church* 46, no. 2 (1977): 151–70.

Mitchell, Broadus. "Alexander Hamilton, Executive Power, and the New Nation." *Presidential Studies Quarterly* 17 (1987): 329–43.

Morgan, Edmund. "George Washington: The Aloof American." In *George Washington Reconsidered*, edited by Don Higginbotham, 287–308. Charlottesville: University Press of Virginia, 2001.

Muñoz, Vincent Phillip. "George Washington and Religious Liberty." *Review of Politics* 65, no. 1 (2003): 11–33.

Myers, Minor, Jr. *Liberty Without Anarchy: A History of the Society of the Cincinnati*. Charlottesville: University Press of Virginia, 1983.

Nelson, Eric. *Monarchy and the American Founding*. Cambridge, MA: Belknap Press of Harvard University Press, 2017.

Newman, Richard S., and Roy E. Finkenbine. "Black Founders in the New Republic: Introduction." *William and Mary Quarterly* 64, no. 1 (2007): 83–94.

Newman, Simon P. *Parades and the Politics of the Street: Festive Culture in the Early American Republic*. Philadelphia: University of Pennsylvania Press, 1999.

———. "Principles or Men? George Washington and the Political Culture of National Leadership, 1776–1801." *Journal of the Early Republic* 12 (1992): 472–507.

Norton, Charles Eliot. "The Intellectual Life of America." *New Princeton Review* 6 (November 1888): 312–24.

Norton, Mary Beth. *Liberty's Daughters: The Revolutionary Experience of American Women, 1750–1800*. Ithaca, NY: Cornell University Press, 1996.

Onuf, Peter S. *Jefferson's Empire: The Language of American Nationhood*. Charlottesville: University Press of Virginia, 2000.

Padover, Saul K. "George Washington: Portrait of a True Conservative." *Social Research* 22, no. 2 (1955): 199–222.

Peterson, Merrill D., ed. *Thomas Jefferson: Writings*. New York: Library of America, 1984.

Phelps, Glenn A. *George Washington and American Constitutionalism*. Lawrence: University Press of Kansas, 1993.

Pointer, Richard W. "Religious Life in New York During the Revolutionary War." *New York History* 66, no. 4 (1985): 357–73.

Powell, Walter A. *A History of Delaware*. Boston: Christopher Publishing House, 1928.

Rakove, Jack. *Original Meanings: Politics and Ideas in the Making of the Constitution*. New York: Vintage, 1996.

———. "Thinking Like a Constitution." *Journal of the Early Republic* 24 (2004): 1–26.

Ralph, Julian. "The Centennial Celebration." *Harper's Weekly*, 1889, 375–80.

Rapport, Mike. *The Unruly City: Paris, London, and New York in the Age of Revolution*. New York: Basic Books, 2017.

Ray, John. "George Washington's Pre-Presidential Statesmanship, 1783–1789." *Presidential Studies Quarterly* 27 (1997): 207–20.

Richardson, James D. *A Compilation of the Messages and Papers of the Presidents, 1789–1897*. Vol. 1. Washington, DC: Published by Authority of Congress, 1898.

Rigal, Laura. "'Raising the Roof': Authors, Spectators and Artisans in the Grand Federal Procession of 1788." *Theatre Journal* 48, no. 3 (1996): 253–77.

Roosevelt, Franklin D. *The Public Papers and Addresses of Franklin D. Roosevelt. 1939 Volume, War and Neutrality (Book 1)*. Ann Arbor: University of Michigan Library, 2005. http://name.umdl.umich.edu/4926579.1939.001.

Safire, William. "On Language: Marking Bush's Inaugural." *New York Times*, February 5, 1989, SM10, 12.

Schwartz, Barry. "George Washington and the Whig Conception of Heroic Leadership." *American Sociological Review* 48 (1983): 18–33.

———. *George Washington: Making of an American Symbol*. New York: Free Press, 1987.

Sedgwick, Jeffrey Leigh. "James Madison and the Problem of Executive Character." *Polity* 21 (1988): 5–23.

Shy, John. *A People Numerous and Armed: Reflections on the Military Struggle for American Independence*. Ann Arbor: University of Michigan Press, 1990.

Silverman, Kenneth. *A Cultural History of the American Revolution*. New York: Columbia University Press, 1987.

Smith, Billy G., and Paul Sivitz. "Identifying and Mapping Ethnicity in Philadelphia in the Early Republic." *Pennsylvania Magazine of History and Biography* 140, no. 43 (October 2016): 393–411.

Smith, James Morton, ed. *The Republic of Letters: The Correspondence between*

*Thomas Jefferson and James Madison,
1776–1826.* New York: W. W. Norton,
1995.

Smucker, Isaac. "A Great Event of a Century
Ago: Washington's Inauguration and
Inaugural." *Magazine of Western
History,* May 1889.

Sparks, Jared, ed. *Life of George Washington.*
London: Henry Colburn, 1839.

Still, Bayrd, ed. *Mirror for Gotham: New York
as Seen by Contemporaries from Dutch
Days to the Present.* New York:
Fordham University Press, 1994.

Stillman, Damie. "Six Houses for the
President." *Pennsylvania Magazine of
History and Biography* 129, no. 4
(2005): 411–31.

Storing, Herbert J., ed. *The Complete
Anti-Federalist.* Vol. 2. Chicago:
University of Chicago Press, 2007.

Syrett, Harold, ed. *The Papers of Alexander
Hamilton.* Vol. 2. New York: Columbia
University Press, 1962.

Thach, Charles C., Jr. *The Creation of the
Presidency, 1775–1789: A Study in
Constitutional History.* Indianapolis:
Liberty Fund, 1923, 1969.

Thompson, Mary V. *In the Hands of Good
Providence: Religion in the Life of George
Washington.* Charlottesville: University
of Virginia Press, 2008.

Thompson, Robert. "The Lessons of Yesterday
Can Shape a Better Tomorrow." *Seattle
Post-Intelligencer,* July 31, 1989, A7.

Towner, Ausburn. "Our First President's
Inauguration." *Frank Leslie's Popular
Monthly (1876–1904)* 27, no. 4 (1889):
385–96.

Trees, Andrew S. *The Founding Fathers and the
Politics of Character.* Princeton:
Princeton University Press, 2004.

Twohig, Dorothy, ed. *The Papers of George
Washington: Revolutionary War Series.*
Vol. 6, *August 13, 1776–October 20, 1776.*
Charlottesville: University Press of
Virginia, 1994.

Vile, John R. "American Views of the
Constitutional Amending Process: An
Intellectual History of Article V."
American Journal of Legal History 35
(1991): 44–69.

Waldstreicher, David. *In the Midst of Perpetual
Fetes: The Making of American
Nationalism, 1776–1820.* Chapel Hill:
University of North Carolina Press,
1997.

Washington, George. "Farewell Address." In
*The Writings of George Washington from
the Original Manuscripts, 1745–1799,*
vol. 26, edited by John C. Fitzpatrick,
483–96. Washington, DC: United
States Government Printing Office,
1931.

White, Shane. *Somewhat More Independent:
The End of Slavery in New York City,
1770–1810.* Athens: University of
Georgia Press, 1991.

Whitman, Walt. "Crossing Brooklyn Ferry." In
Selected Poems, edited by Stanley
Appelbaum. Mineola, NY: Dover, 1991.

Wills, Gary. *Cincinnatus: George Washington
and the Enlightenment.* New York:
Doubleday, 1984.

Winterer, Caroline. *American Enlightenments.*
New Haven: Yale University Press,
2016.

Wood, Gordon. *The Creation of the American
Republic, 1776–1789.* Chapel Hill:
University of North Carolina Press,
1969.

Zimmerman, John. "Charles Thomson, 'the
Sam Adams of Philadelphia.'"
Mississippi Valley Historical Review 45
(1958): 464–80.

INDEX